Entering the Way of the Great Vehicle

Entering the Way of the Great Vehicle

Dzogchen as the Culmination of the Mahāyāna

Rongzom Chökyi Zangpo

TRANSLATED AND INTRODUCED BY

Dominic Sur

SNOW LION
BOULDER
2017

Snow Lion
An imprint of Shambhala Publications, Inc.
4720 Walnut Street
Boulder, Colorado 80301
www.shambhala.com

9 8 7 6 5 4 3 2

Printed in the United States of America

♾ This edition is printed on acid-free paper that meets the American National Standards Institute Z39.48 Standard.
♻ Shambhala makes every effort to print on recycled paper.
For more information please visit www.shambhala.com.

Shambhala Publications is distributed worldwide by Penguin Random House, Inc., and its subsidiaries.

Designed by Gopa & Ted2, Inc.

Library of Congress Cataloging-in-Publication Data

Names: Rong-zom Chos-kyi-bzang-po, 1012–1088, author. | Sur, Dominic, translator.
Title: Entering the way of the great vehicle: dzogchen as the culmination of the Mahāyāna / Rongzom Chökyi Zangpo; translated and introduced by Dominic Sur.
Other titles: Theg pa chen po'i tshul la 'jug pa. English
Description: First edition. | Boulder: Snow Lion, 2017. | Includes bibliographical references and index. | Translated from Tibetan.
Identifiers: LCCN 2016019345 | ISBN 9781611803686 (hardback: alk. paper)
Subjects: LCSH: Rdzogs-chen—Early works to 1800. | Mahayana Buddhism—Doctrines—Early works to 1800. | BISAC: RELIGION / Buddhism / Tibetan. | RELIGION / Buddhism / Sacred Writings.
Classification: LCC BQ7662.4 .R6613 2017 | DDC 294.3/420423—dc23
LC record available at https://lccn.loc.gov/2016019345

Contents

Acknowledgments

THE STORY OF my involvement with Rongzom begins with James Gentry, who introduced me to Rongzom in the fall of 2009 and suggested that I might be interested in *Entering the Way of the Great Vehicle*. I am very grateful for all the help and encouragement James has given me, before and since. His example of Tibetological scholarship has been an inspiration. Before that time, and since, many other people have also assisted and collaborated with me and I would like to thank several in particular.

First, I'd like to thank my parents, especially my mom, Maggie—who never quit on me. And I would like to thank the Di Zinno and Sur families for the support they've offered over the years.

Within the Tibetan Buddhist tradition, I would like to thank my first teacher, Khenpo Lama Chönam of Golog, a scholar, poet, and practitioner for whom I have the deepest admiration. Also, let me offer my sincere gratitude to some of the many people who gave their time and assistance to this project: Matthieu Ricard introduced me to Khensur Tsering Dorji Rinpoche, who transmitted *Entering the Way* to me and answered many questions. Khenpo Sangye Phuntshog and my good friend, the Venerable Gelong Tenzin Jamchen (Lama Sean Price) of Shechen monastery, were also very generous with their time and erudition. The Venerable Sean, in particular, has been very generous and deserves my thanks. I must also thank Pema Tharchin Rinpoche and Khenpo Gaden of Serlo Monastery for their hospitality and much-needed help in translation. I must also express gratitude for the help of Sogan Rinpoche (Tulku Pema Lodoe of Golog). I also owe many profound thanks to Khenpo Tsultrim Lodoe and Tenzin Gyatso of Serta Larung Gar monastery, for taking time to answer my questions about Rongzompa's *Entering the Way*. Additionally, Khenpo Nawang Jorden of the Sakya International Buddhist Academy, Geshe Tashi Dhondup, and Lama Kunkhen of Kopan Monastery deserve my thanks.

My old friend Geshema Namdrol Phuntsog, of Kopan Nunnery, was also generous with her time and erudition.

Within academia, I must thank David Germano, my primary academic advisor at the University of Virginia. The time and advice he has given me in both personal and professional terms has been invaluable. In my time at UVA, David has time and again gone out of his way to help—and I am thankful to him for it. I would also like to express my gratitude to several other teachers at the University of Virginia: Karen Lang and Kurtis Schaeffer. I would also like to express my gratitude to several scholars who helped me while I was studying at Harvard Divinity School: Leonard van der Kuijp, Charles Hallisey, and Janet Gyatso each deserve thanks. A number of other scholars—José Cabezón, Orna Almogi, Dorji Wangchuk, Andy Francis, Douglas Duckworth, David Higgins, William McGrath, and Michael Sheehy—also deserve my thanks, as do Ravi Gupta, Tammy Proctor, and all my colleagues in the Department of History at Utah State University.

Much of the work that made this translation possible was accomplished while on a Fulbright-IIE grant to Nepal (2012–2013), which I was grateful and honored to receive.

I also want to extend my thanks to my oldest friend, Jayme Burtis, the Bridges family, and Richard Josephson. These people, precious longtime family and friends, have supported me through many years of study. Without their support and encouragement, my life, which I am immensely grateful for, would look nothing like it does now.

Thanks is certainly owed to the folks at Shambhala Publications, Nikko Odiseos and Michael Wakoff, in particular. My thanks for their patience and expertise in bringing this wonderful text to print.

Whatever value there is in this translation, it comes about as the consequence of my collaborations with others. Whatever flaws there are herein are mine alone. And while my translation of Rongzompa's *Entering the Way of the Great Vehicle* may be the first for the English-speaking world, it most certainly will not be the last. As such, I can only hope that this first effort supports further explorations and a more refined understanding of Rongzom, *Entering the Way of the Great Vehicle*, and Himalayan Buddhism's intellectual history and culture.

Finally, I am incredibly fortunate to have a partner, Me Sur, who enriches my life and, during the course of this project, picked me up and dusted me off through many ups and downs.

June 2016, Idyllwild, CA

Entering the Way of the Great Vehicle

Translator's Introduction

The Audacity of Rongzom's Work

The third chapter of *The Blue Annals*,[1] a chronicle of Tibetan religious history attributed to Gö Lotsawa Zhönnu Pel (1392–1481),[2] recounts an interesting story about the author of *Entering the Way of the Great Vehicle*, the translator Rongzom Chökyi Zangpo (hereafter Rongzom or Rongzompa). According to the story, at a gathering of Buddhist scholars from the Four Horns of Central Tibet,[3] a group of intellectuals decided to confront and censure Rongzom over his prodigious and therefore unseemly literary output.[4] These men thought it unacceptable that a person born in Tibet, like Rongzom, had composed such a large number of commentarial and scholastic treatises (*śāstra*, *bstan bcos*). Yet after seeing and discussing each treatise with the author, they were so impressed that each subsequently offered to serve Rongzom as a disciple. A remarkable turnabout from their initial hostility.

The story is worth bringing up in an introduction to one of Rongzom's most important treatises because it suggests that Rongzom flourished at a time in Tibet when there was immense skepticism, if not antagonism, toward autochthonous compositions of Buddhist literature. Moreover, the fact that these would-be censors changed their minds about Rongzom's work only *after* seeing and engaging in discussion of each treatise (*bstan bcos re mthong zhing gsung glengs re mdzad pas*) suggests just how hostile the environment was toward Tibetan composition: these translators and interpreters of Buddhism were ready to censure work they had not even examined, on the basis of the birthplace of the author. Considering that Tibetans have since become prolific authors of a wide variety of authoritative Buddhist literature, we may wonder why, in Rongzom's time, there was a very different attitude.

The Context for Rongzom's Work

Another story found in the Tibetan traditions reports that in 842 CE a Buddhist monk named Lhalung Pelgyi Dorjé assassinated the last Tibetan emperor, Langdarma. Buddhism first penetrated the Tibetan plateau during the Tibetan empire (650–850 CE), and Langdarma's assassination is traditionally said to mark the beginnings of Tibet's "Dark Age," in which the light of the Buddha's teaching nearly goes out. After the assassination, an ensuing struggle for control left a power vacuum that meant that no centralized Buddhist institutions or overarching civic administration would gain any foothold in Tibet again until the late tenth century. That is, after the assassination of the last emperor, an event that precipitated the mid-ninth-century implosion of the Tibetan empire, more than one hundred years of shifting clan alliances and political instability ensued.[5] With no central institutional and administrative authority, a variety of religious movements flourished among various Tibetan communities, clans, and families.

In the eleventh century, an economic and political resurgence was accompanied by an astonishing transmission of religious literature and media into Tibet. This deluge of new transmissions and translations from Indian Buddhism concerning religion, philosophy, art, medicine, and a variety of Indian ritual, contemplative, ethical, and institutional practices, as well as an equally extensive profusion of visionary revelations, began to flood the Tibetan plateau and transform the cultural and political landscape. It was an era of increasing religious diversity in Tibet, when Buddhist institutions began to take root, sharp sectarian boundaries began to emerge, and the scholastic mode of discourse incorporating the newly imported South Asian nomenclatures became de rigueur.

The many ensuing religious divisions were organized at a higher level into an overarching bifurcation into the "Old" (*rnying*) and "New" (*gsar*), which ignores the other religious tradition of historical Tibet, called Bön. Some promulgators of the new lineages of Buddhist practice imported into Tibet, which are traditionally categorized as the "New Schools" by virtue of the fact that their transmission into Tibet stemmed from the renaissance, largely dismissed the religious lineages that existed in Tibet prior to the eleventh-century infusion of religious and intellectual civilization from the south as "old," which suggested decadence, decay, and irrelevance. Adherents to religious traditions that existed in Tibet prior to the eleventh century, however, embraced their identity as the "Old School" (*rnying ma*), which for them implied tradition, ancient pedigrees, and association with a glorious Tibetan imperial past. In fact, Rongzom goes as far as to declare that Tibetan translation of scriptures dating to the Imperium are superior to those given in the New School transmission for six reasons.[6]

The revival of Tibet's religious culture in the renaissance period emerged with two main factions—a group of monastics in the East and the rise of an aristocratic house in the West. In the Western court, the ruler, Yéshé Ö, claimed that tantric Buddhism had been misunderstood and misrepresented in Tibet. He felt that the village Buddhism active in the "Dark Age" was riddled with problems. According to Yéshé Ö and a scion of his royal house Podrang Zhiwa Ö, Tibetans also engaged in the worst type of fabrication by composing their own tantric texts during the Dark Age in order to give textual justification for their wrong views and behaviors, which were said to be mistaken at best and murderous and licentious at worst. In order to establish authoritative lines of religious dispensation—and establish the Western court as a site of emerging political power—Yéshé Ö and Podrang Zhiwa Ö composed formal ordinances containing criticism and charges of fraudulence against the teachers active in village religious communities. The ordinances declare a large number of texts that were eventually codified in Tibet's Old School of Buddhism to be unacceptable and inauthentic works "fabricated" by Tibetans. As such, proponents of the renaissance and its New Schools of Tibetan Buddhism saw these works as dangerous—causes of the degeneration and abuse of the Tibetan Buddhist culture that thrived during the Imperium. These ordinances identify, as objects of their criticism, the "teachers, tantrists living in villages who have no connection with the Three Ways and yet who claim 'We follow *the way of the Great Vehicle*'" (Karmay 1998, 9 [English], 14 [Tibetan]).

Rongzom was an established teacher with a large group of disciples. Such communities were objects of concern for the ascendant political faction in the West keen to claim the mantle of the arbiters of *true religion* in Tibet and to extend control over a wide domain where religious institutions were hitherto largely absent and religious authority was decentralized. One text produced through this effort is Atiśa's famous *Lamp for the Path to Enlightenment*, which formulated a sanctioned relationship between tantric and nontantric Buddhist practice in ways that facilitated a newly emergent, and soon to be dominant, interpretive framework championed by the New Schools of Tibetan Buddhism. For the emerging kingdom in the West, which was intent on establishing a network of Buddhist institutions, criticism of these village masters and their religious communities was part and parcel of their expansionist agenda, which concerned, in part, assimilating (read: bringing under control) these religious communities who might not otherwise join the newly emerging monastic institutions of scholastic learning favored by the rulers in the West and promulgators of the New Schools.

As one of the earliest defenders of the lineages and practices transmitted through the Old School, we may presume that Rongzom was aware of these ordinances. We may nevertheless wonder if his work was responding to or was otherwise inspired by them. While there is no conclusive evidence that can be presented here, it is interesting to note that the Tibetan title of Rongzom's text contains the same phrase—"way of the Great Vehicle"—that is used in the ordinance. That is, the ordinance attributed to the Western ruler Yéshé Ö claimed that the problem with Tibetan religious culture in the Dark Age stemmed from the practitioners of tantra in Tibetan villages who were merely paying lip service to following "the way of the Great Vehicle." In Rongzompa's *Entering the Way of the Great Vehicle*, itself a defense of the Old School, we find textual sources used that were in fact criticized in the ordinances. Thus, we may wonder if the title is meant to be, say, one that resembles and recalls Shantideva's famed eighth-century Mahāyāna classic *Entering the Way of the Bodhisattvas* or whether the title was meant to challenge the notion that the lineages and practices passed down by proponents of the Old School were somehow not authentic Buddhism. Certainly that was among the charges leveled in the ordinances. The ordinances were an attempt on the part of the authors to project temporal and religious power and fashion themselves as guardians and patrons of true religion. We may never know, but another interesting fact beyond the title and its resemblance to the object of criticism named in the ordinance is seen when we recognize that much of the work cited in Rongzom's *Entering the Way of the Great Vehicle* as authentic Buddhist literature is found among works listed as fraudulent in Podrang Zhiwa Ö's ordinance. Rongzom exhibits no self-consciousness about using these works and mentions no ordinance. Moreover, although there are strong clues that the text was written to be read by proponents of the New School,[7] it does not itself contain any explicit references to an intended audience beyond an obscure reference to a request from Lhogom in the colophon and the more explicit reference to "people who are obsessed with treatises on grammar and logic," a phrase that itself causes us to remember that the renaissance in Tibet was accompanied by the lionization of the idea that discourse on the Buddhist path must be logically and linguistically coherent. In any case, Rongzom and his work, particularly *Entering the Way of the Great Vehicle*, should be seen as a product of a transformative time in which an influx of new religious media facilitated the rise of new religious orders.

While esoteric forms of Buddhism based in the scriptures known as "tantras" were common to both the New and Old schools, the lineages and forms were quite different. The New and Old schools also diverged on the issue of the importance of exoteric schools of Buddhist philosophy and the relevance of monastic institutionalism. The New schools embraced monasticism and exoteric Buddhist philosophical systems, both of which were rapidly developed and assimilated into particularly Tibetan forms. In contrast, the Old School, in these early centuries, tended toward lay, often hereditary lineages outside of monastic institutions. In response to the New School's ascendancy, the Old School also engaged in literary production. Apart from the work of Rongzompa, however, this literature most typically took the form of visionary revelations, whose content was primarily esoteric thought and practice, or narrative tales of a glorious past.

In this turbulent religious landscape of the eleventh century, Rongzompa is not only one of the most brilliant intellectuals on the Tibetan plateau but he is also a unique figure who straddled the emerging boundary between the New and Old schools. Rongzom was deeply versed in the "old" esoteric traditions; but he was also a master of the new dispensations—and his personal compositions brilliantly ranged over both with creative and compelling lines of inquiry given in a snappy prose often employing distinctive images and metaphors. His corpus includes commentaries on important New School literature, such as his *Commentary on the Difficult Points of the Sarvabuddha-samāyoga-ḍākinī-jāla-saṃvara-tantra* (Rong zom chos bzang 1999d), and literature associated with the Old School tantras, such as his commentary on the most important text for the Old School, the *Guhyagarbhatantra* (Rong zom chos bzang 1999b). His work is indeed remarkable among Old School figures of the time in that the majority of these figures confined their literary output to the esoteric traditions of their past, whereas Rongzom also engaged extensively with the New School literature and philosophy and its contemporary Indian imports. The text translated in this volume exemplifies this aspect of his work as it is structured around a systematic analysis of various types of Buddhist thought and practice that situates them in relation to the Old School's distinctive Great Perfection tradition. But before venturing into the subject of the text, let me say a few words about the man himself.

The Story of Rongzom's Life

Rongzom is reported to have lived and worked with his wife and two sons in Narlung rong, a district in Rulak in the western Tibetan region of Lower Tshang.[8] While Rongzom's precise dates remain uncertain,[9] what is not disputed is the formative nature of the time in which he flourished—circa the late eleventh century; and nobody today disputes his place among the luminaries of Tibet's Nyingma, or Old School, tradition of Tibetan Buddhism.[10]

According to traditional accounts,[11] Rongzom demonstrated a remarkable, almost spontaneous intelligence and aptitude for language and scholarship from a young age. This did not stop him, however, from being a rowdy little boy. While studying with a teacher in the Lower Tshang region of Central Tibet, Rongzom gained a reputation among his classmates as rather wild and talkative. When word of this reputation reached Rongzompa's father, he went to the teacher and sheepishly offered to remove his son from the school. The schoolmaster replied that no such thing should be done because the boy's intellect was so impressive. He seemed to soak up his teacher's instruction almost instantly from just one lecture. After class, he would go to recess on the playground, where he would recite from memory the day's lesson as he frolicked in play.

Rongzom was said to have easily mastered the major and minor domains of classical knowledge, such as language, grammar, medicine, technology, logic and epistemology, and Buddhism proper, known as the *inner sciences*.[12] So remarkable was his ability to learn and memorize the details of his subjects that Rongzompa is remembered as an emanation of Mañjuśrī, the bodhisattva of wisdom. According to these traditional accounts, Rongzom mastered the Buddhist art of dialectical philosophy by age eleven, and he completed a comprehensive course of Buddhist study by age thirteen. It is said that Rongzompa learned Sanskrit in the same fashion: quickly and seemingly without effort. This may have helped shape his reputation in Tibetan intellectual history as a reincarnation of the Indian translator and Buddhist master Smṛtijñānakīrti, an important figure for the Old School dispensation. In the traditional biographies of him, he is not only known for his many compositions on a variety of subjects but also for his unique and penetrating analyses. Gö Lotsawa Zhönnu Pel marks him as a unique figure, whose theories were different from, and superior to, all others (*lta ba mchog tu gyur pa kun las khyad par du gyur bas*); and Rongzom is remembered as a deft intellectual capable of drawing out the most subtle of philosophical distinctions, "whereby a given word might apply to a given shade of meaning" (Dudjom 1991, 705). Rongzom was not only a consummate translator of sutric and tantric teachings classically attributed to the Buddha along with technical exegetical treatises (*śāstra*) but also an important author in his own right, treating diverse subjects from Sanskrit grammar to epistemology to the Buddhist *sūtras* to dairy farming, from the ethnographic to the phenomenological. As a child, Rongzompa relished the company of Indian masters and understood their Sanskrit materials after the most cursory of readings. His talent for languages was said to go beyond human languages and extend to that of animals.

It is often said in traditional accounts of his life that Rongzompa met the great Indian (Bengali) master Atiśa, who died in Tibet in 1054. On that occasion, Atiśa, author of *Lamp for the Path to Enlightenment*, was said to be so impressed as to wonder aloud what spiritual advice he could possibly have for the polymath.[13] While this anecdote might suggest an early-eleventh-century birth date, reports that Rongzom gained a scholarly reputation by age thirteen offer the possibility of his meeting the renowned master in his youth—perhaps because of his precocity.

What becomes clear through the sometimes dense hagiographical fog of these idealized biographies is that Rongzom is remembered as a unique intellectual, flourishing in a transformative time. His literary output and the quality of his work was so high that people described him as a genius,[14] an accomplished tantric adept endowed with profound and therapeutic spiritual insight.[15] All of his literary works are said to be qualified by their refined language, refined meaning, and "unadulterated expressive style" (Dudjom 1991, 705). His writings on tantra, moreover, are considered so powerful that anyone looking at them receives a profound blessing as a result—even if they have not received the proper transmission, which is considered the imprimatur of the traditional transmission. Moreover, his important work on Great Perfection, *Entering the Way of the Great Vehicle*, which is translated in this volume, has been described by figures such as Dudjom Rinpoche, as "inexpressibly profound and of vast significance" for Buddhists (ibid.). In short, Rongzompa is considered an all-knowing master of the Buddhist religion, one respected for his work on both sides of the Old School/New School divide.

Rongzompa's *Entering the Way of the Great Vehicle*

Entering the Way of the Great Vehicle is a philosophical text; it is also more. It is a text about the practice of Buddhist philosophy—about the conceptual conditions that structure the very possibility of doing philosophy—and, most especially, the place of the Great Perfection within philosophical discourse. This is not a text meant for beginners or those new to Buddhist philosophy. Rather, *Entering the Way of the Great Vehicle* is a highly sophisticated and advanced philosophical text whose agenda is best understood when we look, as we did briefly above, at the historical and cultural context of its production—eleventh-century Tibet. This work represents one of Rongzom's most important works. It is a masterly exposition of Buddhist doctrine organized around a constellation of core issues within a sustained argument about the nature of emptiness, appearance, and illusion—perhaps three of the most crucial philosophical topics in Buddhist discourse and philosophy.

The formal title of the text is *The Exegetical Treatise Entitled "Entering the Way of the Great Vehicle."* The Tibetan word for "exegetical treatise" is *tenchö*.[16] This term is the Tibetan equivalent of the Sanskrit term *śāstra*, which derives from the Sanskrit verbal root (*dhātu*) √*śās*, meaning "teach," "instruct," "rule," and so on. According to *The Princeton Dictionary of Buddhism*, the term *śāstra* indicates

> works contained in the various Buddhist canons attributed to various Indian masters. In his sense, the term is distinguished from SŪTRA, a discourse regarded as the word of the Buddha or spoken with his sanction. In the basic division of the Buddhist scripture in the Tibetan canon, for example, the translations of ŚĀSTRA (BSTAN 'GYUR) are contrasted with the words of the Buddha (or a buddha) called BKA' 'GYUR. . . . In the Buddhist context, the genre is typically a form of composition that explains the words or intentions of the Buddha. (Buswell and Lopez 2013, s.v. "śāstra")

According to one scholar, Paul Griffiths, "a Buddhist *śāstra* is typically an ordered set of descriptive and injunctive sentences, together with arguments to ground and defend them, taken to give systematic and authoritative expression to Buddhist doctrine."[17] Because the Tibetan renaissance was predicated, in part, on the idea that true religion—that is, real Buddhism—originated only in India, it is notable that Rongzom's text, by virtue of containing the word *śāstra* in its title, can be understood to be projecting an almost unquestionable religious authority. That is, the fact this text contains the word *śāstra* in its title suggests that it is an authoritative interpretive commentary on Buddhist discourse that may be raised to the level of canon. This fact becomes more interesting when we turn to *Entering the Way of the Great Vehicle* itself.

The words *Great Vehicle* correspond to the Sanskrit word *mahāyāna*. Ordinarily, the Sanskrit term *mahāyāna* would refer broadly to one of two fundamental religious orientations discussed in the Himalayan Buddhist world; the other is known by the polemically charged label *hīnayāna*, or *Lesser Vehicle*, which would presumably include the Śrāvaka and Pratyekabuddha, or those Buddhist traditions whose authoritative literature is given in the Pali language. In this traditional context, the phrases *the Mahāyana* and *the Great Vehicle* both signal a large constellation of exoteric and esoteric doctrines and practices organized around the teaching of emptiness and the active and altruistic figure of the bodhisattva, given in scriptures written, for the most part, in Sanskrit. Unlike the hearers (*śrāvaka*, *nyan thos pa*) and mysterious solitary buddhas (*pratyekajīnas*, *rang rgyal ba*) who are traditionally said to seek their own peace through the exhaustion of discontent (*duḥkha*, *sdug bsngal*) known as the *nirvāṇa*, bodhisattvas actively turn away from that serene state and vow to delay full enlightenment in order to remain in *saṃsāra*, the cycle of existence characterized by birth, old age, sickness, and death, and driven by karma. Bodhisattvas vow to remain active within this realm of suffering[18] in order to work for the benefit of sentient beings (*sattva*, *sems can*), an imperative driven by the bodhisattva's radical altruism, *bodhicitta*, which spontaneously and naturally motivates his or her every act.

As chapter 1 opens with a brief discussion of the Mahāyāna, or Great Vehicle, Rongzom seems to be evoking a standard Great Vehicle orientation. But then the text quickly shifts the rhetorical register of the discourse in such a way that it suggests a very different nuance for the meaning of the term *Great Vehicle* as it is used in this text. He begins by describing the Great Vehicle as a form of Buddhist life signified and instantiated by what is disclosed in the transformative realization that *all phenomena are illusory* in character and thereby all are essentially equal in some fundamental, significant sense. This description fills a key qualification Rongzom advances for realization and actualization of the spiritually liberated state associated with the Old School's highest practice, the Great Perfection (*rdzogs chen*):

> Entering onto the Great Vehicle (*mahāyāna, theg chen*) path is something enabled through the realization of the illusory character of all phenomena. The authentic assimilation and consummation of the realization that all phenomena are basically the same in being illusory is the Great Perfection approach to the path.[19]

In Rongzom's text, then, the term *Great Vehicle* is an all-embracing rubric that includes exoteric scholasticism as well as tantric and posttantric traditions. Thus, for him, the Great Vehicle includes the cosmologies of the Perfection of Wisdom sutras *and* the tantric Kālacakra, the epistemologies associated with Abhidharma and *pramāṇa* (that is, Indian logical epistemology) and the ontologies described in Yogācāra and Madhyamaka text traditions, as well as the phenomenology associated with the theory and practice of the Great Perfection.

In the first chapter, the Tibetan term *thekpa chenpo*—"Great Vehicle" or "Mahāyāna"—appears in the first and last sentence of the chapter. This is no accident; the term signifies one of the chapter's central rhetorical concerns: establishing an inclusive path structure that marginalizes differences traditionally said to obtain between varying practices such as the Perfection of Wisdom Sutras (*prajñāpāramitā*) revealed in India and the esoteric Tibetan discourses associated with the Great Perfection. The first sentence of *Entering the Way of the Great Vehicle* states quite simply: "I am going to explain a little bit about entering the way of the Great Vehicle."[20] This is a rather surprising opening to one of Rongzom's longest and most elaborate texts. The last sentence of the same chapter reads: "Those who desire to enter the way of the Great Vehicle should recognize that there is no real entity of affliction to be eliminated and that all phenomena are taught to be fundamentally equal insofar they are illusory."[21]

The next use of the phrase *Great Vehicle* after these two incidents is found in the first sentence of the third chapter, which is entitled "Distinguishing the Great Perfection from the Other Vehicles That Retain the Nomenclature of Illusion." There, Rongzom correlates accessing the way of Great Perfection (*rdzogs pa chen po'i tshul la 'jug*) with entering the Great Vehicle;

the only distinction that the author strikes between the two approaches figures around the qualification that all phenomena are rendered basically equal (*'go mnyams pa*) by the realization that they are illusory. According to *Entering the Way of the Great Vehicle*, insight into the illusory nature of reality discloses the Mahāyāna way, which recognizes that all phenomena, including nirvana, are *illusory*;[22] in contrast, the way of the Great Perfection (*rdzogs pa chen po'i tshul*) is described as the culmination (*mthar phyin pa*) of that disclosure, which simply adds a recognition of the total equality of all phenomena in their illusory nature, whether positive or negative, pure (for example, nirvana) or impure (for example, saṃsāra), and so forth. One senses here that, for Rongzom, Great Perfection is a way of reading or understanding Buddhist doctrine rather than being a completely different self-enclosed doctrinal system altogether that is to be juxtaposed with other, different systems. Thus, an important element of Rongzom's project in the third chapter is to articulate and distinguish a particular discourse on the illusory nature of things that is unique to the Great Perfection way yet is genealogically elemental to other Buddhist discourses that teach all phenomena to be *illusory*, *akin to an illusion*, or *illusion-like* (*māyopama*, *sgyu ma lta bu*). Here, Buddhist discourse on the *illusory* constitutes an important rhetorical foundation in the text—a basic philosophical ground on which the text can build its particular world. On this ground, *Entering the Way of the Great Vehicle* objectifies itself through symbolic associations. That is, one function of the text is to symbolically associate Rongzom's Great Perfection discourse with other, traditionally authoritative Buddhist discourses. He accomplishes this by drawing on their common associations around the well-known Buddhist trope that "the nature of reality is illusory." For, according to Rongzom, all schools of Buddhist philosophy agree that the things of ordinary, conditioned life are not what they seem to be—that is, they are illusory. *Entering the Way of the Great Vehicle* simply expands this common ground, and the discourses predicated upon it, to include the Great Perfection as an overarching hermeneutic—a way to read Buddhist discourses, the best way to read them. We note here that Rongzom uses the terms *thek chen* ("Great Vehicle") and *dzok chen* ("Great Perfection") in such a way that they are simultaneously closely related yet also in contrast to one another. This is really the first hint that readers of this text have concerning Rongzom's rather inclusive theory of the Buddhist doctrine of the path.[23]

Before looking at the particulars of Rongzom's text, a few words on the place of this work in Tibetan intellectual history. *Entering the Way of the Great Vehicle* concerns doctrinal systems, a common topic for authors of the time. When the eleventh-century renaissance began in Tibet, important political players in the emerging political kingdom in western Tibet "launched a campaign of denunciation" against Tibetan religious traditions associated with earlier Imperial-era lineages and translations (Wangchuk 2002, 266). The conviction that some of those traditions were not authentic partially motivated western Tibetan rulers to send a group of monks to India and Kashmir in order to find and bring back true religion to Tibet. What was brought back to Tibet in fact forms the basis of Tibet's New Schools of Buddhism.

Proponents of the Old School in Rongzompa's time were not writing texts like *Entering the Way of the Great Vehicle*, which is a synthetic treatise exploring the doxographical systems of Indian Buddhism and offering systematic formulations of how they relate, which includes utilizing the Great Perfection—an object of criticism for some proponents of the New Schools—as a lens into those doxographical systems, the most powerful lens. *Entering the Way of the Great Vehicle* is unique because it often explores the hierarchy of Indian Buddhist philosophical systems using the Tibetan Great Perfection as a lens through which to resolve tensions between these putatively conflicting philosophical positions. The fact that Rongzom uses Great Perfection as a way to interpret Buddhist discourse that resolves different philosophical systems that are traditionally said to be in conflict with one another makes this work unique.

Summary of Chapter 1

Chapter 1 of *Entering the Way of the Great Vehicle* explores the ways in which different philosophical systems conceptualize the nature of affliction and bondage in saṃsāra. The chapter opens with a question concerning the status of suffering. In brief, Buddhists widely accept that sentient beings are bound in the conditioned existence of saṃsāra, a cycle of life and death driven by karmic activity. A question may be raised about the status of bondage in saṃsāra: is the bondage of affliction (*kleśa*, *nyon mongs*) real or is it the case that bondage is not real and we merely *appear* to be trapped in saṃsāra? The remainder of the chapter explores a variety of Buddhist theoretical approaches to analyzing the reality of saṃsāra and the afflictive states of mind commonly thought to bind us there. This exploration surveys five principal Indian Buddhist systems—Śrāvaka, Pratyekabuddha, Yogācāra, Madhyamaka, Guhyamantra (i.e., tantra), and the Great Perfection.[24] In each of the different sections, Rongzom uses each of the Buddhist systems to drive home the point that bondage in saṃsāra is not real. Here, Rongzom's philosophical method is to include the varying systems within an overarching framework such that each resolves to the same view: bondage is not actually real. This *inclusive* approach, found throughout the text, works to temper sectarian hostility by privileging a framework for knowledge that combines traditional (and nontraditional) theory and discourse by embedding the vast variety of different Buddhist practices within his overarching framework of inclusivity. The aim of this chapter is to demonstrate that although a variety of Buddhist paths accept and penetrate the illusory nature of reality (that is, that all is not what it appears to be), that realization—and its soteriological significance—is fully manifest only through the Great Perfection. This chapter introduces us to the author's doctrine of appearance, his inclusive philosophical method, and his reliance upon the writings of Tilopa in forming his view of equality.[25] This chapter, as well as several others, also contains Rongzom's critical comments on the folly of insisting on logical criteria as the sine qua non of authoritative religious discourse.

Chapter 1 is organized around a fivefold framework—a normative hierarchy of doctrines and views typically representing differing approaches to Buddhist theory and practice. In this chapter, however, each doxographical heading does not signal an expositional excursion into the system named. Instead, each heading constitutes a main section and a new philosophical context in which to situate the chapter's overarching aim: to show that when illusory appearance is taken as the basis of analysis—this is Rongzom's starting point precisely because all Buddhist philosophical schools agree that things are illusory insofar as they do not exist the way in which they appear—all phenomena, whether traditionally considered "pure" or "impure," are seen to be fundamentally equal. As a whole, the chapter consists of brief introductory remarks, followed by five main sections and a conclusion. The chapter's five main sections and their topical concerns are as follows:

1. The "Hearer" or Śrāvaka approach to the path (*nyan thos kyi tshul*) concerning the four noble truths (*catvāri āryasatyāni*, *'phags bden bzhi*)

2. The "Solitary Buddha" or Pratyeka-jīna approach to the path (*rang rgyal ba kyi tshul*) concerning the twelve links of the Buddhist theory of interdependence (*pratītyasamutpāda, rten cing 'brel bar 'byung ba*)
3. The "Practitioners of Yoga" or Yogācāra approach to the path (*rnal 'byor spyod pa kyi tshul*) concerning the three natures (*tris-vābhava, mtshan nyi gsum/ngo bo gsum/rang bzhin gsum*)
4. The "Middle Way" or Madhyamaka approach to the path (*dbu ma'i tshul*) concerning the pacification of discursive schemes (*prapañcā-upaśānta, spros pa nye bar zhi ba*)
5. The Madhyamaka and "Secret Mantra" or Guhyamantra approach to the path (*dbu ma dang sangs sngags kyi tshul*) concerning the five exemplars of illusion (*pañca-māyā-upamā, sgyu ma'i dpe lnga*)
6. Conclusion, summing up the folly of philosophical certainty

Throughout, each philosophical framework, whether drawn from the Śravaka, Madhyamaka, or another, functions to let Rongzom explicate the primary theme of the chapter concerning the status of affliction—that is, there is no real entity constituting the bondage of affliction within saṃsāra. Thus, this chapter centers around the doctrine of the *kleśas*—"defilements," "afflictions," "afflictive states of mind," and so forth—which are said to disturb the minds of all sentient beings. More specifically, chapter 1 is titled "The Reality of Affliction." The term for *reality* is the Sanskrit *lakṣaṇa*, a polysemous term used broadly in South Asian and Tibetan religious discourse.[26] Afflictions (*kleśa, nyon mongs*) are themselves the subject of detailed examinations in Buddhist philosophy (*abhidharma*).[27] In the *Madhyāntavibhagakārikā*, one of the Five Works of Maitreya,[28] a text of critical importance for the Yogācāra text tradition, we find nine types of characteristics of affliction (*nyon mongs mtshan nyid rnam dgu*). Rongzom's phrase "the character/reality of afflictions" nicely intertwines three domains of discourse: ontology (what there is), epistemology (how we know what there is), and psychology (how we respond to what there is in mental and emotional terms). It is ontological and epistemological because this discourse concerns knowledge of reality (*mtshan nyid*) and phenomenal character (*mtshan nyid*) in combination with the psychological doctrine of affliction (*kleśa*) and the Yogācāra doctrine of the three natures (*trilakṣaṇa*). All three are themselves the subject of Buddhist epistemological logic (*pramāṇa, tshad ma*). This doctrinal amalgamation—ontology, epistemology, psychology—provides

Rongzom the rhetorical and conceptual ground for his unique discourse. A tantric element is suggested by Rongzom's insistence that all phenomena, whether afflicted or pure, are basically equal because they are illusory. Thus, while the doctrine of affliction is generally emphasized within Buddhist worldviews that entertain ontological binaries such as *pure* and *impure phenomena*, in *Entering the Way of the Great Vehicle*, the ontology of Buddhism's doctrine of affliction is given within the tantric context in epistemological terms.

Summary of Chapter 2

Chapter 2 of *Entering the Way of the Great Vehicle* is entitled "Objections and Replies." Its interrogation of reality constitutes a mostly rational argument against the distinction between real and imaginary phenomena posited in traditional epistemologies.[29] In a dialogical fashion that is well known in Buddhist discourses, this chapter treats particular philosophical issues connected with Rongzom's Mind-Only–inspired doctrine of appearance. The chapter begins by stipulating the truth of the illusory nature of appearance and questioning its rational implications. For Rongzom—and Buddhist philosophers generally—all phenomena are like an illusion, a mirage, a dream, a reflection, and an emanation; but this does not entail that the psychophysical aggregates constituting a person and, for example, a mirage, are utterly and in all ways the same. According to Rongzom, all ordinary appearances have sources. The force and duration of a given appearance, Rongzom writes, derives from the power of its source. That is, everything is illusory; but some illusions are more powerful and effective over the long term than others.

Rongzom's view of reasoning is useful to understand here. Reasoning, on his view, is, like appearance itself, naturally flawed but useful. This approach to the doctrine of the nature of appearance has implications for Rongzom's concept of buddhahood, which has been examined in detail by Orna Almogi (2009). Almogi has shown that Rongzom's conception of buddhahood, when drawn from literal and close readings of his texts, denies that buddhas have gnosis; and it maintains that buddhahood is simply the purified expanse of reality (*dharmadhātu, chos dbyings*).[30] In short, Rongzom's view gives rise to numerous conceptual tangles that Almogi unravels under three points; that is, if a buddha in fact has no gnosis that would (1) "devalue" teachings that state otherwise, such as those that refer to the

Buddha as "all-knowing," and so forth; if a buddha in fact has no gnosis that would (2) render moot "all efforts at gathering the immeasurable accumulations of beneficial resources and gnosis"; and if a buddha in fact has no gnosis that would (3) render the Great Vehicle conception of buddhahood the same as the Śrāvaka conception and thereby render the Great Vehicle a redundant and superfluous enterprise (Almogi 2009, 173). It is the second concern, in particular, that affords insight into chapter 2's agenda.

If buddhahood is simply purified reality devoid of gnosis, how, in the absence of any basis or substrate, could a buddha act benevolently in the world in accordance with the variety of intellectual capacities of sentient beings? Given Rongzom's apparent position on the subject—a buddha's gnosis is a mere appearance and not real—his use of the concept of gnosis is all the more remarkable. Yes, gnosis is simply one more appearance for sentient beings and thus, in Rongzom's view, is delusive. However, within the samsaric domain of unenlightened existence, it appears to sentient beings that buddhas are actually qualified by their gnosis—their own enlightened mind. This appearance, however, does not correspond to the true nature of enlightenment. For Rongzom, the very possibility of enlightenment is structured by the absence of any and all appearance. The difficulty of this philosophical position lies in accounting for the qualities of buddhahood that are espoused in the Great Vehicle, such as unimpeded compassionate salvific activity for the benefit of sentient beings, in the absence of any gnosis, which would function as a real basis or "substrate" for such activity. The example Rongzom turns to throughout the text to explain his position, particularly in chapter 2, is the figure of the sage (*ṛṣi*, *drang srong*), a holy being. According to Almogi, Rongzompa employs the figure of the sage to justify, or account for, a buddha's salvific activity that emanates for the benefit of others in the absence of any qualifying gnosis. Almogi (2009, 173–74) writes:

> [Some Buddhist philosophers] reject the need for a substratum, and employ the example of *ṛṣi* (that is, "sage"; *drang srong*), whose resolutions or aspirational wishes come about even after his death, without, that is, the need for the *ṛṣi* as a substratum that is endowed with capabilities, and even without any other substratum to which the capabilities have been transferred. In the same manner, [these Buddhist philosophers] argue, the qualities appear for the sake of disciples, even though no nonconceptual

> gnosis exists to serve as their substratum. The buddhas appear to be endowed with qualities, since compassion and resolutions have been previously respectively attained and made. They do acknowledge, however, the possibility that the qualities appear on account of the continuity of another substratum to which the capabilities have been transferred, such as in the case of a *ṛṣi* who leaves behind a wooden splint to which the power of the *garuḍa* mantra attained by him had been transferred, and which is thus endowed with the power to cure poisoning long after the *ṛṣi*'s death. In this case, the qualities can arise on account of their having been previously transferred to another substratum.

On this view, sentient beings and a buddha are basically equal in nature. All phenomena are empty, naturally beyond sorrow, and naturally luminous (*rang bzhin bsal ba*). All phenomena are perfectly awakened from the beginning (*yas nas sangs rgyas pa*), though sentient beings do not experience this because they do not have a view of equality that renders all phenomena basically the same because they are illusory appearances. The continuum of whoever realizes the object in this manner comes to consist in the purified *dharmadhātu* and is thus indistinguishable from a buddha.

Chapter 2 of *Entering the Way of the Great Vehicle* thus engages several philosophical issues. The chapter is organized around four issues implied by various views that are broadly connected within the generally accepted Buddhist axiom that all phenomena are "illusory," "like an illusion," or otherwise "illusion-like" (*māyopama*, *sgyu lta bu*). The chapter is technical and sophisticated, employing subtle philosophical logic, allegory, and striking metaphor, and makes several interesting and diverse references that range over topics such as

- Abhidharma ontology,
- a Hindu epic,[31]
- an allegory recalling a Greco-Roman myth,
- techniques of mirror divination associated with *Kālacakratantra*,
- the Buddhist doctrine of interdependence,
- the status of conventions,
- the origin of gnosis,
- cosmology, and
- epistemology (the basis of confusion and error).

Several rhetorical concerns mark this chapter. The primary theme around which objections and responses are raised is *nangwa*, or "appearance" (*pratibhā, snang ba*). The term is subtle and straddles the line between objective and subjective. In objective terms, it is rendered into English as "appearance" and refers to a percept that a conscious being may be aware of. In subjective terms, this word may also be rendered as "perception." While it is impossible to consistently render *nangwa* into English in a way that captures the very useful bivalence of the term, the reader of Rongzompa's text is edified by being aware of the ways in which the word can be used to play on both senses of this technical term.

In general, chapter 2 works to persuade the reader of the durable power and fundamental equality of the appearances we perceive. The discourse given in this context also accounts for the efficacy of a holy being's previous aspirations and how, through the force of his or her aspirations, a holy being may continue to emanate effects in the world, actions that can ripen and function in the distant future to profound effect even after the holy being has passed from this world. Appearances, though illusory, are effective. According to Rongzom's second chapter, the reality of a projected appearance correlates with the potency of its source. On Rongzom's view, since it is well known—read: accepted—that, for example, the aspiration of a great sage to work to benefit beings in the future will come to fruition even after that sage has passed from this world, there can be no doubt that the aspirations of enlightened beings, who are obviously superior to a sage, can exert profound effects on the world long after they are gone from it. To that rhetorical end, Rongzom's second chapter evokes examples from a variety of scenarios in which appearances vary in nature and potential. Rongzom argues that particular appearances, such as those that emanate in the world as the result of aspirations made by a holy being, work in the absence of any real substrate that might be asserted to be its basis or source at the time of the appearance. Such a view invokes Rongzom's sparse conception of enlightenment as the thoroughly purified dharmadhātu with no qualified gnosis involved. In short, buddhas have no "knowledge" or cognitive operations. Such phenomena are said to be totally precluded from the domain of enlightenment.[32] On this view, the positive qualities of a buddha are not connected with any nonconceptual gnosis qua basis or source. To persuade his readers of the sagacity of this point in chapter 2, Rongzom describes the aspirations of a sage that may manifest and function even after the sage has passed from this world.

In the chapter's concluding remarks, Rongzom invokes a triad of subjectivity he terms the "three aggregates" of mind (*vijñāna, sems*), intellect (*buddhi, blo*), and cognition (*vijñapti, rnam par rig pa*). He discusses the dreamlike unreality of the phenomena operating within "time" and "space." These two cognitive dimensions are both correlated with the confusion wrought by ordinary appearances that distinguishes a sentient being from a buddha. Here, *Entering the Way of the Great Vehicle* also provides its first reference to its most-cited text: *Bodhicittabhāvanā* (*Meditation on Bodhicitta*), which is attributed to Mañjuśrīmitra, an important figure in the transmission of the Old School's Great Perfection tradition.[33] In addition, except for the fifth chapter of *Entering the Way of the Great Vehicle*, which treats the Great Perfection, chapter 2 contains the greatest number of citations from other works overall.

Summary of Chapter 3

Chapter 3 of *Entering the Way of the Great Vehicle*, entitled "Distinguishing the Perfected System of Illusion in the Great Perfection from the Other Vehicles That Retain the Nomenclature of Illusion," aims to carve out a particular rhetorical and tropical niche for discourse on the Great Perfection, one that distinguishes it from other Buddhist philosophies, all of which discuss the nature of illusion. Chapter 3 is organized around three main philosophical issues, with a fourth and final section discussing the nature of the Great Perfection. In the first of the three philosophical issues, *Entering the Way of the Great Vehicle* treats the epistemological status of appearance and confusion. That is, after Rongzom argues in previous chapters for the fundamental equality of illusions, emanations, and the like, the first question he asks himself through the interlocutor in chapter 3 is whether or not these illusions are in fact phenomenologically significant objects—that is, are they objects observed by the mind (*dmigs pa*). This leads to a discussion, known in the Old School tradition as Rongzom's "Black Snake Discourse," of the nature of the Buddhist doctrine of the two truths. This passage contains a striking comparison of the different degrees of fixation on appearance that occur, according to Rongzom, in connection with various theoretical approaches to the spiritual path. That is, according to the "Black Snake Discourse," one's perception of reality or unreality is largely structured by the philosophical view to which one adheres. One's philosophical stance determines the degree of reality one attributes to whatever appears within one's experience.

While comparisons between different views are often given in Buddhist treatises in terms of their view of ultimate reality or their view of valid conventional phenomena, the basis of comparison that Rongzom uses is a false appearance—and not simply a false appearance but the appearance of a false image. The example Rongzompa gives is, of course, "the appearance of a black snake's image in water." Rongzom's purpose in using this example is to show how the minds of people who adhere to different doctrinal orientations to the path experience and act on a different realization of the two truths. By means of this example, Rongzompa is also suggesting just how the teaching of the illusory is effectively different from system to system. By "distinguishing between the varying degrees of fixation on appearance" (*dngos por zhen pa che chung gi bye brag*) that accompany a given philosophical stance, Rongzom interrogates the hierarchy of views (*lta ba mthon dman*, literally "higher and lower views"), each of which traditionally purport to be the *only* view to clearly elucidate and evince the path.

In the second issue of chapter 3, Rongzom interrogates the nature and scope of logical reasoning, affirmation, and negation. This discussion is the longest in the chapter. It contains a discussion of the basis of various theoretical views found among non-Buddhists and in Śrāvaka, Yogācāra, Madhyamaka, and Guhyamantra, and within the Great Perfection. The section also outlines the biases that broadly structure the philosophical enterprise, generally; and it offers a rather visceral metaphor for dangers involved in insisting upon philosophical precision.

A third philosophical issue explored in chapter 3 of *Entering the Way of the Great Vehicle* is the nature of imputation, conceptuality, appearance, and the teaching of the two truths. There is also a fourth section of the chapter, which has two parts. The first is itself a cursory explanation of the distinctions between different approaches to the path. That is followed by a presentation of the status of Great Perfection as a broadly conceived concept that subsumes several important technical Buddhist rubrics. Great Perfection, according to Rongzom, is many things: a vehicle (*yāna, theg pa*), a transmission (*āgama, lung*), a discourse (*pravacana, gsung rab*), the deepest intention lying behind tantric discourse (*abhiprāya, dgongs gzhi*), and the core of all esoteric precepts (*upadeśa, man ngag*). This passage, in particular, encourages the view that, for Rongzom, Great Perfection is not, strictly speaking, a traditional Buddhist system that may be set over and against other systems.

Turning to the specific issues and themes that animate the chapter, we find four sections in chapter 3, given as follows:

- Introduction: The Great Perfection approach to the path
- Issue 1: The epistemological status of appearances
- Issue 2: The scope of logic and reasoning and the character of philosophy in the systems of non-Buddhists, Śrāvakas, Yogācāra, Madhyamaka, and Guhyamantra
- Issue 3: The nature and scope of imputation, conceptuality, and the two truths
- Section 4: Distinguishing the limitations and potential of various approaches to the Buddhist path—Śrāvaka, and so on—and explicating the status of Great Perfection within the broader structure of Buddhist teachings

At the close of chapter 2, there is discussion of the "reversal," "collapse," or "overcoming" (√*log*) of fixation on appearance. Summing up there, Rongzom writes:

> There is no real entity whatsoever to be eliminated outside of what is simply labeled by the term *thoroughly afflicted*. There is no real entity to be established outside of what is simply labeled by the term *utterly pure*. Nevertheless, when [the illusory nature of phenomena is] not recognized, the process of confused appearance nevertheless pertains accordingly to appearance alone.[34]

Rongzom ends chapter 2 by discussing the intimate relationship obtaining between confusion and appearance for those whose understanding of reality is based upon anything other than the fundamentally illusory nature of phenomena. With that issue in mind, chapter 3 begins. The opening of chapter 3 connects the view of equality (*samatā, mnyam pa nyid*)—an important thesis for the Great Vehicle proponents of emptiness (*śūnyatāvāda, stong nyid smra ba*),[35] the Yogācāra especially—to the Great Perfection. As mentioned above, the Great Vehicle approach to the path, Rongzom writes, is truly revealed through recognizing the fundamental equality of all phenomena, which is shown by their illusory nature. Penetrating the illusory nature of reality is the doorway to the Great Vehicle's path to total buddhahood, which is perfected through "the authentic assimilation and consummation" (*rtogs pa tshad du chud cing mthar phyin pa*) or perfection of that primary recognition.

Typically, the doorway to the Great Vehicle of the Mahāyāna is described in the context of the bodhisattva path to buddhahood, which is broadly characterized by a radical form of compassion called *bodhicitta*. To be sure, the view of equality described here suggests a compassionate stance. Rongzom's description, however, is totally organized around the view of equality, which is attained through perfectly assimilating one's realization of the illusory nature of phenomena. In this way, Rongzom situates the Great Perfection as the consummation of the basic Great Vehicle path, its natural outcome.

Summary of Chapter 4

Chapter 4 of *Entering the Way of the Great Vehicle* is entitled "The Great Perfection Approach Is Not Undermined by Reason." This statement should not be understood as a truth statement about reality. In fact, at the outset of chapter 4, Rongzom admits (albeit tacitly) that Great Perfection is illogical. Nevertheless, the chapter tries to persuade its readership that the way of Great Perfection is not undermined by logical reasoning. It cannot be, because the rationalist project cannot by definition encompass the Great Perfection. It is, in fact, smaller in scope than Great Perfection. In this chapter, we encounter a powerful survey of the predicative nature of language, grammar, and concepts, which functions as a broader critique of the Buddhist premium on rational soteriology, one that sets limits on the efficacy of logic in the context of the path.

The opening of this chapter contains a remarkable passage in which Rongzom states unequivocally that the Great Perfection can be penetrated through faith alone.[36] Yet, he continues, people who are "obsessed with the logical and grammatical treatises" have advocated the rejection of the Great Perfection on the basis that it is irrational (*rigs pa dang 'gal*). Notably, Rongzom does not deny this charge. As our author has argued, any effort at forging a conceptual framework is by definition based in biases—that is, structured by attitudes of acceptance and rejection—and therefore cannot perfect the realization of the illusory nature of phenomena. Great Perfection is not ratiocinative in nature. Logic and grammar are anchored in bias. Thus, in a move analogous to Nāgārjuna's famous claim, in a dispute among proponents of different views, to be faultless by virtue of professing no view,[37] Rongzom claims, at a time of disputes among proponents of rationalist doctrines, that Great Perfection is faultless by virtue of not being a domain of experience connected with the efforts of intellectual inquiry. Just as Nāgārjuna's "middle way" is understood as the perfection of view itself—that is, the pure view—Rongzom's Great Perfection is the perfection of the path—that is, enlightenment. The end. Thus, in a move not unlike one made by Wittgenstein, who rejected the notion of philosophy as a cognitive discipline as nonsense,[38] Rongzom rejects the notion that Buddhist enlightenment is cognitive in nature—that it consists in, or emerges (in the end) from *getting better at "knowing."* Knowing is about discriminating "this" from "that." Enlightenment is facilitated and structured by the absence of that type of possibility for discrimination. The idea that enlightenment is, strictly speaking, rationally construed is conceptually analogous to the idea that "the pain I'm having right now does not hurt,"[39] which would be, obviously, nonsense. The point is that becoming a buddha is not an act or activity or transformation of the ordinary thematic mind (*citta*, *sems*). In buddhahood, the ordinary mind is not transformed into something it is not. The conditions for its possibility are dissolved. The state of enlightenment is not the jurisdiction of the intellect. Buddhahood it is not a cognitive act. People with simple faith may penetrate Great Perfection through their faith alone. The opening of chapter 4 reads:

> When this Great Perfection approach to the path is taught in a condensed manner, it is said that the bases of all phenomena are included simply within mind and mental appearance; the nature of the mind (*citta*) itself is awakening (*bodhi*) and thus referred to as *the mind of awakening* (*bodhicitta*). There is nothing to be taught other than this. People with faith in the Great Perfection approach realize and penetrate it through being shown this alone. People who are obsessed with treatises on grammar and logic have abandoned the Great Perfection approach to the path, which is like a wish-fulfilling jewel. They are fixated on various trinket-like philosophical tenets and tend to think: "These philosophical tenets of ours are established through grammatical points and reason. The Great Perfection approach to the path is in conflict with reason; and that which is in conflict with reason ought not to be accepted."[40]

What faith alone means in this context is not clear. Perhaps it refers to faith in the teacher or teaching such that uncritical acceptance characterizes the disciples' attitude toward religious instruction. Faith may in this case refer to a stance that is simply opposed to one constructed philosophically. Being faithful may also be about relationships with teachers, deities, a particular ritual cultus, and so forth, thus invoking a type of Gadamerian openness, a *being-susceptible-to*. In any case, on Rongzompa's view, those who superordinate a soteriology emphasizing linguistic and logical precision in discourse on the path are not unlike to those who would treasure costume jewelry over a wish-fulfilling gem: while the former looks nice—shiny, sparkly, lots of bling to attract the eyes of the unsophisticated—it is, relatively speaking, ineffective, of little worth, and given simply for show. This approach to the path is, according to Rongzom, missing the soteriological forest for the ideological trees.

Who are these people, mentioned by Rongzompa, who are obsessed with *treatises on logic* (*yuktiśāstra, rigs pa'i bstan chos*) and *treatises on grammar* (*śabdaśāstra, sgra'i bstan chos*) and what do these terms refer to? In general, both terms are used to refer to the epistemological discourse connected with the tradition founded by Dignāga (fifth to sixth century) and Dharmakīrti (sixth to seventh century).[41] Further, it appears that Rongzom uses the term *yuktiśāstra* to refer to canonical texts that employ the so-called four principles of reasoning (*yukti catuṣṭuyam, rigs pa rnam pa bzhi*), such as *Saṁdhinirmocanasūtra*, *Śrāvakabhūmi*, *Abhidharmasamuccaya*, and *Mahāyānasūtrālaṃkāra*. The term *śabdaśāstra* reminds us of the well-known term *śabdavidyā*, which names one of the five Indian Buddhist sciences or domains of knowledge (*pañcāvidyāsthāna, rigs gnas lnga*), the locus classicus of which is given in the sixtieth verse of the eleventh chapter of the *Mahāyānasūtrālaṃkāra*.[42] *Śabdavidyā*, according to van der Kuijp (1994, 393), "not only [references] (Sanskrit) grammar, but also its ancillary sciences of poetics, prosody, lexicography and dramaturgy." This term is commonly used to describe Thonmi Saṁbhoṭa's eight grammatical treatises. It is also used to describe exegetical texts that are considered authoritative or valid (*pramāṇa, tshad ma*) and that emphasize accounts of the world given in terms of agent (*kartṛ, byed pa po*), activity (*kriya, bya ba*), and instrument (*karaṇa, byed pa*).[43]

In the context of the present chapter, however, it appears that Rongzompa uses the term *śabdaśāstra* most specifically to refer to the tradition of logical epistemology (*pramāṇa, tshad ma*) of Dignāga and Dharmakīrti. It would seem that strict adherents to this tradition rejected Great Perfection on the grounds that it is irrational. Based on the opening of this chapter, this group of "logicians" appears to be one audience of *Entering the Way of the*

Great Vehicle's fourth chapter. Rongzompa states from the outset that his chapter sets aside the rhetoric of Great Perfection and its unique technical terminology in order to survey some of the logical approaches to the path. One reason for this rhetorical strategy might be that this comparison will be taken more seriously if given in the idiom of Indian Buddhist logicians; alternatively, the chapter may be seen as a primer on the logical methods of the proponents of the pramāṇa system. In any case, Rongzom states:

> For the benefit of such people, here I will set aside the idiom renowned in the Great Perfection approach to the path, which uses such terms as *sphere* (*bindu*, *thig le*), and *greatness* (*che ba*). Instead, I explain some facets of the system of logic using a more broadly accepted nomenclature.[44]

The opening passage's juxtaposition of faith and the condensed teaching of the Great Perfection on the one side, and the rejection of Great Perfection as irrational on the other, is remarkable. The condensed teaching of Great Perfection consists of two parts. The first is the statement that all things in our experience participate in the mental. This is Rongzom's Mind-Only–oriented framework. The second is an explanation of the term *bodhi-citta* as "ordinary thematic mind (*citta*) is itself awakening (*bodhi*)."[45]

At face value, such a statement seems to collapse the basic Buddhist distinction between sentient beings and buddhas; below, Rongzom will explore whether or not this move is palatable to Great Vehicle logicians for whom the premium is on a logically coherent description of the path. Resolution of this apparent conflict is found in Dharmakīrti's ideas concerning subject and predication. No chapter in Rongzom's *Entering the Way of the Great Vehicle* is particularly easy to read, but chapter 4 is Rongzom at his most detailed and difficult; it introduces or extends the following topics:

- unity and identity
- the relationship between *bodhi* and *sattva*
- the structure of existential and predicative statements
- implicative and nonimplicative negation
- holistic and atomizing types of cognitive awareness
- the nature of verbal signification
- the nature of ontological and epistemological distinction
- the nature-and-distinction model itself

- consolidation versus preclusion as criteria for logical proofs
- the four logical procedures proving sameness and difference
- the nature of ideas or conceptual generalities (*samanya*, *spyi*)

Summary of Chapter 5

The fifth chapter of Rongzompa's *Entering the Way of the Great Vehicle*, entitled "Writings on Great Perfection," is the longest and most esoteric in the text. It is explicitly dedicated to an exploration of early writings on the Great Perfection. As such, it is, among other things, a window into the intellectual history of Great Perfection as it develops into a systematic tradition that culminates in the fourteenth-century work of Longchenpa.

Chapter 5 is organized by the author into three sections: (1) the fourfold rubric of Great Perfection teachings, (2) the textual tradition of the Great Perfection, (3) and methods for settling bodhicitta. Section 1 concerns the nature (*rang bzhin*), greatness (*che ba*), twenty-three points of deviation and seven types of obscuration (*gol sgrib*), and methods for consolidating bodhicitta. Additionally, six great spheres (*thig le chen po drug*) are treated; and there are sections on three types of predication, three types of certainty/confidence/assurances (*gding*), three fundamental roots of intimate advice or esoteric precepts (*upadeśa*, *man ngag*), textual sources for the teaching, impediments to concentration, mastery of bodhicitta, signs of "warmth," and the qualities of bodhicitta.

The first is a very short section outlining a fourfold rubric for Great Perfection discourse organized around the concept of bodhicitta. Rongzompa states that this fourfold rubric is his own; and the chapter opens by framing itself in terms of his fourfold interpretive scheme in the following manner:

> Here, we should disclose something of the actual writings (*gzhung nyid*) of the Great Perfection. Any and every writing that discloses the system of the Great Perfection is included in four types of teaching. That is, writings on Great Perfection teach (i) the nature of bodhicitta, (ii) the greatness of bodhicitta, (iii) deviations and obscurations connected with bodhicitta, and (iv) methods for "settling" or "consolidating" (*gzhag thabs*) bodhicitta. Teachings on the deviations and obscurations, in fact, become teachings on the nature of bodhicitta. In the teaching on [its] nature, greatness is penetrated and devi-

> ation and obscuration are eliminated. Therefore, even though there is no such fourfold organizing rubric in writings on Great Perfection as such, [the discourse in the writings] does not go beyond it.[46]

The second and third sections are roughly the same length as the first. The second section, on the writings of Great Perfection, is organized around Rongzompa's treatment of twelve tropes, or statements, common in the writings of Great Perfection. The twelve tropes are as follows:

1. All phenomena are considered awakened in the intrinsic nature of bodhicitta.
2. All confusing appearances are to be considered the play of Samantabhadra.
3. All sentient beings are considered as the profound field of awakening (*zab mob byang chub kyi zhing*).
4. All domains of experience are considered to be naturally arising gnosis (*rang byung gi ye shes*).
5. All phenomena are considered to be naturally perfected as the five types of greatness (*che ba lnga*).
6. All phenomena are enumerated in terms of being considered to be naturally awakened as the six great spheres (*thig le drug*).
7. The thirty deviations and obscurations (*gol sgrib gsum bcu*).
8. Removing the hindrance of doubt via the three types of being (*yin pa gsum*).
9. Determining the final view (*dgongs pa'i rting gcad*).
10. Comprehending the basis of esoteric precepts/intimate advice (*upadeśa, man ngag*).
11. Resolving all knowables by means of bodhicitta within a single great sphere (*bindu, thig le*).
12. Resolving how the ground of the indivisible Samantabhadra is disclosed spontaneously without effort in the present state because of the greatness that constitutes the fact that everything, everywhere, is at all times already perfect (*yas nas sangs rgyas pa*).

A large portion of this section is also devoted to a survey and treatment of the points of deviation from, and obscurations to, the view of equality. These deviations and obscurations are said to hinder an individual in penetrating the view of equality at the heart of Great Perfection's reading of the Buddhist doctrine of illusory appearance.

In the third section of chapter 5, on "settling" or "consolidating" bodhicitta (*byang sems gzhag thabs*), we find a discussion of meditation and the relation between mindfulness and equanimity in the system of Great Perfection as well as in the writings that explicate them, and we find discussion of the critical impediments to concentration and the mastery of bodhicitta.

In the time I spent translating *Entering the Way of the Great Vehicle*, I had an opportunity to work with several scholars and teachers from the Old School tradition of Tibetan Buddhism. In each and every case, when turning to chapter 5 of Rongzompa's text, these scholars and masters of Tibetan Buddhism strongly intimated that chapter 5 was so laden with deep significances embedded within esoteric symbolic associations that a detailed description of it should be left to traditional scholars to explain within the traditional context. This may indeed be the case in some sections of the chapter, particularly with respect to its treatment of particular elements of the Sanskrit language, which I do not fully understand. That said, what should be stressed about chapter 5 and the system of Great Perfection it articulates can be summed up in two words: Mind Series (*sems sde*). In fact, if one were to sum up Rongzompa's presentation of Great Perfection in one phrase, it would be Mind Series. But what does that mean? According to David Germano, the Mind Series genre represents the most diverse "literary canon" of the Great Perfection's seven traditions. The Mind Series, he writes, is

> a very loose rubric covering the majority of developments prior to the eleventh century, and their subsequent continuance by conservative authors. The texts that fall under this sub-rubric were thus authored over a lengthy time period, and are bound together (taking for granted the characteristic Great Perfection motifs and terminology) primarily by a common rejection of practice of any type, as well as by their rejection of funerary Buddhism. (Germano 2005, 10)

The Mind Series is one of three "divisions," "trends" or "genres"—along with the Space Series (*klong sde*) and Intimate Instruction or Esoteric Precept Series (*man ngag sde*)—traditionally structuring the discourse on Great Perfection. It is often said that all Great Perfection tantras can be subsumed under one of the three divisions. Tradition often traces this threefold rubric to the Indian figure Mañjuśrīmitra; among academics, however, there is also the view that the division originates with the work of the Zur clan (Kapstein 2009).

In the broadest terms, the Mind Series is described as Great Perfection literature that emphasizes "the immediate presence of the enlightened mind, and the consequent uselessness of any practice that is aimed at creating, cultivating or uncovering the enlightened state" (van Schaik 2004, 165). Set in contrast to the other two divisions of Great Perfection tantras, the Mind Series literature "emphasizes luminosity of the basic mind (*rig pa*) in its natural state" thus emphasizing a positive subject, gnosis, while the Space Series "emphasizes the expansive or spacious mind in its natural state" otherwise known as the negative phenomena called emptiness (*śūnyatā, stong nyid*); and the Intimate Instruction Series "emphasizes the indivisibility of the two" (Buswell and Lopez 2013, s.v. "klong sde"). The renowned Old School luminary, Longchenpa (1308–1364), describes the Mind Series as a teaching on the primacy of the mind that "is for preventing the mind from being distracted from" naturally arising gnosis; the Space Series as a teaching focusing on, and preventing distraction from, "the expanse of Samantabhadrī, the ultimate nature" (*dharmatā, chos nyid*); and the Intimate Instruction Series as a teaching for "ascertaining the crucial point of the nature of what it is" (Tulku Thondup 1989, 43–44).

According to Sam van Schaik (2004, 185), Mind Series literature is "on the nature of mind, identifying it with wisdom, and referring to this as bodhicitta." Rongzom's Mind Series–based presentation of Great Perfection, put succinctly, states that "the nature of the ordinary mind (*citta, sems*) is awakening (*bodhi, byang chub*) and thus it is called 'the mind of awakening' (*bodhicitta, byang chub kyi sems*)." Questions about why Rongzompa's presentation emphasizes the Mind Series and makes no mention of tantras from either the Space Series or the Intimate Instruction Series must be answered elsewhere.[47] My summary of chapter 5 concludes here with an outline of the specific categories treated in chapter 5, given in the order of treatment:

- the nature of bodhicitta
- the greatness of bodhicitta
- deviations and obscurations
- methods for settling bodhicitta

- from the writings of Great Perfection
  - twelve Great Perfection tropes or rubrics
  - phenomena seen to be perfected within the single sphere of bodhicitta
  - confused appearances seen as the play of Samantabhadra
  - sentient beings seen as the profound field of awakening
  - all domains of experience seen as naturally occurring self-appearing gnosis
  - phenomena seen as perfected within the nature of the five types of greatness
  - the six great spheres (*thig le*)
  - the elimination of deviations and obscurations by means of the thirty deviations and obscurations
    - Worldly
    - Śrāvaka
    - Pratyekabuddha
    - Prajñāpāramitā
    - Kriya tantra (the general approach of tantra)
      - The suchness of the self
      - The suchness of the deity
      - The suchness of the recitation
    - Ubhaya tantra
    - Yoga tantra
    - Mahāyoga tantra
    - Anuyoga tantra
    - Atiyoga tantra
  - twenty-three points of deviation
    - the seven obscurations
    - three deviations from the essence of awakening
    - three deviations from concentration
    - three deviations associated with causality
    - four deviations from the path of actual reality
  - the seven obscurations
  - the three beings
  - the three great certainties or assurances
  - the three fundamental esoteric precepts
  - resolution through bodhicitta
  - what is resolved in Great Perfection

    - the disclosure of methods for consolidating bodhicitta
    - disclosing those points through scriptural sources
- on critical impediments to concentration
- criteria for the attainment of mastery over the ordinary mind
- on the signs of warmth
- on the qualities of bodhicitta

Summary of Chapter 6

The full title of the sixth and final chapter of *Entering the Way of the Great Vehicle* has a polemical edge to it. It reads: "Instructions on Paths Encountered through Methods Connected with Effort for Those Who Are Unable to Remain Effortlessly within the Natural State according to the Great Perfection Approach." Here, Rongzompa offers an essay, for the most part descriptive in nature, on methodical approaches to the Buddhist path that are associated with effort. A primary theme of the Great Perfection is the natural and effortless state. This is typically contrasted with "lower paths" that require effort—anathema in the Great Perfection—such as the effort to generate wisdom that is espoused in the Perfection of Wisdom (*prajñāpāramitā*) textual tradition. The chapter title suggests that there are alternative approaches to the Buddhist path for those of us unable to ascend to the zenith of Great Perfection without help. Chapter 6 has eight sections:

1. Methods for improving the mind in the system of the *pāramitās* or Guhyamantra as doors to Great Perfection
2. Six faults connected to concentration or meditative absorption (*bsam gtan*)
3. Conceptuality (*kalpanā*, *rtog pa*)
4. Nine obscurations associated with the path
5. The eightfold concentration that eliminates the five faults
6. Six-limbed yoga
7. Five signs of stability
8. After attaining signs of mental stability

A ninth section may be added corresponding to the verses of poetry that close *Entering the Way of the Great Vehicle*. Within these explicitly stated subjects, chapter 6 discusses several topics:

- deity yoga
- the basis-of-all (*kun gzhi*)
- *śamatha* and *vipaśyanā*
- spiritual corruption
- cognitive confusion
- intellectual grasping
- the nature of the breath
- the emanation and absorption of lights
- the nature and types of deities

The treatment of these categories, including deity yoga, is respectful in tone. For example, Rongzom states that being contemptuous of other theories creates obstacles on the path. The chapter reads like a primer on exoteric and esoteric methods of Buddhist meditation. If I were to sum up the chapter in just a few words, I would say this: for those of us unable to simply rest in an unfabricated state because of our want of discrimination and so on, Rongzom describes a group of practices in sympathetic turns and exhorts the practitioners to connect these practices to the view of equality valorized in Great Perfection. If so, then that practice, for example, deity yoga, becomes qualified by skill in method and therefore a doorway leading to Great Perfection. The chapter opens with the following statement:

> Now, I am going to explain the cultivation of paths that employ effort for those unable to remain in the natural state as it is given in the Great Perfection, because [these paths] should be embraced via the view of the Great Perfection since the great bliss of bodhicitta is the fundamental dharma that works to alleviate all the maladies connected to the bondage of conditioned existence. As it is stated in *Meditation on Bodhicitta*:
>
> > Any virtuous dharma possible that is not encompassed by Samantabhadrī—
> > Even the practice of Samantabhadra—is the work of Māra, and thus it will eventually diminish;
> > They are indeed the work of Māra, though proclaimed to be the practice of a bodhisattva.
>
> Even methods to improve the mind in the Pāramitā and Guhyamantra vehicles appear as many doors to the path. In these cases,

> a "path to liberation" emerges that is a meditative absorption (*dhyāna, bsam gtan*) consisting in the elimination of the five faults and the removal of the ten obscurations. There is also a "path to liberation" constituted by concentration (*samādhi, ting nge 'dzin*) that is qualified by the eight applications that eliminate the five faults (*pañcadoṣā, nges pa lnga*) to śamatha. There is also a "path to liberation" constituted by the concentration that overcomes grasping, imagination, negation, and differentiation with respect to the psychophysical aggregates (*skandha, phung po*), constituents (*dhātu, khams*), and bases (*āyatanam, skye mched*). There is also a "path to liberation" that emerges in terms of the six qualities of disciplined recitations and concentrations for the mind that is naturally difficult to tame. There is also a "path to liberation" that emerges in terms of concentration that takes mind, body, and deity as an objective support. While there are many methods such as these that are taught for improving the mind, all of them cannot be fully explained here—they are explained only in part.

Thus, from the onset, in chapter 6, the shortest in the text (50 percent shorter than the next-shortest chapter), Rongzompa's agenda is clear. Chapter 6, among other things, is a primer for various practices given in the context of the Great Perfection as a strategy for interpreting those practices. The chapter is remarkable not only for its pithy descriptions of well-known Buddhist rubrics, some particularly connected with the New schools, but also for its striking comparisons and references to, inter alia, animals. In chapter 6, Rongzom makes the following comparisons:

- The confused mind is like a bird at night: hidden.[48]
- Beings fixated on a state of concentration are not unlike a baby sparrow who remains in the nest, unwilling to move onto a path of maturity.
- On the path of Great Perfection, goal and effort are lost, not unlike an arrow that has disappeared into its target.
- The desire to attain supernatural powers along the path is not unlike a farmer who, in his desire for pure butter and from his reliance upon dairy cows, becomes fond of milk and yogurt and therefore never actually tastes real butter.

- Thinking one has become deeply profound, taking pride in one's spiritual accomplishment, and denigrating other theories is not unlike the spoiled children of a king or minister who do not apply their minds to the advice of holy beings.
- A person who fixates on the psychophysical aggregates is not unlike a greedy monkey.
- The designation of conventions is not unlike a thieving cat.
- The psychophysical aggregates are not unlike an empty house. When the senses are disciplined, it is not unlike the cracks, crevices, and windows of that house being closed.
- The mind-basis-of-all is not unlike a source of medicine inside a pot of poison, gold obscured by turquoise, and a precious jewel concealed in mire.
- The ordinary mind is not unlike a monkey that does not engage in its own affairs but gets involved in what are not its affairs.
- The ordinary mind is not unlike the waves in the great ocean.
- The ordinary mind is not unlike a trickster (*sgyu can*).
- A person who tends to his or her spiritual business is not like a monkey.

These analogies are unique and striking. In sum, chapter 6 confirms Rongzom's inclusivist approach to Buddhist philosophy and argues that the lower practices and theories that require effort on the part of trainees may in fact be recognized as doors to the Great Perfection. Such a view makes sense in the context of Rongzompa's metaphor of the path in which all the different spiritual paths ultimately empty themselves into the ocean of the Great Perfection.

On the English Translation

Rongzompa's text, it should be said, is not written for beginners. Commentarial and interpretive Buddhist treatises (*śāstra*) such as *Entering the Way of the Great Vehicle* are works often written by, and for, an educated audience of elites. Although the title, *Entering the Way of the Great Vehicle*, might connote an introductory subject, this work presumes a great degree of knowledge on the part of the reader concerning the Buddhist (and, occasionally, non-Buddhist) doctrines and philosophies. The Tibetan prose is often arcane. The grammar and syntax are often complex, sometimes containing metaphor and wordplay that are not easily translatable. For example, the Tibetan term I have rendered throughout as "appearance," *nangwa* (*pratibhā, snang ba*), has a subjective and objective bivalence that is impossible to bring out if the translation is to be consistent. In the subjective context, *nangwa* means *perception*; in the objective context, it means *appearance*. Mindful readers might benefit from keeping both valences in mind.

My intention in translation is to provide readers an accurate *and* readable English-language text. To that end, I have sometimes rendered active-voice sentences in the passive voice (or vise versa), and I have often split up long, unwieldy sentences into smaller practicable ones. In all cases, I have endeavored to retain the sophisticated tone and character of Rongzompa's composition, while striving to avoid the use of any unnatural "hybrid English."

The Commentarial Treatise Entitled *Entering the Way of the Great Vehicle*

Rongzom Chökyi Zangpo

1. The Reality of Affliction

I AM GOING to explain a little bit about entering the way of the Great Vehicle (*mahāyāna*). First and foremost, it makes sense for those who wish to be freed from the ocean of saṃsāra and accomplish unsurpassable awakening to scrutinize the character of the afflictions. This is because it is well known from the general teachings of the Buddha that beings bound by affliction (*kleśa*, *nyon mongs*) are adrift on the ocean of saṃsāra. After that, it makes sense to seek out the superior path, which is an antidote, and act to cultivate it. This is because without a thorough understanding of afflictions, they cannot be eliminated. If they are not thoroughly understood, there can be no recognition of the method that ought to be cultivated—and therefore no opportunity for obtaining liberation will be found.

It is because of these points alone that everything knowable is understood because the recognition of the nature of mind just as it is, the circumstance of the confused mind, and the circumstance of the unconfused mind includes everything knowable. Thus, there would be no generation of an incomplete entry into a state of spiritual freedom like the awakening of the Śrāvaka and Pratyekabuddha. To that point, I will explain the investigation into the character of the afflictions.

Here, it may be asked if the character of so-called affliction is actually a real entity (*dravya*, *rdzas*) binding sentient beings within saṃsāra. If not, is it the case that the affliction to be gotten rid of on the path is not a real entity and beings yet appear as if bound by it?

We recognize that the afflictions that are to be eliminated are not real entities.

The Śrāvaka System

According to the Śrāvaka system, one is said to have attained *the fruit of an arhat* once one has rid oneself of the whole of the three realms' afflictions by means of the paths of seeing and meditation, having thereby severed all the fetters of conditioned existence. Given the fact that arhats eliminate afflictions, when we analyze the statement that there are a variety of types of afflictions to be eliminated, we may ask how it is the case that no real entity of affliction is found upon examination. For the moment, should we assume that, apart from the afflictions that are eliminated through seeing the truth of suffering, the afflictions eliminated through seeing the truth of suffering's origin, and so on, pertain to a single real entity of affliction? On the other hand, if we examine the statement that afflictions are present as different and specific real entities, then, in that case, *everything* would be eliminated simply through seeing the truth of suffering. In that case, meditation on another path would be rendered pointless.

What if, on the other hand, one were to say afflictions are present as different, specific entities? In that case, since everything knowable, when summarized, is nothing other than what is divided into the aspects of the four truths, the number of afflictions to be eliminated would unquestionably be multiplied by four through the force of being the perceptual basis qua object for the four truths. In that case, there could be no decisive reckoning of the divisions of what is knowable. Accordingly, the truth of suffering—recognized in terms of the four aspects of the first noble truth—impermanence, dissatisfaction, the empty, and the selfless—pertaining as it does to a *receptiveness that recognizes* [or *is able to endure* penetrating the truth of] the attributes of suffering,[1] would thus, through the force of that assertion, entail that seeing the truth of suffering would multiply each of the afflictions to be eliminated by four.

If someone suggests that these multiple afflictions are identical to the character of suffering and thus would not be multiplied, then true origins would not be anything beyond true sufferings since all karmic processes (*saṃskāra*, *'du byed*) are characteristic of suffering; and anything qualified as a sensation is explained by superiors as suffering. This is not unlike the theory held by non-Buddhist extremists who postulate a creator as a cause wherein the effect is not contingent upon a cause. Given the activity of the eternal cause as such, it is like saying that an effect is indeed not manufactured by a function.

This is unlike the view postulated by Buddhists for whom phenomena emerge on the basis of relations in which, in fact, the cause is contingent upon the effect and where the effect, too, is contingent upon the cause. Thus, through a process of karmic maturation, the state of the five acquired psychophysical aggregates constitutes burden-like embodiment that is not unlike an injury that, given the fact it is characterized by suffering, occasions the manifestation of suffering in the future. That state is thus a characteristic of a true origin of suffering. Thus, with the five psychophysical aggregates as an objective basis, realizing the selflessness of phenomena will, without doubt, rid one of all afflictions. Further, everyone who makes distinctions beyond count of what is knowable will undoubtedly eliminate all afflictions when they have produced the realization of the selflessness of all phenomena.

In one sense, if a person's father is killed by a piece of wood, the person might generate hatred toward that piece of wood. If the person generates hatred toward that piece of wood, then afterward, if the person feels hatred for a second or third piece of wood [because they remind him or her of the wood that killed his or her father], would those [additional] instances of hatred all comprise one single entity of hatred? Or would it be the case that each instance of hatred for each specific stick is a distinct entity of hatred? If those instances of hatred comprise a single entity of hatred, then inasmuch as the piece of wood were burned to ashes, it would seem reasonable that all instances of like hatred would be correspondingly eliminated—but that is not the case. If the instances of hatred are specifically distinct, an enumeration of them could not be reckoned even by the end of an aeon; and to the degree that those instances of hatred are eliminable, each instant eliminating each instance of hatred would not in fact achieve an exhaustive end.

If numerous afflictions were able to be eliminated through a single path, then meditation upon a variety of paths would be rendered pointless. If a single affliction were able to be eliminated by means of numerous paths, then the Buddha's teaching of a variety of afflictions would also be rendered pointless. If it were the case that various paths could not weaken afflictions even a little, many paths would also not eliminate them. If they did, it would not be the case that afflictions pertain to one single entity. If that were so, there would be no decisive reckoning of entities in regard to affliction. Thus, according to the Śrāvaka system, there is no real entity given in connection with afflictions.[2]

Nevertheless, when we describe how it is that arhats have eliminated affliction, it is said that arhats realize the selflessness of persons. Because of that, the delusive view of the transitory collection is pacified and the magical projection of all affliction simply abates automatically. However, when the view of the transitory collection is encompassed by aspiring bodhicitta, it is transformed into an illimitable collection of merit. When it is conjoined with insight into selflessness, the blemishes of affliction are transformed into pure appearance. It is not, in any case, that there is a real entity that is impure. For example, while a dream within a dream appears in dependence upon the dream, and an illusion within an illusion, too, depends upon the illusion, insofar as both are devoid of real entities and yet appear as if present as real entities, they are seen as if basically equal.

The Pratyekabuddha System

According to the way of the Pratyekajina Superiors, profound actual reality (*dharmatā, chos nyid*) is realized by means of the twelve limbs of interdependent origination on the paths of seeing and meditation. Thereby, all afflictions of the three realms that are to be relinquished are totally eliminated. This is said to be the attainment of the *fruit of self-awakening*.

Thus, inasmuch as afflictions are held to be real entities that are distinct, through the force of the [taking each of] the twelve limbs of interdependent origination [as objects qua perceptual bases], the uninterrupted path and the path of thorough liberation would be doubled, and a single affliction that is to be eliminated would be multiplied by twelve. Furthermore, each of those individual limbs is in fact characterized by the four truths. This is because, in this context—with actualizing karmic processes conditioned by ignorance, and so on—anything akin to a burden and injurious by nature, such as the ordinary body, pertains to true suffering. Such things as consciousness conditioned by karmic processes actualize a state of suffering in the future. Thus, they pertain to true origins. Because such things as karmic processes are halted when ignorance is negated, they pertain to true cessations. And since meditation on the character of interdependent origination halts karmic processes, it pertains to true paths.

Thus, even a single affliction that is to be eliminated would be rendered into forty-eight because of the influence of the [view of the] four truths. According to this path system, however, there can be no decisive reckoning of afflictions obtained in connection with any real entity of afflictions.[3]

The Yogācāra System

According to the philosophical position asserted in the system of the path of the Yogācāra, mind and mental factors associated with the three realms—the character of which are false conceptions (*abhūtaparikalpa, yang dag pa ma yin pa'i kun tu rtog pa*)—function neither as the apprehended nor the apprehender. They are defined as empty of duality, simply one's own awareness. Therefore, they stand in conflict with the character of the afflictions because the arising of an object is something marked by a type of error.

In any case, a well-known philosophical position of the Yogācāra states, for example, that earth, gold, and the earth element appear to the mind perceiving gold ore. In this case, the perception of gold as earth is false, perceiving it as gold is correct, and the earth element is included in both. Similarly, and in connection with the character of dependent phenomena (*paratantra, gzhan dbang*), perception in terms of apprehended and apprehender—that is, duality—is a false perception, perception of it as perfected (*pariniṣpanna, yongs grub*) is correct perception, and dependent phenomena are included in both.[4] Within dependent phenomena, no real imagined or perfected entity is found.

Accordingly, we might say that when a fire-brand, a wheel, and luminosity appear to the mind and we perceive a fire-wheel,[5] the fire-brand appearing as a wheel is a false perception, perceiving it as a fire-brand is correct, and that luminosity is included in both. Here, only insofar as the fire-wheel and the fire-brand are considered to be real entities is the presence of luminosity acceptably included within both. Thus, if it is suggested that the fire-wheel, which is something totally imagined (*parikalpita, kun btags*), is a real entity, while the fire-brand, which is something perfected, is not, then luminosity, which is something dependent, would pertain to the imagined fire-wheel and yet be absent in the second factor—that is, the perfected fire-brand.

When we consider the fire-brand to be a real entity, however, there is no real fire-wheel. At the point when the imagined fire-wheel is perceived, the perfected fire-brand has progressively been occluded as a single object because the fire-wheel has no basis in reality; the dependent luminosity—that is, the glow of the fire-brand—therefore pertains to the fire-brand alone and thus is not included in the second factor—that is, the imagined aspect.

It is a similar situation if both the imagined and the perfected are real entities: whether the perfected is a real entity or what is imagined is acceptably included within both, they pertain to the character of one's own awareness such that neither have any basis in reality. What is imagined cannot be established in either. Thus, there is no real entity found constituting affliction that is something to be eliminated.[6]

THE MADHYAMAKA SYSTEM

Accordingly, insofar as the realists[7] will not find any real entity of affliction that is to be eliminated—even in the context of their own philosophical positions—within the Madhyamaka system, there is nothing ultimately established. This should be recognized when, in conjunction with their insistence that conceptual elaborations (*prapañcā*, *spros pa*) are ultimately pacified, it is asked rhetorically in Madhyamaka discourse, "How could there be any real entity found that is to be eliminated?" On this view, it is said that although there is no real entity to be eliminated ultimately, the correct and incorrect conventions perceived by the mind suggest perforce that there is no conflict when someone states that according to correct conventions there exist afflictions to be eliminated. In that case, I would say that when it is asserted that there exists something that is to be correctly established, then however many varieties of conventions are recognized, they too would be correctly established. Yet when it is asserted that there does not exist something to be correctly established, all variety of conventions are rendered basically the same. Moreover, it is said that the setting forth of the division of conventions into correct and incorrect is presented in terms of instances of efficacy or a lack thereof, though [both are] similar in appearance.[8] This is not unlike the fact that the material form of a vase retains water while the material form of a vase's reflection cannot. In such a presentation as this one,[9] though the personal entity is proven to be functional, the phenomenal entity is not.

In that case, one might ask how is the personal entity established? Two points comprising internal and external continua are sketched out here. First, there is the inner continuum consisting in the continuum of a person such as a man or woman, person, god, and so forth, wherein a real entity is retained respectively in each. Yet in the context of the dharma, these are considered the six elements, six sources, and five psychophysical aggregates, the simple collection of which manifests a single mental awareness. There is no real entity of a sentient being, whether person, god, or what have you. Second, in the context of the outer continuum, I am speaking of such things as a pillar, a vase, and so forth, which are of a single concordant, consistent state, in which the natural state of a whole vase or the natural state of a single pillar is retained. Yet in connection with the dharma, even these are simply something composed of the five elements (*dhātupañcakam*, *khams lnga pa*), the six external sense fields (*ṣaḍbahyāyatanam*, *phyi'i skye mched drug*)—and no whole real entity is found that constitutes the natural state of a vase. Thus, the statement that a vase retains water is also something that proves the functionality of a personal entity because in the case of a phenomenal entity, the very appearance of some characterized object to some given conscious awareness is a phenomenon. In such a case, a reflection of a vase appears because of a vase, but only because of the vase's shape and color, which are visually perceptible, not because of the vase's tactility, and so on, which are not visually perceptible.[10] If, however, the function of color, which is associated with the personal entity, were indeed fulfilled by the phenomenal entity's reflection, then insofar as the performance of a phenomenon's activity is presented mostly in terms of the activity instigating help and harm, it absurdly would follow that a representation of sunlight would, on this view, injure one's eyes, a representation of moonlight would bring benefit, and both would scatter darkness.

While that which retains water is something that can be touched, that which acts as color is not. Thus, there is no presentation of a comparison between color and tactility. Distinct phenomena simply perform distinct activities and in this way, on this view, a vase retains water. This assertion that the reflection of a vase does not is simply an assertion in accordance with what is known in the world: that entities of persons perform activities.

Given that personhood is unreal, how could its activity be a real entity? That kind of establishing proof is not unlike someone who, being carried away by the raging waters of a river, seizes upon a rotten root, thinking it will buoy him! In that case, someone might suggest that if no ultimately establishing proof is insisted upon, and one is content not to analyze mere conventions, since, when analyzed, conventions cannot withstand the burden of proof, there would be no conflict, or contradiction, when conventions are negated through reason. Yet if reasoning is unnecessary for an establishing proof that is merely conventional, isn't the statement that they are similar in appearance and that correct and incorrect conventions are arranged by virtue of distinctions in efficacy, or a lack thereof, itself a reason?

On this view, positive affirmation too is appropriate even if it only affirms something but for a moment. If, however, a convention cannot even withstand the burden of its own validating criteria per se, how can a mere convention even be real? For example, if, unlike an elephant [of war] spurred by a metal whip to eradicate an enemy while bearing a host of soldiers, a cow working to plow a field while wearing a yoke is not even able to bear being spurred by the prod of a goad, how would the convention "working to plow a field" even apply? And then what would be the distinction between such an ineffective creature in the context of "working to plow a field" and, say, a drove of castrated goats?

In the same way, while unable to withstand the burden of proof needed to establish something as an ultimately real entity—and given that whatever can be proven to be a real entity is, moreover, merely a correct convention—just how is it that the conventional expression "correct convention" is applied? And then what would be the distinction from, say, the view of an ordinary mundane individual?

Holding such a dislocated view as this is quite a boggling state, indeed. A case in point is Anantayaśā, the ancient *cakravartin* sovereign whose unending personal aspirations took him to the world of the Trāyastriṃśa heaven,[11] located on top of Mount Meru, where Indra, the Lord of Gods, split his throne in half in order to make a seat for Anantayaśā, who indeed gained resources there equal to those of Indra. This turn of events, however, provoked in him a fierce mind of covetous desire through the force of which he fell from heaven back down to earth, where his confusion caused him to repeatedly ask of the people "Whose country is this?"

"We hear from our elder generations that this land is that of its first sovereign, Anantayaśā," they said. "With an impassioned mind, he died, like a lamp buffeted by winds. Such is what people have heard—that he was born into quite an astonishing state!" they said. "Anantayaśā, who emitted the seven precious stones from the crown of his head, was on par with Indra—no person surpassed him. Yet, dying from an impassioned mind as he did, there was no person lowlier than him. Alas, he surprised us!"

It is just such a stupefied state that is totally unable to conceive of how inapt it is to hold that there is some real entity that has the character of correct convention that should be either given up or adopted while maintaining that there is no establishing proof for anything because all phenomena are, in the end, undisturbed or pacified (*upaśānta*, *nyi bar zhi ba*) qua conceptual elaboration.

In that case, someone might ask, "If there is establishing proof proper, how is it that all conventions are basically the same?" A case in point is when a rope is perceived as a snake—the rope is actually present, and the snake has no basis in reality (*atyantābhāva*, *gtan med pa*). The awareness perceiving the rope is indeed a correct consciousness, and the conscious awareness perceiving a snake is a confused consciousness. The snake per se, being false, does not exist in the manner in which it appears. That being so, the snake perceived by awareness, since it is simply an imaginary imputation—one thing imputed onto another—has no natural identity (*ātmalābha*, *bdag nyid thub pa*) of its own. Moreover, if the rope is carefully scrutinized, it is seen to be a collection of just so many strands of grass or wool. Thus, when the conscious awareness of the rope as something singular and round is dissolved, it exists simply as a collection of its parts. The rope and the snake, then, are basically the same because neither have any basis in reality.

An awareness perceiving a simple collection of parts is a correct cognition (*samyagjñāna*, *yang dag pa'i shes pa*). The awareness of the rope, then, is not unlike the awareness of the snake—that is, both are mistaken cognitions (*bhrāntijñāna*, *'khrul pa'i shes pa*). Moreover, if the grass, or wool, parts are themselves carefully scrutinized and seen to be a simple collection of atoms such that the grass, or wool, strands are also realized to be unreal, the object and conscious awareness of it proceed just as in manner above—that is, they dissolve. Moreover, if conscious awareness distinguishes the atoms themselves, it recognizes that they are not real because at the time of perceiving the existence of the mere emptiness of empty form, all objects, and the awarenesses assuming them, will proceed in just the manner as above—that is, they dissolve. Thus, when emptiness is analyzed, what we refer to as "the empty" positions itself as something contingent upon a thing, since if the actual thing does not exist neither could its emptiness. Whatever is empty, of what quality is it empty? Further, *whose* empty is it inasmuch as it is realized that there is no quality that is established as real and all objects are basically the same in that absence?

In being mistaken cognitions, all conscious awarenesses are basically the same. In not existing as they appear, everything confused is basically the same. Everything that does not exist as it appears is basically the same in not acquiring a natural identity. If something is devoid of an acquired natural identity, moreover, both the object and the conscious awareness of it are devoid of being fundamentally unequal.

In that connection, when at first a snake is perceived, fear, then hostility, is generated. After that, upon seeing the rope, a haughtiness connected with having rid oneself of the hostility emerges; then an awareness that generates fixation emerges. After that, when awareness of the rope is dissolved—after awareness fixating on the rope [as something] singular [and] round is broken off—an awareness connected with the inception of fixation on the simple collection of its parts emerges, because there can be no elimination of the cyclical relation between the realist view and awareness tied up in the delusive extremes of fixation and aversion. Only if the character of an object is properly set forth as unreal would it be on a par with the entity that is set forth for the moment (*re shig par gzhag pa'i rdzas*), because all characteristics are fundamentally equal—excepting what does not deny mere appearance. In such a manner, all variety of conventions appear thus qualified by a common, consistent appearance. Particular variations on this view are as follows:

1. The consistent, or varying, experience of appearances with respect to karmic inheritance[12]
2. Totally pure and totally impure appearances[13]
3. Accessible and inaccessible appearances[14]
4. The falsely appearing and the correctly appearing[15]
5. Appearances qualified by both [false and correct appearance][16]
6. The perception of false appearances marked by error[17] and the perception of false appearances not marked by error[18]
7. Appearances having a basis, those that are baseless, and those that have false bases[19]
8. Efficacious and ineffective appearances[20]
9. Appearing to exist as a real entity and appearing as something imagined[21]
10. Totally imagined and actual appearance,[22] and so on

Thus, just as it is acceptable that all the presentations of various conventional appearances are established as real in accordance with the consensus among specific individual communities, they would all be fundamentally equal in that context.

Here, someone may ask, "What is consistent, or varying, experience of appearances with respect to karmic inheritance?"

Whether in the context of those who talk about the existence of external objects (*bahyārthāstivādin, phyi rol gyi don yod par smra ba*), for whom something such as fire is an instance of form that is real by virtue of common karma, or in the context of those who deny external objects, for whom the appearance of that same instance of fire, by virtue of the karmic imprints of common karma, is seen as the external objectification of the mind-as-such, given that "in" a single fire appearance, which is an instance of form, a single phenomenon qualifies as something commonly established as a substrate (*gzhi*), conflicting varieties of appearances of the world and the beings who reside within it are nevertheless such that when people and ordinary animals come into contact with fire, they appear to burn; and this appears as a state of suffering.

For an animal species called the *fire-cleansed deer*,[23] fire, instead of burning, works to bathe the fur and thicken the coat of the animal. Thus, here fire does the work of water. Also among animal species is the fire-dwelling mouse, for whom a home is constantly made amid wild fires. It enters into places alight with flames. In this case, fire here does all the work of a home and food. There are, among types of hungry ghosts, the female fire hungry ghost;[24] and among types of divinities, there are the divine *ṛṣis*,[25] fire gods who receive burned offerings from the brahmin caste. Their bodies are rumored to be something made from the fire element. Cases such as these qualify as consistent appearances that are experienced with respect to karmic inheritance. Not only that, but something such as grass, which, for most animals, appears as a source of enjoyment that sustains life, does not appear in that way for most people. The reason for that is that it does not directly provide sustenance to us. This, too, is an instance of consistent, or varying, appearances that are experienced with respect to karmic inheritance. Furthermore, when a sentient being is in hell, such as the Land of Burning Iron or the Groves of Mount Shalma, it is in a state of suffering. When a sentient being is in the heavenly realms, it appears to be in a state of enjoyment, as if all its wishes were magically fulfilled. These appearances are not simply particular manifestations for an individual, but they are real for those under the influence of common karma or under the influence of common karmic imprints—especially for beings wandering in saṃsāra who are human—for whom the mind-as-such appears as the object. In any case, it is not because of each specific appearance's influence that the conditions for personal happiness or suffering are brought about. What is more, while people's food, drink, clothes, and so on, can actually be real and commonly enjoyed, the enjoyment is, for many, not self-determined since some part of such enjoyments might typically be under the control of some powerful lord or some such other controlling factor. For others, enjoying a degree of autonomy means enjoying anything one desires. Things like this constitute a variety of appearances, experienced as consistent or varying, with respect to karmic inheritance.

Here, someone may ask, "What are totally pure and totally impure appearances?"

To that it may be said that the whole river Ganges is located at one terrestrial point for both humans and pretas and appears to both as an enormous flowing river. In that sense, it does not comprise a different basic subject for either party. Nevertheless, for pretas, the state of the water appears impure, as something like pus. It appears as something thoroughly incapable of being enjoyed. To people though, the state of the water appears as water, appearing to be pure and unpolluted, capable of being enjoyed. Furthermore, the pure field of the Bhagavan Śākyamuni,[26] the four continents of this world itself, is reputed to be an utterly impure field. For that reason Śāriputra said, "I have seen this field of the Bhagavan's filled high and low with ravines, precipices, and grime." On his return from the Buddha Field beyond Sorrow (Aśokakṣetra, Mya ngan med pa'i zhing), Brahma Jaṭil remarked, "Venerable Śāriputra, don't utter such words. For it is only in your mind that there is high and low.[27] In the Bhagavan's field, there is nothing utterly impure. I see this field of the Bhagavan as pure, like the divine abode (*surālaya*, *lha'i gnas*) of the Paranirmatavaśa,[28] with a perfectly structured ground of precious stones."

At that moment, the Bhagavan, having made this buddha field—that is, this world of Jambudvipa—appear to all around like the eastern pure buddha realm [called] Arrayed with Jeweled Ornaments, said to Śāriputra, "What impurity attributed to the sun and moon causes the blind not to see them?" Śāriputra replied, "The sun and moon are not flawed; the blind are flawed." The Bhagavan said, "Likewise, this buddha field of mine, like the eastern pure buddha realm arrayed with jeweled ornaments, is always like this—that is, perfect—yet you don't see it. For example, even though *devaputra* demons ingest nourishing nectar from a single jeweled vessel, there would be varying experiences of the taste that accords with each individual's accumulation of merit. Likewise, even for those born into a single buddha field, whether it is seen as pure or impure depends on the degree to which their karma is purified." That being so, it is not that appearances such as these manifest differently to everyone. They appear as a single basis. And it is not that appearances are consistent for everyone; apparent variety is a matter of pure and impure vision. Appearances such as these are varieties of appearances that are utterly pure and those that are not utterly pure.

Here, someone may ask, "What appearances are accessible and inaccessible?"

In this case, take two beings wandering through saṃsāra, people who live together. One is drunk (*matta*, *ra ro*), passed out—dispossessed of sensation or accessible discriminations. One is in a state possessed of mindfulness and introspection.[29] When both are touched in the same measure by fire, it is as if one seems not to experience the dissatisfying touch of fire while the other seems to. Yet both experiences pertain to consistent appearances that are experienced with respect to karmic inheritance. That being so, the word *burn* is warranted in both cases; and in this way a variety of accessible and inaccessible appearances may be recognized.

Here, someone may ask, "What is a false appearance?"

It is like the appearance of a fire-wheel in connection to a spinning fire-brand.

If someone asks what is a correct appearance, I say that it is the appearance of any object just as it actually is.

Here, someone may ask, "What are appearances that are qualified by both false and correct appearance?"

When a rope is seen as a snake, a rope image does appear to the sense consciousness. The consciousness, accompanied by discursive recognition—that is, "Snake!"—is marked by the appearance of a snake image; and in this way there is a so-called appearance qualified by both false and correct appearance.

What if someone were to ask what is a perception of a false appearance marked by error? It is akin to spinning a fire-brand in front of those who are children.

If someone were to ask what is a perception of false appearance accompanied by veracity, I say it is not unlike spinning a fire-brand in front of a scholar.

Here, someone may ask, "What are those appearances that have a basis?"

The appearance of a fire-wheel by virtue of a spinning fire-brand, the appearance of a double moon for one with cataracts, and the appearance of a moving mountain to one who is sitting in a boat.[30]

Here, someone may ask, "What are appearances without bases?"

The appearance of falling hairs to one with cataracts and the appearance of the sky filled with needles to one who has ingested downy datura.[31] Furthermore, it is from the karmic imprints connected with the manifestation that different appearances manifest. Thus, another example of a baseless appearance concerns the march of a sovereign's army of soldiers upon the road: they march to the beat of their drums. For some part of the distance, the sovereign would accompany them. Once arrived at the enemy front, he will disperse his army's divisions to see whether or not the enemy host has arrived. As long as the enemy host is not physically seen, the drum sound, resounding, continues to be heard. Therefore, since, by force of karmic imprints (*vāsanā, bag chags*) the sovereign does not recognize the appearance qua sound of the drum simply as a resounding drum sound but, rather, as a correct inferential sign inducing knowledge of the absence of an enemy troop, he will, at a distance,[32] think "the enemy host is at a distance from here" while the drum continues to be heard. Here, the appearance having no basis is akin to the mind thinking "the enemy host is unseen" as long as the drum sound resounds.

Perhaps someone will ask, "What is an appearance having a false basis?" I answer that it is akin to the perception of water in a mirage, because a mirage is in fact devoid of a primary element as a basis. Inasmuch as it is devoid of its apparent entity, water, it nevertheless appears to be water.

Because of the consistency and inconsistency connected with these appearances, something that appears capable of acting upon the mind stream of individual sentient beings wandering within saṃsāra might appear to be incapable. The incapable might appear capable.

The apparent presence of a real entity might become the apparent presence of something imagined. The apparent presence of something imagined might become the apparent presence of a real entity.

What appears totally imagined might become the appearance of what is actually real. Therefore, inasmuch as each specific attribute works as a proof of being real, truly proving even one attribute establishes [the qualificand] as existent, as what is in fact a consistent appearance for the ordinary person and a consistent particular appearance, as well. If some such thing were ever validated, then all the various conventions would be capable of being established in accordance with however they are commonly recognized in the world. If the true establishment of some phenomenon is not insisted upon theoretically, then just establishing consistent appearances for people will not establish it as a particular because all conventions are fundamentally equal.

If what is an inconsistent appearance for people functions as proof of the extensive influence of something, even if something truly established is already asserted, [I might say:]

> One appearance removes another
> Thus, no particular is established at all —
> And all are fundamentally equal.

The Madhyamaka and Guhyamantra Systems

Thus, the Madhyamaka and Guhyamantra (*gsang sngags*)[33] systems prove that nothing whatsoever among all phenomena is truly established. Phenomena are described in the context of an innumerable variety of trainees' intellectual capacities and dispositions. Yet all the various particular things in the world, being characterized by nothing other than their respective apparent criteria [for being perceived], are thus basically the same. This is why, in this context, the form of a dream vase appears capable of retaining water, although the form of a vase's image does not. Nevertheless, except for the dream's scope of appearance alone, given its nature, there is no distinction in actual capacity—or lack thereof—to function. For this reason, all phenomena are proclaimed to be like an illusion, like a mirage, like a dream, like a reflection, and like an emanation.

*Illusions (*māyā, sgyu ma*)*

Here, someone may ask, "What is the character of an illusion?"

On this view, an illusionist who has made an effigy from such things as pebbles, sticks, grit, and so forth, and incanted mantras over the clay figure such that it has been penetrated with the force of applied practice, then causes various forms—that of a man, a woman, a horse, an elephant, whatever—to manifest in the experience of some others. Though from the first moment the images occur, they do not arise from anywhere at all. Even when apparent, since they are an illusion, nothing actual is present at all. Once people are persuaded that they are an illusion, they cease to be; they do not appear. Yet at that moment, [they] have not gone anywhere. In which case, here it is said: "By the force of the circumstance that one has been persuaded that the form is an illusion, it is not present in one's sensory domain. For this reason, it is simply not manifest. Yet it is not set forth that in such an instance a momentary continuum has ceased or been eliminated. Here, while both appearance and nonappearance are, given their absence of character, of the same reality, and given that as long as the conditions remain, the appearance (or perceived object) remains, the character of that appearance as such is perfected. In this sense, since there is no other objective factor that could be established, it is described as an 'utter illusion.'"

*Mirages (***marīci, smigs rgyu***)*

Here, someone may ask, "What is the character of a mirage?"

In a place where sand is present, the sun's oppressive heat is beating down on it, and someone is looking [at it] from a distance, there would be the experience—that is, the appearance—of something like streaming water, which becomes manifest through these conditions. From that first moment, however, it did not arise from anywhere. Even at the moment of appearance, since there is no elemental basis—that is, no water—it does not pertain to anything actual whatsoever. Upon the sun setting, the appearance of a mirage ceases and does not appear. Yet at that moment, it has not gone anywhere. In which case, here it is said, "By the force of the circumstance that the sun has set, the mirage is not present in one's sensory domain; thus it is simply not manifest. Yet it is not set forth that a momentary continuum has ceased or been eliminated. In this case, given their indivisibly characteristicless character, both appearance and nonappearance are of the single reality. Given that, as long as the conditions remain, the appearance—or perceived object—remains, and the reality of the appearance as such is perfected. In this sense, since there is no other objective factor that could be established, it is termed 'a mirage.'"

*Dreams (***svapna, rmi lam***)*

In that case, it may be asked, "What is the character of a dream?"

In a sleeping person's dream, both sources of enjoyment such as pleasure groves, parks, and the like, and sources of discontent such as prisons, jails, and so on, are observed [by the mind] and become something apparent (*dmigs shing snang bar 'gyur*). Yet even from the first moment, neither arose from anywhere. Even at the moment of appearance, since both pertain to a dream, there is no actual reality present whatsoever. Upon awakening, they stop; they do not appear. Yet at that moment, nothing has gone anywhere. In which case, here it is said, "By the force of the circumstance that one awakens, the dream is not present in one's sensory domain; thus is simply not manifest. Yet it is not set forth in the teaching that a momentary continuum has ceased or been eliminated. Though both appearance and nonappearance, given their indivisibly characteristicless character, are of a single character. Given that, as long as the conditions remain, the appearance—or perceived object—remains, the character of the appearance per se is perfected. In this sense, since there is no other objective factor that could be established, it is described as 'a dream.'"

*Reflections (*pratibimba, rmi lam*)*

In that case, perhaps it is asked, "Just what is the character of a reflection?"

In this case, when an undistorted image, such as a face, remains as a clear image upon such a thing as a mirror, there emerges the appearance of a reflection. At that first moment, though, it did not arise from anywhere. Even at the moment of appearance, since there is no elemental basis, nothing actual is present at all. Any partial aggregation of conditions means the reflection stops; it will not appear. Yet at that moment, it has not gone anywhere. In which case, it is said, "By virtue of incomplete circumstances, the reflection is not present in one's sensory domain; thus it is simply not manifest. Yet it is not set forth that a momentary continuum has ceased or been eliminated. Though both appearance and nonappearance, given their indivisibly characteristicless character, pertain to a single reality. Given that, as long as the conditions remain, the appearance, or perceived object, remains, and the character of the appearance as such is perfected. In this sense, since there is no other objective factor that could be established, it is called 'a reflection.'"

*Emanations (*nirmāṇa, sprul pa*)*

Someone may ask, "What is the character of an emanation?"

In this case, I consider emanations connected with gnosis (*jñāna*, *ye shes*), emanations connected with concentration (*samādhi*, *ting nge 'dzin*), and those which are neither—that is, emanations achieved in connection with knowledge mantras (*vidyāmantra*, *rig sngags*). When mantras are incanted over a white flower that is then cast into the sky, there appears something approaching a thousand tathāgatas. Likewise, when mantras are incanted over a golden flower that is then cast into the sky, there appear numerous arhats. Incanting mantras over a red flower that is then cast into the sky, there appear numerous divinities. Incanting mantras over a blue flower that is then cast into the sky, there appear numerous *yakṣas*[34] and *rakṣasas*.[35] Though from the first moment they occur, they do not arise from anywhere at all. Even when apparent, since they are emanations, nothing actual is present at all. Once persuaded that they are emanations, they cease to be; they do not appear. Yet at that moment, they have not gone anywhere. In which case, here it is said, "By the force of the circumstance that one has been persuaded that the form is an emanation, it is not present in one's sensory domain. Thus, it is simply not manifest. Yet it is not set forth that a momentary continuum has ceased or been eliminated. In this case, given their absence of character, while both appearance and nonappearance pertain to the same reality—and given that as long as the conditions remain, the appearance, or perceived object, remains—the character of that appearance itself is perfected. In this sense, since there is no other objective factor that could be established, it is described as 'an emanation.'"

In this way, all the appearances of various internal and external things, as well, manifest as appearances so long as there are karmic imprints within the continuum of the individual sentient being connected with ideas about the objective apprehended and the subjective apprehender. Yet from the very first moment, though, they do not in fact arise from anywhere. Even at the point of appearance, nothing actual is present at all because of its being something that appears due to the influence of karmic imprints. When the karmic imprints of both apprehended and apprehender are exhausted, the appearances of both stop; they do not appear. Yet at that moment, they have not gone anywhere. In which case, it is said, "Since they do not pertain to the domain of nonconceptual gnosis, which is devoid of conceptions of apprehended and apprehender, they simply are not manifest. Yet it is not set forth that a momentary continuum has ceased or been eliminated. However, given their indivisibly characteristicless character, both appearance and nonappearance are of a single reality; and given that as long as the conditions remain, the appearance, or perceived object, remains, the character of mere appearance is perfected.

In this sense, since there is no other objective factor that could be proven, all phenomena are thereby proclaimed to be like an illusion, like a mirage, like a dream, like a reflection, and like an emanation. Therefore, because all things characterized in this way are characterized by error, there is no actual real entity of affliction constituting a *something* to be eliminated along the path.

Conclusion

On this view, given that we have observed the fallacy of philosophical systems that posit the existence of an entity that is to be eliminated—affliction—this reasoning, which demonstrates that there is no real entity of affliction constituting something to be eliminated, is not presented with the intention of undermining someone else's philosophical system through conflict and contradiction. Rather, it is a description of the perception that may cause the collapse of one's own philosophical position through one's own philosophical position alone. This is not unlike, for example, when a damaging wind rises in a dense woods. The thick trees of the woods would, at that moment, become something that works to protect the woods so that not too much damage is done. When, however, a damaging fire occurs as a result of the wind, the wood provides no shelter. It is consumed until not even a trace remains.

If it is said that someone proves any from among those self-defeating philosophical theories, this would only reference a flawless establishing proof for proponents of [that particular] philosophical theory—that is, those who perceive their own dialectical procedure to be flawless. Yet, from the point of view of those with deep and expansive awareness, philosophical proof is nonetheless a perception that is fabricated as one's own experience, which is comparable to turbid water. For example, in the past, the Brahmin named Terrestrial Flower[36] said to the Brahmin named Undying:[37]

> Alas, O Brahmin, your
> Totally faultless methods,
> When seen from my point of view,
> Taint and habituate you with every word.

Just as it has been stated that what is said by the Brahmin named Undying, who perceives his own method to be faultless, is, from the point of view of the Brahmin called Terrestrial Flower, like something tainted that is corrupting Undying's perception, it also follows that the insistence found in the Śrāvaka system—that is, that associated with afflictions are actually a number of real entities to be eliminated—perforce functions to manufacture a number of classifications. And because the assertion itself has fabricated certainty regarding the number, it is thus something tainted in having manufactured a debased assertion concerning real entities. Within the Yogācāra system, the insistence upon a real entity to be eliminated has fabricated categories of attributes. Thus, like something tainted, it has manufactured something self-debasing. Within the Madhyamaka system, these special classifications fabricated concerning correct and incorrect conventions are simply stated to be as if something tainted, self-debasing.

This is not stated because the Madhyamaka system is said to be in conflict with the system of the Unexcelled Secret (*guhyānuttara*, *gsang ba bla na med pa'i tshul*). [The Mādhyamika] would not be seen to be undermined because he or she is clinging to his or her own philosophical position for protection, even though [the position] has already been problematized here. Describing the perception of someone who appears to have conquered himself or herself by means of his or her own philosophical position comes about when one's philosophical position is *consumed until not a trace remains*. For that reason, these faults described above were discussed.

Those who desire to enter the way of the Great Vehicle should recognize that there is no real entity of affliction to be eliminated and that all phenomena are taught to be fundamentally equal insofar as they are illusory. This is the end of chapter 1.

2. Objections and Replies

First Objection: Concerning the Reality of Illusions

Here, our issue is the Buddhist teaching proclaiming all phenomena to be illusory (*māyopama, sgyu ma lta bu*). Especially in the context of all composite phenomena being impermanent and all phenomena being devoid of a personal self, the phrase *illusory* applies.[1] When all phenomena are proclaimed to be devoid of any essential nature and "illusory" because of being generated by different causes and conditions, this is done with three features in mind:[2] (1) the selflessness of phenomena, (2) the selflessness of persons,[3] and (3) the three natures (*trisvābhava, ngo bo nyid rnam pa gsum*), which have no inherent nature. Since all phenomena are devoid of any ultimate nature, they are proclaimed to be "illusory" even though correct conventions are asserted to be real entities.[4] Yet, it is not the case that the two—illusion and the aggregates—are utterly equal. How is this so? An illusion appears only for a moment, whereas the aggregates of sentient beings wandering in saṃsāra appear stable for some duration of time. An illusion is not something that is completely fashioned by mind and mental factors. It is also not something accessible in terms of sensation and conscious discrimination. Yet the psychophysical aggregates of beings wandering in saṃsāra are completely fashioned by mind and mental factors and are accessible by sensation and discrimination. Therefore, it would not be right to fundamentally equate the two.

Response to the First Objection

I explain that instances of appearance such as those discussed above are indeed counted among illusions—emanations, too. In the case of emanations, especially, we find that there are emanations of the Tathāgata and those of bodhisattvas who are tantric initiates that manifest for the benefit of beings wandering in saṃsāra. These emanations may exist working to accomplish the deeds of a buddha for up to an aeon or longer. Some try to establish a proof for the deeds of a buddha for only a year, month, a day, for as long as the sun shines, a morning, or an hour. For some, the deeds of a buddha seem to be fashioned by gnosis though they are established as unfashioned by gnosis. For others, they appear to be fashioned by gnosis and establish the fashioning itself. For still others, they appear to be unfashioned by gnosis and nevertheless establish the fashioning itself. And for some, the deeds of a buddha appear to be unfashioned by gnosis yet are established as fashioned.

Nevertheless, given the absence of any real distinction between the character of illusions and emanations, they are basically the same. A pure maiden may look into a mirror incanted with a *prasena* mantra and perceive the image of a female thief in it while an ordinary person will not. Yet given the character of the image, there is no distinction between it and an illusion. In dreams, too, people may, because of the influence of a particular deity, see and predict things in the future. For ordinary people, however, this is not the case even though there is no difference between the character of a dream and an illusion. Take mirages, as well. Some, because of their conditions, work to obscure perception of the road, whereas others do not. Nevertheless, given the character of a mirage, there is no difference between it and an illusion. Even when it comes to illusions that are influenced by the level of genuine power connected with esoteric mantras associated with illusions, some might remain for a moment or for some longer duration in time. Some might appear as just a color or shape; some appear as scent, flavor, or even something tactile.

In just such a case as this, the magician called Good Illusion-Maker[5] wanted to test whether the Conqueror was all-knowing or not. In order to find out, he magically issued forth a magical projection of a multitude of delectables and then invited the Conqueror, along with his community of Śrāvakas, for a midday meal. The Conqueror, knower of the three times and others' mind streams, accepted the invitation. There, he transformed Good Illusion-Maker's illusory issuance by the force of his power to effect the minds and experiences of others.[6] The illusory delectables in fact remained constant in reality. And the Buddha and his retinue enjoyed them for lunch and ended the meal with an aspiration (*praṇidhāna*, *smon lam*), in which the Buddha said:

Whosoever gives, whatsoever is given,
Gives just such without objectification—
That alone is the very essence of equal charity;
May that come to completion for one who is good.[7]

Thus, there are even illusions that can bring about the twofold accumulation. That is to say, whereas the transformative power of Good Illusion-Maker's secret mantra was feeble and thus his magical issuance was incapable of any constancy in appearance, the true transformative power of the Conqueror's unsurpassable faculty is his capacity to project appearances that persist for a long time. Nevertheless, given the character of illusion, they are fundamentally equal. Appearances in the experiential domain of others that are not appearances completely fashioned by the mind or one's own experience are capable of enduring in time for a long period, though they are no different.

They emerge from the great power of the mantras of illusionists. Take, for example, King Ramacandra's son Bali. His mother, who had left to go to a village on an errand, entrusted him to a sage to be taken care of. At some point while she was away, the sage noticed that the boy was no longer tagging along with him. Having lost him, the sage searched all over for the boy but did not find him. With nothing else at hand, he fabricated an illusion—in a likeness similar to Bali's. This doppelgänger endured within reality.

When [Bali's mother] the goddess Sita returned,[8] the boy also returned—from his maternal grandmother's—to his home, where he remained. [Upon seeing them both,] the mother was not able to recognize which one was her son. She thought that one boy was a pretend and one her son by birth but could not tell which was which. So she took them both before the king and reported all that had happened to him. The king, too, did not recognize his son; and for a long time, both acted as princes. In this case, especially, because the power of the sage is superior to that of the illusionist, his projected illusion is all the more stable in appearance. Similarly, because the relative power of the secret mantra of illusionists is weak, the projected appearance is simply unable to appear stable. The power of karma and affliction is still greater than that. Karmic projections and afflictions appear to endure for quite a long time for that reason.

Imagined forms (*parikalpitarūpa*, *kun brtags pa'i gzugs*), and mastered forms (*vaibutvikarūpa*, *dbang 'byor ba'i gzugs*) are a similar case, as well. At one time in the past, there was a person who wished to practice yoga and went to a master (*ācarya*, *slob dpon*) for a dharma transmission. The teacher first wanted to check whether or not this person had any capacity to meditate. So rather than giving him any transmission, he said, "Meditate on the presence of excessively large buffalo horns on your head." Upon hearing this, the person went home, meditated resolutely, and sooner or later attained concentration such that something like a direct perception of buffalo horns became clear to him, though they did not appear in such a way that he was able to touch or hold them by hand. At that point, the horns are an *imagined form*. By meditating in that manner over the long term, at some point the horns became tactile. The person then thought, "I should ask the master if I have accomplished the buffalo horns and if so what I should do next." As the person prepared to walk out, he could not get through the door and summoned the villagers. "Raze the door!" the person said. The villagers, after they had arrived, remarked on the beautiful horns present upon the person's head and proceeded to raze the doorway. Now freed, the person went before the master who, also astonished, gave the transmission. Thereafter, the person attained success in the Great Seal (*mahāmūdra, phyag rgya chen po*). Horns capable of producing such an incident in and of themselves are mental objects called *mastered forms*. When they are present in the ordinary sensory domain of all beings, they are termed *real forms* (*pariniṣpannarūpa, grub pa'i gzugs*), which are no different from the type of appearing form that is the maturation of previous karma.

Even a physical body that is not one's own idea can be actualized through the aspirations of others. In the past, there was a weaver (*tantuvāya, tha ga ba*) who went to the forest to cut down a tree to make a loom. Among the finest trees, the weaver thought to himself, "it would not be right to cut down such fine trees for my simple loom." So the weaver continued searching in order to find an appropriate tree from which to make the loom. The difficult search took the weaver all around the forest, but to no avail. Then a forest goddess appeared before the weaver and, seemingly pleased, said, "Man, since yours is fine work, it is good that you did not cut down fine trees to do it! What boon do you desire for such a virtuous choice?"[9] The weaver, not knowing what to request, asked a friend—a friend who happened not to be very intelligent—who said, "Being weavers, wouldn't it be great if we could weave from both our front and back sides." After hearing this, the goddess appeared before them. "Bestow upon me the capacity for weaving with both my front and back," the weaver said. "May it be so," answered the goddess. Immediately after, the whole of the weaver's body and senses were transformed: two additional hands and feet emerged behind him, manifesting the semblance of an unhuman body.[10] When the weaver went back to his village, the villagers cried, "There is a demon here upon us!" and set upon him with stones, killing him. After his death, his ordinary viscera and body became evident to the people, who cried out, "Kyé-ma![11] The slayed demon has a human corpse—what is this?" All the flesh, blood, bones, and faculties, too, were those of a human albeit with additional limbs; and they found out that this was in fact an accomplished weaver who was well known to them.

In this case, especially, the appearance produced through the power of another's aspirations is not really different than a body that will be brought about through the maturation of karma. If there is a slight difference, it would be that the force of karma and affliction appears at a later time (for example, a later life), the great force of meditative equipoise (*samāhita*, *mnyam par bzhag pa*)[12] brings about perceived phenomena (for example, in this lifetime), and that the force of sincerely uttered aspirations appears immediately (for example, in the next moment). In these cases, what is common between the three is that they are nothing other than various appearances because of the influence of contingent causes and distinct conditions.

The Tibetan term for illusion, *sgyu ma*, when analyzed etymologically, is traced to the Sanskrit term *māyā* and indicates something deceptive or incorrect. The Sanskrit term for emanation, *nirmāṇa*, renders the Tibetan term *trül-pa* (*sprul pa*), which indicates a projection that is not a totally distinct entity from its source. As such, all things that appear do not obtain their own state as an entity. They are simply deceptive, false objects appearing because of the influence of different causes and conditions. Thus, everything that appears should simply be recognized as basically being the same as an illusion and emanation.

Second Objection: Concerning the Reality of Causality

Yet someone might try to argue that these things that appear as cause and effect are not simply reducible to appearances that remain constant over a long period of time because the continuum of momentary causes and effects appears to pure worldly gnosis (*śuddhalaukikajñāna*, *dag pa rjig rten pa'i ye shes*)[13] and because the continuum of momentary causes and effects is never severed or eliminated. For if it were said to be severed, the argument goes, that would be postulating a form of nihilism.

Response to the Second Objection

The Conqueror indeed proclaimed that phenomena arise as dependent relations (*pratītyasamutpāda, rten cing 'brel bar 'byung ba*). On this view, if a cause is present, a result will arise; and if cause and condition are interrupted, its result will also be prevented. Just this alone was proclaimed by the Buddha to be the great pathway to freedom that dispels the two extremes.

It was not in fact proclaimed by the Buddha that the continuum of causes and effects is never severed. Accordingly, the special seal impressed upon all the dharma discourses (*pravacana, gsung rab*)[14] given by the Conqueror and all the bone relics of the Buddha's body, on the worldly sciences (*śāstra, gtsug lag*) and objects of worship, is the essence of interdependence (*rten 'brel gyi snying po*):

> *ye dharmā hetuprabhavā hetuṃ teṣāṃ tathāgato hyavadāt* |
> *teṣāṃ ca yo nirodha evaṃ vādī mahāśramaṇaḥ* ||

All the above mentioned should be recognized as being stamped, impressed with this, the Buddha's seal. As to its meaning, it is rendered either as

> All phenomena arise from causes;
> Those causes were pointed out by the Tathāgata;
> The great *śrāmaṇa* taught this [and]
> Proclaimed that which is their cessation,[15]

or as

> Of phenomena that arise through causes,
> The Tathāgata taught the causes;
> The great śrāmaṇa also stated
> The manner of their cessation.[16]

It is explained on this view, which is in accordance with the explanations given by the teacher of the world (that is, the Buddha), that phenomena are not produced by a creator, are not emanated by Iśvara, have not arisen through self-nature, are not transformed by time, and have not arisen causelessly. Thus, this teaching that phenomena arise from causes and conditions is that of the Tathāgata, and none other. The teaching that when the cause of a given phenomenon is interrupted, its effect is obstructed, too, is that of that great śrāmaṇa, the Buddha, Conqueror of the world along with its gods—and no one else's. And to be clear: it was not proclaimed that the continuum of causes and effects is never severed.

In a different sūtra,[17] there is an explanation of the fact that phenomena arise as dependent relations, the purport of which is similar. It states: "Just as it is proclaimed by the chief expounder of the superiority of liberation, who declared that he himself had knowledge of the state beyond the suffering of birth, old age, and decay: the world is something formed in connection with karma and affliction; knowledge brings about the causes that prevent karma and affliction." This also corresponds to the meaning of the teaching that states: "Monks, when this is present, that comes to be; from the production of that, this arises; and in this way, with ignorance as a condition, karmic processes come to be" up to "and the perennial heap of saṃsāra comes to be." Also, the teaching which states: "When this is interrupted, that ceases to be; because of the interruption of ignorance, karmic processes cease to be" up to "the perennial heap of saṃsāra ceases to be." Thus, it was not proclaimed by the Buddha that the continuum of causes and effects is never severed. The two extremes are in fact dispelled: The extreme of eternalism (*śāśvatānta, rtag pa'i mtha'*) is dispelled by the fact that nothing personal transmigrates. Thus, it is stated:

> By means of [analogy to] orality, lamp, mirror, and stamp,
> Sun-crystal, seed, the sour, and sound,
> The wise ought to realize the aggregates qua (re-)connection
> Rather than transmigration.[18]

The extreme of nihilism (*ucchedānta, chad pa'i mtha'*) is dispelled by the fact that production derives from causes and conditions. Thus, it is stated:

> Whosoever imagines that even the subtlest entity (*śūkṣmabhava*) ceases,
> That fool does not see what it means to arise conditionally (*pratyayotpannārtha*).[19]

It is not in fact taught that "the extreme of nihilism is dispelled because the continuum of causes and effects is never severed." The continuum of causes and effects appears to pure worldly gnosis; it appears to the pure worldly gnosis of bodhisattvas because of the power of the two fixations (*dvayagrāha, 'dzin pa gnyis*) that result from karmic imprints that remain in the bodhisattvas' continuum.

Exploring the question of whether or not tathāgatas are, in fact, possessed of a pure worldly gnosis is another issue altogether.[20]

That said, a person who holds a philosophical position like the one described above is like a doubtful bird. When a doubtful bird is flying above the path looking down, it is examining it carefully. When the doubtful bird sees that the footing of the path has shifted a bit, doubts stop it. It moves off the major established path fearful and looking for protection. Because of this, the doubtful bird moves off the path, to the edge (*mtha'*)[21] of the path. There, he is tormented by the splinters offered by the thick wood encircling the path. Likewise, the Conqueror proclaimed that given the fact that phenomena arise interdependently—as dependent relations—when causal conditions are interrupted, their effects will be obstructed. On this traditional *great path to liberation* that dispels the two extremes of nihilism and eternalism, the doubtful bird, because of its fear of falling into nihilism vis-à-vis the causal continuum being interrupted and its shunning the extreme of an external causal continuum, moves to the extreme edge of the path and is thus tormented there by the [intellectual] splinters of realist views.[22]

Third Objection: Concerning the Reality of Pure Phenomena

Even if it is true that in the impure realm of totally afflictive phenomena (*saṃkliṣṭa, kun nas nyon mongs pa*) causal effects are obstructed inasmuch as their causes are interrupted, the appearance of a fully matured buddha body (*vipākakāya, rnam par smin pa'i sku*), the display of a totally pure field, and a perfectly encompassing ornament consisting in the inexhaustible continuum of enlightened body, speech, and mind actualized through illimitable collections of merit and wisdom would be unceasing.

Response to the Third Objection

While it is true that the collections of merit and wisdom would be the causes and conditions for the apprehension and appearance of a completely pure body and domain, they are not the fundamental (*maula, dngos gzhi*) causes of that appearance. How so? The occasion of merit accumulation is also a context in which harm can occur through force of turbulent (*duṣṭhulya*, *gnas ngan len*) karma. At that time, meritorious karma indeed appears as something beneficial. For example, this is not unlike the fact that, in the absence of a fundamental base, a white cloth (*śuklaḥ paṭa*, *ras yug dkar po*) may be infused (*vāsita*, *bsgo*) with stains, cleansed by washing, and again infused with a fine color. Similarly, if earth, water, and time elements are present, seeds will give forth their fruit. Otherwise, if water is absent, nothing can grow. Likewise, when the underlying basis marked by karmic imprints of the two fixations is moistened by the water of craving, the seeds of karma will grow. When devoid of just the water of craving, the seeds of karma will not grow. Accordingly, because they are devoid of the moisture of grasping even though they remain on the ground of conceptuality, holy arhats do not generate fully mature aggregates (*vipākakāya*, *rnam par smin pa'i lus*) even by meritorious karma. This is not unlike the fact that a boat works to advantage as long as the danger of a river is present, but once the danger is no longer present and one proceeds onto dry land, at that point the boat works to no advantage.[23] Likewise, as long as the danger of turbulent actions is present, meritorious karma works to one's advantage, and at the moment that there is no harm from turbulent actions, meritorious karma is of no benefit. The Buddha even proclaimed the fact of being divorced from all benefit and harm to be "awakening." Here, it is stated:

> Take as an example that which traverses
> To the other shore of a rising river,
> Composed from grasses and wood and the like;
> Equipped to cross the water,
> One gets in; once having crossed,
> Cast it aside and go on happily.
> The path across saṃsāra
> Is like that since, once generated,
> What is and is not dharma is eliminated
> And awakening is happily attained.[24]

Similar to that is another proclamation:

> The creator, who emits and gathers
> All illusion-like entities,

That one, thence, has no evil.
Merit is like that, too—
To be without merit and sin,
That is indeed proclaimed to be awakening.[25]

In definitive terms, the reality of awakening is simply the pacification of both sin and merit. It is not unlike the teaching that awakening is characterized as peace, beyond sorrow. Thus, while treatises on language (*śabdaśāstra*, *sgra'i bstan chos*) give *nirvāṇa* as a term for the extinguishing of a flame, it is also the name of the Buddhist monk who is beyond sorrow; and *nirvāṇo-a-ga* is a term for the extinction of a flame. In this manner, the expression "fire extinguished" simply refers to the pacification of an actual blaze. It has not gone anywhere; it does not remain anywhere at all either. Thus, the term *nirvāṇa* is used. The term *nirbaṇo bhikṣu* is the name of a monk who is beyond sorrow. Accordingly, the term indicates an ideal monk who has simply pacified the fires of attachment (*rāga*, *'dod chags*), aversion (*dveśa*, *zhe sdang*), and delusion (*moha*, *gti mug*). In actuality, they have not gone anywhere; they do not remain anywhere at all and thus the term *nirvāṇa* is used.

Therefore, while meritorious karma is indeed a condition for the purification of appearances, it is not an actual causal and conditional basis of it. Neither is the accumulation of wisdom (*jñāna*, *ye shes*), which, in due course, pertains to nonconceptual gnosis (*nirvikalpajñāna*, *rnam par mi rtog pa'i ye shes*) that is obtained after generating bodhicitta and through the power of one's own spiritual disposition and guidance from a teacher. The accumulation of wisdom is the continuum composed of an immeasurable root of virtue that takes the expanse of reality (*dharmadhātu*, *chos kyi dbyings*) as its objective basis (*dmigs pa*). It is also something born of the faculty of mindfulness (*smṛtīndriya*, *dran pa'i dbang*). Yet because gnosis actually arises divorced from concepts of apprehended and apprehender, it is not a conducive condition for appearance. Take, for example, the blazing fire at the end of an aeon,[26] which is not conducive for bringing together the conditions of conceptual construction. Pure worldly gnosis, too, is qualified by dualistic appearance, and its emergence is contingent upon a basis of virtue in which the three spheres are completely purified. Thus, it is generated in dependence upon appearances. That said, though its character is qualified by erroneous appearance, it is characterized by correct perception. It is, for example, not unlike spinning a fire-brand in front of discerning folks. Thus, it is not a conducive condition for appearances. For example, when, after piling up a lot of kindling, a fire is lit, there is some kindling that is burning, some that is not burning, and some that is about to start burning. While it is the case that fire is generated in dependence upon the wood, fire is nevertheless not a condition that causes the wood to remain for a long period of time and spread; it is, rather, a condition that depletes it.[27]

Pure worldly gnosis, as well, is similar: it is qualified by seeds along with their appearances, which result from a timeless karmic propensity for clinging. It is generated in dependence upon a basis of virtue in which the three spheres are completely purified. It thoroughly understands all phenomena to be like an illusion and an emanation absent any inherent nature, empty of name and reason, and generated only from causes and conditions. Thus, pure worldly gnosis is not a conducive condition for the proliferation of the continuum of appearances. There is, moreover, no phenomenon that is generated in the absence of causes and conditions or any phenomenon that is generated from incompatible causes and conditions. Thus, no other cause and condition for the generation of pure worldly gnosis is found when the consciousness to which appearances manifest is transformed.

First Objection

Here, someone might object: if the production [of utterly pure appearance] is not asserted ultimately, it is not contradictory for [pure appearances] to appear to emerge as only illusory conventional phenomena.

Response to the First Objection

That phenomena have no ultimate nature does not conflict with the fact that conventional phenomena are produced. If there were such a conflict, the distinguishing mark of the Buddha's teaching—that is, that phenomena arise as dependent relations—whether asserted ultimately or conventionally, would be such that there would be no conflict between the continuum of conditions being severed and an effect of that continuum being observed. If that were the case, then conventional phenomena—even as mere illusions—would be nonexistent, without even so much as an ontologically viable trace. Therefore, it is not proper to say that "the continuum of utterly pure appearance, too, is unceasing because it has 'immeasurable collections' as a cause." Moreover, here it is suggested [that buddhas are] qualified by a *fully matured* buddha body that is an embodied basis for great gnosis; but after having eliminated the view of the self along with its karmic imprints,[28] how could one cling to the body, which is a burden, and remain within a conditioned state?[29]

If it is not viable for the continuum of appearances to remain, how is it established that tathāgatas are possessed of pure worldly gnosis? Again, if the issue is scrutinized with a discerning intellect, establishing that tathāgatas are possessed of even a state of nonconceptual gnosis seems inappropriate because of the emergence of nonconceptual gnosis when bodhisattvas are in meditative equipoise (*samāhita, mnyam bzhag*).

According to the texts in which bodhisattvas postulate a collection of eight consciousnesses, the emergence of nonconceptual gnosis is contingent upon a fundamental consciousness (*ālayavijñāna, kun gzhi rnam shes*)—fully matured, untransformed, containing all karmic seeds—that generates a mental consciousness. If it emerges through a seed that is the collection of an illimitable basis of virtue and takes the real expanse of reality as it objective basis, if it generates insight and concentration born from a faculty of mindfulness free from any state of self-grasping and is divorced from conceptual appearances of apprehended and apprehender, if it is an uncontaminated mind that obtains the label *transcendent mind* or *gnosis*, if the fully mature fundamental consciousness is transformed, then contingent upon what causes and conditions does a consistent type of gnosis like that nonconceptual gnosis of bodhisattvas emerge?[30]

When exhaustively analyzed, it is difficult to know whether the transformed state of the fundamental consciousness is itself mirror-like gnosis (*ādarśajñāna, me long lta bu'i ye shes*) and thus nonconceptual gnosis; or whether in that fundamental basis, mental consciousness generates a transformed individually discriminating gnosis (*pratyavekṣaṇajñāna, so sor rtogs pa'i ye shes*) that is an ultimately real subject. In that case, it would contradict transmigration (*gnas 'pho ba*).

Second Objection

If someone says "it is an inconceivable phenomenon," then it would become imperative to prove all imputed phenomena.[31] If someone were to say that nonconceptual gnosis emerges from that ordinary mind and mental consciousness, then—along the lines of the discussion of pure worldly gnosis above—there would be a need to locate its causes and conditions.

Response to the Second Objection

According to texts of those who postulate a single consciousness, for example, when a stone containing gold flecks is smelted, the gold flecks are extracted. First, the appearance of a rock is perceived, after which, when gold is perceived, it is thought about in conventional terms as the valuable rock from which gold is obtained. If scrutinized with a discerning intellect, the two are not naturally cause and effect of one another; rather, both the gold flecks and the stone share in the single character of earth element. Through fire, the underlying stone, the undesirable element, is extracted after which there is a desirable remainder.

For most folks, the undesirable element is thought of as stone. When the desirable element is manifest, they would think of it as something from which gold particles are obtained. From that, since the manifestation of natural gold conditions the manifestation of the undesirable element, people think that rust emerges from the gold. After that, upon the manifestation of a yellow mineral in which no impurities are found, folks think: "gold flecks!" In a similar way, when training occasions the convergence of insight and concentration within a single consciousness, an undesirable element is extracted after which there is a desirable remainder, which, in conventional terms, is labeled, respectively, the ordinary mind (*citta*, *rnam shes*) and gnosis. Moreover, given the variety of conditions in which purities and impurities manifest, we find gnosis designated in terms of *nonconceptual* and *pure worldly*. According to this system, though, there is no separation between the desirable and undesirable elements. The gold flecks, moreover, are extracted through smelting that refines it and attenuates impurities; and in the end, both are consumed. Similarly, ordinary mind, which is undesirable, and gnosis, which is desirable, are of a single element of consciousness. Thus, according to this system, especially, there is no *good element* that is something separate from a *bad element* because, in the end, there would be no appearance of either.

Even if the collection of eight consciousnesses is asserted, one is not freed from this fallacy (*bādha*, *gnod pa*). Since stainless awareness arises when all the karmic seeds in the fundamental consciousness are destroyed, there is no reason whatsoever to think that some extra karmic seed remains that generates cognitive awareness. Again, neither system can establish that nonconceptual gnosis is itself something that transcends the character of cognitive awareness, for gnosis emerges either in conjunction with sensation or divorced from it. If it is qualified by sensation, how could it be nonconceptual? If it is divorced from it, how could it be cognitive awareness?[32] If it is independent of sensation, how is it that the convention *inanimate* (*jaḍa*, *bems po*) is not applied? Thus, if it is maintained that it is divorced from sensation, there is no need for debate.

Third Objection

Some even state that nonconceptual gnosis emerges from the karmic imprint of actual reality.[33] Some also state that it emerges from its own substantial cause (*upādānakāraṇa*, *nye bar len pa'i rgyu*).

Response to the Third Objection

Are karmic imprints of actual reality infused[34] by something distinct or are they not so infused? If they are so infused, how is it [actual reality] feasibly actual reality at all? If they are not so infused, how can one avoid postulating its [actual reality's] own nature as its cause? Further, is the substantial cause something dependent upon a contingent condition or not? If not, how could phenomena arise as dependent relations? How could one avoid, moreover, postulating a cause for a self-governing causal agent? If actual reality is dependent on such [causal factors], what distinction is there between its general causal conditions and its nature? When it is said, in this case, that this is proven through the reasoning on reality (*dharmatāyukti*, *chos kyi rigs pa*),[35] there is no need for proof via another form of reasoning. As to the notion that there is nothing at all that entails a fallacy, we shall analyze the object, criteria, consequences, and so on, of the reasoning on reality below. Thus, it is not possible to prove that "the continuum of causes and effects that appears as totally pure phenomena (*vyavadānikadharmāḥ*, *rnam par byang ba'i chos*) is unceasing." In fact, all phenomena are basically the same insofar as being illusory.

Fourth Objection

If that is so, it might be asked, "If all phenomena are akin to an illusion, how is it that the ultimate character of awakening and the uncompounded character of the peace associated with nirvāṇa is set forth as akin to an illusion?"

Response to the Fourth Objection

The reality of awakening is divorced from conventional description. Beings wandering in saṃsāra nevertheless recognize and take as an objective basis that "there is an awakening to be achieved that is the attainment of an uncompounded actuality." Thus, considering that existing as an objective basis entails being an existent object, awakening is illusory. Along these lines, it is said,

> Consciousness is like an illusion;
> Awakening, too, is akin to an illusion;
> For example, some illusionists
> Incant mantras over a figurine, after which
> The finely crafted form is
> Penetrated through the force of applied practice;
> To the captivated mind, such forms as
> A quadruped and others appear.
> Similarly, the mind cultivated through the
> Collection of merit and gnosis
> Manifests in the imagination of
> Sentient beings as unexcelled awakening.[36]

Also, as it is said, "If there is some phenomena that is either greater than or superior to nirvāṇa, that too is like an illusion, like a dream."[37] Thus, of everything that can possibly be set forth as an object of designation, none are not illusory.

When nirvāṇa is discussed in the context of its absence of true nature, there is no illustration that may be offered that establishes its illusory character. Such phrases as "all phenomena are like an illusion," and so forth, occur in discourses in which the words proclaimed are applied definitively—and in some that are said to teach in excessive terms. Proclaimed in definitively applied terms, it is stated:

> All rivers flow in zigs and zags,
> All women are illusive, flattering,
> Everything included as the forest,
> Is undoubtedly taken to be wood,
> Everything made is impermanent,

Anything produced is dissatisfying,
All phenomena are illusory.[38]

And just as it is proclaimed in excessive terms:

All rivers flow in zigs and zags,
The Nerañjarā river, however, runs straight;
All women are illusive, flattering,
Female arhats are not,
Forests are all determined to consist of wood,
A forest of precious jewels is not wood,
Everything made is impermanent,
The exalted body (*kāya*, *sku*) of one who has gone to bliss
constantly resides.
Anything produced is dissatisfying and
Emergent nonconceptual gnosis is bliss;
All phenomena are illusory.

Thus, whatever is present and holds its own character is called a *phenomenon* that is feasibly established as an entity; and whatever is said to be characterized by its absence of character—for example, nirvāṇa—is thus something that simply must be imagined.

Fifth Objection

Here, someone might suggest that if the continuum of great gnosis alone is not a perceptible referent of the mind, then there would be no basis upon which a buddha's deeds of great compassion could arise. Thus, how could peace in the form of a partial nirvāṇa be avoided? How could the term *nonabiding nirvāṇa* (*apratiṣṭhanirvāṇa*, *mi gnas pa'i mya ngan las 'das pa*) even be applied?

Response to the Fifth Objection

Along those lines, if at a determined point in time—through the force of the collective karma of beings wandering in saṃsāra—processes manifest that are themselves precipitated by previous actions (*karma*, *las*), and if accordingly they are actually capable of projecting periods of destruction, formation, vacuity, and subsistence of the arena that comprises the world during a great aeon, what about buddhas? From generating the exalted mind of bodhicitta up to experiencing diamond-like concentration (*vajropamaḥsamādhi, rdo rje lta bu'i ting nge 'dzin*) and through the force of accomplishing great waves of enlightened activity for the benefit of migrators by means of the ten perfections, they are capable of projecting unimpeded compassionate activity. So what point is there in being astonished?

Sixth Objection

Here, as well, someone might suggest that the formation of the physical world is the existing force that emerges as something manifesting in accordance with the karma of the unbroken continuum of beings wandering in conditioned existence.

Response to the Sixth Objection

If that were the case, how would the world form during the period of vacuity?

Seventh Objection

Further, it might be said that the world is actualized from, in equal parts, projecting karma from the past and presently occurring karma.

Response to the Seventh Objection

If that were the case, after arising as an arhat, how could the body of someone who has reached nirvāṇa avoid destruction immediately upon attaining the uncompounded? What holy body relics would subsequently be left over? Thus, what is precipitated through intensely powerful karma of the past need not rely upon presently occurring karma; and even if the intense energy of karma happening currently was present and it was capable of preventing the maturation of previous karma, there would still be no contradiction.

On this point, moreover, if the power of some sage's aspirations, which can remain for perhaps a hundred or even a thousand years after the sage passes away, can project the manifestation of virtuous good and malevolent negativity wherever that sage has made aspirations, then what about the capacity of buddhas to project the emanations that manifest conducive to whatever the needs of trainees, the capacity for which is accomplished from first taking up the aspiring mind on through the limitless aspirations that are finally perfected aspirations on the ninth bodhisattva ground? How could such a state be impossible? And what source is there for astonishment?

Eighth Objection

It might also be suggested that the objective basis for the sage's aspirations and sentient beings are set forth in virtue of being *blessed* [literally: "transformed through majesty"] (*adhiṣṭhita, byin gyis brlabs pa*).

Response to the Eighth Objection

In this system, compassionate activity is unimpeded. If it does not rely on the continuum of the aspirant, then the wish itself is something that has a basis in sentient beings. Accordingly, the object of compassion is indeed sentient beings and therefore it is stated:

> For as long as the afflictions that sicken migrators are not healed,
> There is no curing the compassion of bodhisattvas.

It is also stated in *The Teaching on the Limits of Aspirations*:[39]

> However far the utmost limit (*paryanta, mthar thug*) of space,
> The bounds of sentient beings, too, are like that;
> Whatever the utmost limit of karma and affliction,
> The bounds of my aspirations, too, are like that.

This, as well, is taught: "Into each and every atom of the world that is the environment, into each and every pore of the sentient beings who are its inhabitants, the innumerable blessings of compassion enter." Teachings such as these amount to nothing more than reasonings, many elucidations of which appear in sūtras of definitive meaning.[40] This is also taught here:[41]

> One brought forth by the uncompounded,
> Is a noble person.

This is also taught when it is stated:[42]

> Do not view a buddha as form;
> Do not study a buddha in terms of name, race (*gotra, rigs*) or family (*anvaya, rgyud*);
> A buddha is not explained as sound,
> A buddha is not brought forth by mind, consciousness, or intellect;
> That which is actual reality—that is the Conqueror.

This is also taught when it is stated:[43]

> Insofar as someone classifies characteristics,
> They are in a child's domain of experience;
> Such a person does not perceive
> The ineffable buddhas.

This is also taught when it is stated:

> The virtuous, uncontaminated quality of a tathāgata,
> Is the supreme dharmakāya, in which
> There is no suchness per se, no being-in-suchness;
> Like a reflection, a tathāgata appears in worlds.

This is also taught when it is stated:[44]

> A tathāgata is a phenomenon forever unarisen (*anutpāda, skye med*);
> All phenomena are akin to a sugata;
> Childish minds, fixated on characteristics,
> Act on phenomena not present in their worlds.

Or where it is stated:[45]

> Whosoever perceives me as form,
> Whosoever understands me as sound,
> Engages in a mistaken effort;
> That person does not perceive me.
> The guide (*nāyaka, 'dren pa*) is the dharmakāya;
> One should see a buddha as actual reality.

Passages such as these thus proclaim in detail the buddha's own nature, which both authoritative scripture (*āgama*, *lung*) and reasoning (*yukti*, *rigs pa*) show to be utterly pure dharmadhātu. In that case, sentient beings and a buddha are equal in nature, and all phenomena are empty of nature. All phenomena are naturally beyond sorrow (*prakṛtiparinirvṛta*, *rang bzhin gyis mya ngan las 'das pa*). All phenomena are naturally luminous. All phenomena are manifestly perfectly awakened from the beginning.

Whoever realizes the object in this manner, his or her intelligence is indistinguishable from a buddha. Regardless of the fact that the five psychophysical aggregates of a person are illusory, when possessed of the intelligence of the state of the tathāgata, they pertain to the supreme path, because what does not pertain to the supreme path is any perceived distinction between sentient beings and buddhas. Such a mode for objects is not simply the purview of the guhyamantra system alone. It is also proclaimed in the sūtras of definitive meaning in accordance with the *Āryagaṇḍavyūhasūtra*,[46] which proclaims:

> I and the buddhas—and anyone—
> Naturally abide in equality;
> And those who do not, who do not *get it*,
> Will yet become sugatas.
>
> Form, sensation, and discriminations,
> Consciousness, intentions;[47]
> They will become mahāmunis—
> Tathāgatas beyond count.

Those who deprecate the tantric teaching that the ordinary psychophysical aggregates are, in reality, the Jina's *maṇḍala*[48] will also deprecate sūtras that teach this. Moreover, for those who assert this teaching to be a merely imagined meditation intended as an antidote for the sake of the path, I would remind them of such things as the imagined and mastered forms mentioned above. As for the character of conceptuality and imputation, they will be explained below.

Fourth Objection: Concerning the Reality of Saṃsāra

Some might say that even if there is no real entity of affliction to be eliminated and all phenomena are naturally beyond sorrow, wanderers within conditioned existence, who are bound, nevertheless experience various dissatisfactions drifting upon the ocean of saṃsāra.

Response to the Fourth Objection

To that, it should be said that although there is nothing real restraining beings, it is from the appearance of seeming to be bound that the appearance of the experience of suffering comes to be. Take, for example, a young prince or householder's son whose immaturity drives his out-of-control behavior.[49] One day, he remains at home to play. In the family storeroom, he stuffs a jewel wrapped in a red cloth into an already overflowing basket. It thus overflows more and spills some drinks inside. The basket cord, as well, frays. Strands fall into leftover cooked rice, which spills. After a while, his play stirs up his appetite. Once hunger is upon him, he searches the storeroom for food. When he looks toward the basket and sees the rice and frayed basket cord, he perceives a snake and leaves the storeroom frightened and with no food. Growing thirsty, he begins to search for something to drink. In the storeroom, he perceives the spilled drinks as blood because of the red glow of the jewel. Again, the boy leaves the storeroom frightened. Pained by his thirst and hunger, he is reduced to tears and wailing until a servant (*antevāsin/upasthātṛi*, *nye gnas*) arrives, who asks, "Boy, why are you crying?" The boy answers, "When I went looking for food and drink because I was hungry and thirsty, there was a snake in the cooked rice and blood in the drinks. I got scared; and though famished and parched, I was not able to get any food. So I was crying."

Thereafter, the servant without even offering the slightest bit of advice[50] to the boy, says to him, "Boy, do not cry. I will get rid of the snake and clean up the blood and give you some clean food." He removes the cord and the jewel, cleans up, and gives the boy some food and drink. The boy thinks, "This servant has cleaned up what is foul and given me clean food and drink!" With such thoughts in his mind, the boy is freed from his suffering.

If there was even the smallest point of advice that could be given to the youth, one would simply say this: "What *is* the snake here? *This* is the cord *you* placed there. What *is* the blood here? It is the light from the jewel *you* placed here."

Once the youth recognizes the food and drink to be clean from the beginning,[51] he would be freed [from any discontent]. In the same manner, although all phenomena are like an illusion, sentient beings, not recognizing this to be the case, appear—because of the influence of a realist view—to be bound by afflictions and appear to experience discontent. Accordingly, [sentient beings] are obsessed with appearances of illusory phenomena; because of that, they are fixated on characteristics.

Thence the emergence of the attachment to ambitions (*smon chags 'byung*) in which affliction completely disturbs the mind and by force of which the various karmic processes of conceptual construction manifest. It is in that context that these aggregates, which are in the nature of suffering, come to be. Especially under the influence of appearance, the emergence of obsession with things, and so on, comes to be, as I discussed above.

First Objection

It might be suggested that while the nature of things is such that the character of afflictions, karma, and discontent (*duḥkha, sdug bsngal*) emerge only through a causal process, that process itself is a real entity. In that case, if there is no need to search for a distinct actual basis in what appears as any given thing, or if there is no need to search for a distinct factor of the actual basis, or if there is no need to search for other qualitative factors, and no need to search for a distinct fundamental basis, then what distinct actual basis should be sought?[52]

Response to the First Objection

That is like saying, for example, that when a blue cloth is perceived, there is a need to recognize something outside the consciousness itself appearing in a blue aspect that is the real entity present—something distinct that is the actual objective basis, the causal efficacy of which qualifies a real object whose own character in this case is derived from a primary element. In that case, what distinct factors of the actual basis are there to be validated? What is said, here, is this: what appears is merely the blue of the cloth. Different factors of blue such as lapis lazuli (*vaiḍūrya, bai ḍūrya*), sapphire (*indranīla, in dra ni la*), ink (*pattra, lo ma*), and so on, and different factors of the cloth's blue itself, as well, appear so long as obscurations do not hinder them; and there is a different recognition when a factor of blue is not seen by those for whom [perception] is hindered.

In that case, what distinct qualitative factors are there to be validated? What is said is that only the cloth's color and shape are perceived. Other things, however—its type (*kula, rigs*), cause (*hetu, rgyu*), source (*ākara, 'byung khungs*), manufacturing (*śilpa, bzo*), weight (*gurvī-laghvī, lci yang*), texture (*mṛidukā-karkaśatvam, 'jam rtsub*), quality (*nus, śakta*), value (*argha, rin thang*), and so on—are recognized.

In that case, what distinct basis is there to validate? What is said is that when blue ink is perceived in the appearance of the blue cloth as the blue of the cloth, it is the blue ink that is the actual basis. Yet in this case, there is something else that is not recognized that should be recognized. Accordingly, the philosophical validation of distinct characteristics comes about because of an insistence upon the existence of entities of persons and phenomena. In that connection, the validation of a distinct factor that is an actual basis and the validation of its qualitative factors each flow from a philosophical insistence upon a personal entity. Both the validation of a distinct actual basis and the validation of the qualities of the basis emerge because of asserting the presence of a real phenomenal entity. Thus, for those who insist philosophically upon a real personal entity, when a cloth appears, different types of things, such as a vase and so forth, are precluded. And since similar types of things such as a second cloth are precluded when the cloth's unified nature is itself something validated as a real entity, its color, tactility and so forth—everything is comprehended as an instance of that nature's quality—thereby remain unperceived as different factors even though one factor of a single quality is being perceived.

Things like vases and other cloths (other things, too) have their own respective natures, even the ones that are themselves blue, since their respective blue colors are distinct from the blue of a given cloth, their blue colors are distinct colors from the blue factor of the cloth, not unlike what was described above. Therefore, when validating a real phenomenal entity because of putting an end to a real personal entity, both factors [the entities of persons and phenomena] are precluded. Accordingly, though it is possible to perceive a blue cloth or blue ink when the perceiving consciousness is generated in a blue aspect, it perceives that object's nature in toto. Given the fact that there is no perception of a distinct factor as an actual basis, there is also no perception of a distinct qualitative factor.

If, in the context of asserting a real phenomenal entity, there is an assertion that external objects are real entities, an actual [that is, objective] basis that is distinct would be validated. For, just as suggested in the discussion above, when a blue cloth is perceived, then except for something besides the mere appearance of consciousness as such as blue, an object, which is itself characterized by efficacy and the presence of a real entity, would be asserted. When external objects are denied as real entities while insisting upon consciousness being a real entity, it is stated that, in accordance with that assertion, when a blue cloth is perceived, it does not exist as some real entity distinct from the consciousness perceiving it. Yet if consciousness itself appears as if blue, then a distinct actual basis of appearance characterized by false conceptions is recognized as the actual presence of some real entity. In the light of such an assertion, the statement would be proved. However, when assertions such as these are not validated, simply labeling the mere appearance of characteristics as the character of a given phenomenon is not to be seen as a fault.

Second Objection

If all phenomena are empty of their own nature, then what source is there for their appearance? What source is there for confusion? Given that appearance entails [an objective] basis of appearance, is it not the case that confusion entails a basis of confusion?

Response to the Second Objection

Although there is no basis for either appearance or confusion, inasmuch as the conditions remain present, appearance and confusion remain possible. The problem lies in supposing that their bases are real, though they are not—just as a mirage initially appears real but ultimately is not. Further, the recognition that bases are devoid of nature is incompatible with things being confusing. Although they are without nature, what conflict is there in not realizing and having become familiarized with that? If it is the case that appearances that are confused do not entail a base, what are their conditions? These two [appearance and confusion] become unified within a single cause because of the influence of nonexistents things that appear; and awareness is confused because of the influence of nonexistents that appear.

If that is the case, which of these two is first? They are basically the same. For example, when an awareness to which nonexistent objects appear existent is generated in a dream, at the very first moment this awareness is generated, it is something confused. At the very first moment that a confused awareness is generated, its generation is accompanied by an image that appears as the object. Therefore, these two are basically the same. Likewise, all sentient beings' confused appearances are basically the same.

If that is the case, what, where, and for how long have these confusing appearances been confused? In the context of mere convention, it is said that if someone is confused, it is sentient beings of the six regions that are confused. In terms of where they are confused, it is in the three realms (*tridhātu, khams gsum*) of saṃsāra. In terms of for how long, it is from beginningless time that they have been confused. This is how it is explained in the context of mere convention, though, in reality, that is not the way it is.

How is it then? The appearances of place, time, and person as such are confused appearances. Take, for example, an instance of the appearance of a nonexistent object that appears as a real object in a dream. Through the appearance of place, time, and person, happiness and discontent manifest in experience. Here, oneself and other people live in places—some of which are agreeable, some of which are not—participating in experiences of happiness and discontent for what appear to be varying durations of time. In the appearance itself, there is no such object, no such person, no time, either; even happiness and discontent are not present. Nevertheless, such phenomena appear as if existent, though they are nonexistent. Likewise, while beings wandering within conditioned existence appear to revolve in saṃsāra under the sway of two types of ignorance from a beginningless point in time, in a single moment of the fundamental mind, its own nature appears as the illimitable world. That is to say, though a reflection appears to reside deep within a mirror, and while it appears to reside upon its surface, since a mirror has no depth, the reflection inhabits no distinct physical point. Likewise, given that it is not something distinct in the mind, it has no [spatial or temporal] dimensions in the world. In a dream, time, too, does not pass—not even an hour. Although one might have a dream that seems to last for an aeon or longer, no prolonged period of time passes, either. When bodhisattvas transform the passing of a week into the passing of a great aeon,[53] the week and the great aeon, as well, are mere appearances to awareness, neither of which comprise any real temporal extension. During the transformation of a week into an incalculable aeon, too, there is no elongation of short moments of time into longer moments of time. Similarly, even those who assert saṃsāra to be without a beginning point in time confuse awareness for time.

If that is the case and all appearances are confusing experiences, by what process does confused awareness appear? This point is explained in *Meditation on Bodhicitta*:[54]

> A thinker's false conceptions are experienced without beginning;
> The intellect is incorrect, conditioned by the force of ignorance, thus
> The happening itself of mind, mental factors, and the three bodies
> appear as objects.

Thus, since the mind of beings wandering in saṃsāra has been overpowered by ignorance, and since it is primordially devoid of inception, it is naturally discursive and corrupted by false conceptions. Under their influence, the happening itself of mind and mental factors as such appears as the three actual bases of objects. Therein, the three actual bases—the happening itself of mind and mental factors—appear as three aggregates. What are the three? Mind, intellect, and cognition (*vijñapti, rnam par rig pa*).

On this point, moreover, those who philosophically postulate a collection of eight consciousnesses insist that the mind is fundamental (*ālaya, kun gzhi*), that intellect pertains to afflicted intellect (*kliṣṭamanas, nyon mongs pa can gyi yid*), and that cognition comprises the collection of six consciousnesses. Those who postulate a single consciousness assert a single cognitive element whose subtle or gross production is distinguished through causes and conditions. For example, the single nature of the ocean is an unwavering state consisting in its moist (*saṃsveda, gsher*) and fluid (*picchilatvam, mnyen pa*) character. By virtue of the condition of its medium (*upādānapratyaya, nye bar len pa'i rkyen*)—that is, water—it is always moving just a little bit; and the quality and quantity of its waves undulate by virtue of external conditions. Not unlike that, what we call *mind* is that very consciousness, which is a natural source for various capacities, that is characterized by cognitive awareness. What is referred to as the *intellect* is that very mind that by nature constantly grasps at an "I" under the influence of its medium. What is referred to as *consciousness* is said to be that very intellect described in terms of giving rise to the various subtle and gross types of awarenesses by means of objects and faculties. In sum, it follows that the actual bases appear as the three objects by force of the three aggregates. In terms of the mind appearing as an object, it is stated:[55]

> When the power of habit grows under the influence of karmic imprints accumulated through various karmic processes,
> The appearance of the mind as such appears similar to an object and body, as if something filled with bones.[56]

Due to the force of conceptual cognition having accumulated karmic imprints connected with the conceptual constructions that are associated with varieties of karmic processes, the power of the mind as such grows, and the mind as such appears as external objects and the body along with its faculties. This is a confused appearance, devoid of a fundamental basis, not unlike the hairs that appear to someone with cataracts, the sound of drums of a ruler's army, and the pile of bones upon which one meditates on the unpleasant, which appear under the influence of internal conditions that are devoid of any external fundamental basis.[57] In connection with the second actual basis of objects [intellect], a text teaches:

> The self generated because of the intellect as an object in the continuum of accumulated karmic imprints is nonexistent.[58]

So the intellect, with its focus on the self and the sense of self-importance connected to the mental continuum associated with karmic imprints, is fixated on a self that does not exist. By the force of that, self and other are differentiated like a snake and its tongue. These are confused appearances that have a fundamental basis, like the appearance of a fire-wheel produced from a spinning fire-brand and the appearance of a snake produced from seeing a rope. As an objective basis, it appears as if qualified by a self. In connection with the third actual basis of objects [cognition], it is stated:

> Cognition is produced from that which is clouded;
> It does not see what is subtle.[59]

Since [cognition is] clouded by the production of coarse processes of cognition and its attendant mental factors, the fixation upon various things as different and distinct is generated apart from [any awareness of] the subtle processual factors [by which] mental objects and sentient beings appear. The mind's objects and sentient beings are generated as the multiplicity of different things that we are attached to. In this case, confused appearance is accompanied by a fundamental basis that is false. For example, whether from a mental state fixated upon water, not knowing it to be a mirage, or the lively play of a small replica animated through illusion, the awareness involved is stimulated by other conditions. At a given point, when attachment and aversion are strongly generated, the appearance of a small replica that one has manufactured, although produced, is perceived as a distinct woman, which is akin to fixating on a thing and producing attachment and aversion.

These three confused appearances, moreover, comprise a unity of condition because cognized objects are not recognized as mental appearances since there is fixation on things as different and distinct. Through various karmic processes, under the influence of a variety of karmic imprints accumulated in the mind, the confused mind appears as objects and sentient beings. Under that influence, the intellect gives rise to the conceit of self and other. Because of the influence of both, cognition forms a basis of comparison because it appears as an object in dependence upon the dualistic projection of self and an other appearing to the mental faculties.

So in dependence on the fixation upon, and the appearance of, various objects, the intellect produces something similar to the view of the transitory collection because of the mental conceit of self, since all minds and mental factors are made to issue forth as contaminated. Under the influence of both, awareness of a variety of selves and a variety of phenomena is generated, because of which the cycle of becoming revolves uninterruptedly.

If one wishes to turn away from confused appearances, all appearances must be recognized as mental appearances per se. Thereby, the peg tethering the tent of self-grasping is pulled out of the ground of ignorance. Upon turning back an obsessive perspective on things and their character, the inaccurate awareness that sees mind-as-self and seizes on object-as-characterized—even with respect to correct appearances—is reversed and the force of turbulent karmas is attenuated. Meritorious karmas, as well, become conjoined with a nonobjectifying insight.

Take objects that appear in dreams, for example. When recognized as a dream because one's sleep has become a bit lighter, this is similar to the inability to generate attachment and aversion because fixation—even with respect to correct appearances—has been reversed. After that, when one has awakened and appearance itself is overcome, how could attachment and aversion be produced? Likewise, divorced from an obsessive perspective on things because appearance as such is overcome through the generation of the power of insight and concentration, how could conceptual constructions brought about by affliction come to be in connection with appearances that are mere illusion? Thus, in simply recognizing or not recognizing the nature of phenomena, we find that there is no real entity whatsoever to be eliminated outside of what is simply labeled by the term *thoroughly afflicted*. There is no real entity to be established outside of what is simply labeled by the term *utterly pure*. Nevertheless, when the nature of phenomena is not recognized, the process of confused appearance pertains accordingly to appearance alone.

Here concludes the second chapter, pointing out objections and responses to the teaching that all phenomena are basically equal in terms of being illusory.

3. Distinguishing the Perfected System of the Illusory in the Great Perfection from the Other Vehicles That Retain the Nomenclature of Illusion

Entering onto the Great Vehicle (*mahāyāna, theg chen*) path is something enabled through the realization of the illusory character of all phenomena. The authentic assimilation and consummation of the realization that all phenomena are basically the same in being illusory is the Great Perfection approach to the path.

First Objection: Concerning the Reality of Confused Appearances

To that, it might be asked whether or not proponents of the Great Perfection approach would assert that the confused appearances described above are perceived by the mind.

Response to the First Objection

Is that supposed to be a question about whether or not these—whatever they are—are appearing or not? Or is that a question about whether or not said appearances are actually real or not? If it is a questions about appearance—and they are said to appear—then what basis of dispute is there to be manufactured between various theories? Nobody at all disputes whether shared appearances do or do not appear to ordinary sense faculties. If it is a question about whether or not appearances are actually real or not and one holds that they are actually real, how then could someone perfectly realize them as illusory in accordance with the Great Perfection?

The hierarchy of views correspond only to greater or lesser degrees of obsession with appearances as solid, real things. Take, for example, the appearance of a black snake's image in water: for some, perceiving the snake as real causes fear; and they try to get rid of it. Similarly, even though the dissatisfying state of things is in fact illusory, the Śrāvakas perceive it as real and attempt to get rid of it. And even though some recognize the image as a reflection, they still perceive there to be a danger in touching it and, thus, practice to apply a remedy.[1] Similarly, the Prajñāpāramitā text tradition approaches phenomena as illusion-like. Yet it also fabricates remedies—generating gnosis concerning the knowable and great compassion—because of its theory that causal efficacy is real. Some who recognize the image as an image, who indeed realize that no injury comes from contact with the "snake," are capable of persuading others who are incapable of touching it themselves because of their fear, which is, in fact, unjustified. Similarly, according to the system of Kriyatantra and Outer Yogatantra, even though vulgar behavior and substances are recognized to be without any intrinsic fault, some practitioners are themselves incapable of simply letting go,[2] so they make offerings to deities, practice austerities, use substances that pertain to spiritual accomplishment (*siddhadravya*, *dngos grub kyi rdzas*), and so on. Some recognize that they will not be harmed by touching it and practice austerities while trampling on it in order to swiftly eradicate others' fear of it. Similarly, to do away with all manner of activities and experience the equality of all phenomena according to the Inner Yogatantra system, one engages in stomping on it and undertakes the austerities in which phenomena are considered neither good nor bad and one consumes foods with no consideration of whether they are pure or impure. Some, whose awareness of the character of the reflection is unmistaken, see the image for what it is and thus see all the above practices as child's play. These people are thereby beyond such unhelpful notions as the real rejection [or elimination] of afflictions as if they were real and that beings are, in reality, bound by them. They in fact perceive trampling on an image as if one is fearless as childish. These people are not capable of generating any conceptual constructions whatsoever that are conditioned by biases. For such an individual, no perturbation of the mind occurs.

Similarly, it is because of realizing and, in the end, assimilating the very basic equality of all phenomena according to the Great Perfection approach to the path that awareness thus remains undeluded by the influence of appearance, incapable of generating conceptual constructions, and unbiased, unmoved, and unexerted. Thus, the perfect realization of the illusory in this context pertains to the penetration, or consummation, of the realization of the indivisibility of the two truths. Further, simply asserting the identical nature of subject (*dharma*, *chos*) and its predicate (*dharmin*, *chos can*) does not count as a realization of the indivisibility of the two truths.

On this view, even in the Śrāvaka system, where the character of karmic processes is asserted to be impermanent, impermanence as such is not asserted to be something distinct from karmic processes. In the Yogācāra, where the character of false imaginations is asserted to be empty of duality, it is not asserted that emptiness is something different from dependent phenomena. Thus, even assertions of actual reality regarding a subject are not asserting reality to be something different than the qualificand, so when Mādhyamikas assert that all phenomena are qualified by an absence of inherent nature, what point is there bringing up any assertion on their part that emptiness is something distinct from the phenomena that it putatively qualifies?[3] Nevertheless, since Mādhyamikas will not let go of the discursive scheme of the two truths, their view is not counted as a nondualistic view. When these appearances of outer and inner things are seen to be totally imagined and basically the same, *that* is proclaimed to be seeing the indivisibility of the two truths.

Second Objection: Concerning Reality in an Illusory World

Illusions, emanations, and the like are brought to mind as mere appearances. Thus, if it is established, or if it is possible, that the appearances of those illusions, emanations, and outer and inner things are basically of the same character, because they are alike in appearance, then what is totally imagined—the eternal self of the non-Buddhists, and so on—is comparable to what has no basis in reality, like a hare's horn (*śaśaviṣāṇa*, *ri bong gi rwa*), which is a superimposed object that is denied. If outer and inner things, which are established through direct perception and nonobservation (*anupalambha*, *mi dmigs pa*)—that is, inference—are in fact generated because of causes and conditions, how can they be basically the same as what is totally imagined? If an actual basis were found in connection with the totally imagined, it might be said their being equal or not can be qualified and indeed possible; but without establishing the actual basis itself in connection with the totally imagined, what precisely would be established as equal to what?

Response to the Second Objection

The illustration *(lakṣya, mtshan gzhi)* that establishes something as totally imagined or in terms of its own characteristics is appearance itself. All philosophical theories—from the non-Buddhist extremists up through the perspective of the Great Perfection—take the character of appearance as their basis; what they dispute between themselves concerns what pertains to the character of appearance and how it exists. What pertains to the character of appearance is established as true; its existence is established as an objective basis. When a given appearance is repudiated as totally imagined by another, it is nonimplicatively and implicatively negated. Through nonimplicative negation (*prasajyapratiṣedha, med dgag*), only what is totally imagined is repudiated. Through implicative negation (*paryudāsa, ma yin dgag*), some characteristic that one asserts to qualify an appearance is validated. Here, the four procedures that negate and establish are only mentioned; they will be explained below.

In this way, the philosophical positions of others are repudiated and one's own are established using the four procedures that negate and establish. Yet all theories are indistinguishable insofar as they consistently assert that causes and conditions give rise to effects that are established through direct perception and nonobservation, from which one's assertions about the actual existence of a given appearance and how it actually pertains [to reality] are established and the similar assertions of others regarding what is actual are disputed as being about what is nonexistent and does not pertain [to reality], because of being established as about what is totally imaginary. Inasmuch as the entire horizon of theories is hierarchically validated in this manner, first, all one's own views are established as true. The views of others are then established as being about what is totally imaginary. When hierarchically established in this manner, eventually whatever is one's own point is the only one that is deemed actual—*the* significant point that does not leave anything unaccounted for.

The Non-Buddhist View

The basis of the non-Buddhist view—the eternalist view, the view of a creator as cause—is given in terms of five types, which is to say: Mahābrahma,

Vaśavartideva, the eternal self, eternal nature, and eternal minute particles. Though these are eternal, they are also causes that are eternal. It is through their power that appearances—outer and inner things that are impermanent—exist as the effects of their emanations. These causes, which are the productive activity of eternal causes alone, never fail to produce their effects. These outer and inner things, which are the productive activity of constant effects alone, never fail to be caused. Accordingly, these outer and inner things exist because of causes and conditions; and the nature of the effects themselves, in addition to being established via direct perception and nonobservation, are seen to be impermanent.

On this view, sages who are endowed with the divine eye once the concentration of meditation is attained (*dhyāna-samādhi, bsam gtan gyi ting nge 'dzin*), having seen the transmigration of sentient beings, see the transmigrating person who is a so-called sentient being, from the body that is composed of minute particles of those who have died to the occurrence of sentient beings who move from one state to another and are born instantaneously; even the birth of corporeal beings whose bodies are composed of minute particles are seen through yogic direct perception. Instantaneously born sentient beings, who do not transmigrate and whose bodies are composed of minute particles, are also seen through yogic direct perception. Therefore, on this view, under the influence of the conception of an eternal sentient being, since all that exists is composed from minute particles that are eternal, the aggregates that are established through the composition of particles are emanated, or fabricated. Thus, since the particles move to another person after a person is destroyed, the assemblage of minute particles is impermanent. Yet the minute particles themselves are permanent—never subject to destruction.

When, moreover, the beginning point of a cosmic cycle[4] is considered through that divine eye, inasmuch as at first there are no other sentient beings, there is a perception of the arisen Mahābrahma; and there is no perception of a time prior in which Mahābrahma was not present. Consequently, the non-Buddhist extremist thinks that the world is formed because it is conceived by Mahābrahma, in accordance with his wishes, who thinks: *the entire world is emanated by me.*[5] Their divine eyes see it in this way. After that, when an end point is considered, given that different sentient beings are seen to die, this world too is seen as perishable. Yet at that point, Mahābrahma is seen to remain undying—and there is no perception of a subsequent time in which Mahābrahma is not present. Given observation through yogic direct perception and nonobservation through yogic direct perception, and given that these also appear as things that are causes and effects, which are themselves established by direct perception and nonobservation, this is considered a view in which things exist just in the manner in which they appear.

The Buddhist Systems

Among Buddhists, and included among the followers of the theories of the Vaibhāṣikas, those such as the followers of Vatsiputra (*vatsīputrīya, gnas ma bu'i sde*) say that Mahābrahma and Vaśavartideva are neither existent nor eternal. They are not causes and their respective selves and nature have no basis in reality. People who are instantaneously born sentient beings exist in an inexpressible relation to the aggregates,[6] similar to the relation of water spirits to water.[7] The transmigration of that which is the person (*gang zag ba*) is like a water spirit fleeing from a barren place. Nevertheless, it is asserted that it exists as a momentary impermanent thing. Minute particles, however, are not subject to momentary impermanence (*kṣaṇānitya, skad cig ma'i mi rtag pa*). They claim that momentary impermanence is real. According to this philosophical position, the non-Buddhists extremist view that Mahābrahma, among others, is permanent *and* a cause is proven by nonimplicative negation to be totally imagined. It is therefore denied. That which is the person is proven through implicative negation to be existent, transmigrating, and indestructible such that ultimate reality is proven to be a real entity of which things may be predicated. More need not be said on the matter given the fact that the Vaibhāṣikas and those in their camp—the Sautrāntikas, as well—and regions such as Kashmir and Madhyadeśa/Maghada are the source of so many conflicting theories.[8]

The Śrāvaka System

To summarize for the moment, in the Śrāvaka system, that which is set forth as real according to the system of the non-Buddhist extremists, these outer and inner things, are totally imagined on the Śrāvaka view and therefore without any basis in reality. [For Śrāvakas, however,] the character of the aggregates, elements, and sources is not like that. These outer and inner things are dual, produced by causes and conditions, and established through direct perception and nonobservation—things with their own character. The how and the what of them are established as ultimately real entities.[9]

What is real according to the yogic direct perception and nonobservation of non-Buddhist extremists is, on their view, devoid of error, even though there are others who do not perceive such. Here, when the state of death ceases,[10] that enables the coming-into-being (*abhinivarta*, *mngon par 'grub*) of the intermediate state (*antarābhava*, *bar ma do'i srid pa*); the cessation of that enables the coming-to-be of the state of birth (*upapattibhava*, *skye ba'i srid pa*) such that the continuity of the five aggregates is without interruption. Given that is the case, when one of the three states of being comes to an end, the view that fixates on the imagined emerges inasmuch as one has failed to realize the reality of obtaining a single birth. In yogic direct perception, there is no confusion. Even the idea of a beginning point and an end point of the self and the world is analogous to that, too.

The Yogācāra System

According to the Yogācāra approach to the Buddhist path, given these appearances of outer and inner things, the Śrāvakas are mistaken in their insistence that (1) external objects are real entities independent of cognitive recognition, which have their own particular characteristics that are naturally capable of being grasped, and that (2) cognitive recognition is itself an internal object, which is also a real entity capable of being grasped. Both these [external and internal objects] are totally imagined, with no basis in reality. Moreover, the Yogācārins work to negate them using nonimplicative negation.

In the Yogācāra system, although false conceptions are [said to be] devoid of duality, they are indeed characterized by their dual appearance. Given that these are generated by causes and conditions and are not, moreover, incompatible with direct perception and nonobservation, is not the actual occurrence of mind and mental factors a reflexive direct perception (*svasaṁvedana-pratyakṣa*, *rang rig pa'i mngon sum*)? Is direct perception as such not knowledge of reality? In that case, what need is there to prove knowledge of reality through some other form of reasoning? Is there some powerful distinct second knowledge of reality that repudiates it [direct perception], establishing the ultimate state as something whose existence and being is substantially real? In the Yogācāra system, nondual cognition is established as a real entity in existential and predicative terms.[11]

Among the schools of Yogācāra, there are Yogācārins who postulate real images (*satyākāravādin*, *rnam bden smra ba*). For them, it is said that, in the end, whatever appears is a real entity. There are also Yogācārins who postulate false images (*alīkākāravādin, rnam brdzun smra ba*). For them, the presence of generated appearances of object and subject—false appearances—if true, are only conventionally true. What is real is said to be characterized by reflexive awareness, which is empty of duality and is, in the end, a real entity. There are also Yogācārins who postulate the nonexistence of images (*nirākāravādin/anākāravādin, rnam pa myed par smra ba*). For them, there is not even a single moment of experience in which there is the generation of subjective and objective images connected with mind and mental factors associated with the three realms, because dualistic appearance pertains to karmic imprints, which cannot be described as either the mind or something other than the mind-as-such (*sems nyid*). Reality (*tattva, de nyid*) is something said to be imagined. Therefore, all obscurations, such as afflictions and the like, in fact pertain to adventitious (*āgantuka, glo bur ba*) karmic imprints, and their character is totally imagined. The mind's own nature, even for a sentient being who is not enlightened, is something radiant, reflexively aware, and inherently real. Even for a superior, there is no enhancement of the mind along the path beyond that of a sentient being and thus the mind's own nature is a natural state of gnosis divorced from images. If there is some small distinction to be made, it would be that, for sentient beings, the mind's own nature is not experienced as radiant. This is because of the obscurations caused by adventitious karmic imprints. At the level of the superior, however, the nature of the mind is said to be experienced as radiant. To sum up, all Yogācārins maintain that whatever is marked by nonconceptual gnosis, the very natural state that is empty of duality, is said to be an ultimately real entity.

The Madhyamaka System

In the Madhyamaka text tradition, it is said that whatever the Yogācārins' theories about whether the character of the ultimate exists [existential statements] and what can be said about it [predicative statements] (*ji ltar rnal 'byor spyod pa rnams kyis don dam pa'i mtshan nyid du yod pa dang yin par lta ba de dag*), they are totally imagined, with no basis in reality and nonimplicatively negated. For a Mādhyamika, there is no establishing an ultimate through implicative negation. Correct conventions, which are just conventional illusions, are generated by causes and conditions. They have the capacity to perform a function, and they make sense only insofar as they are not scrutinized. When scrutinized, they cannot withstand the burden of proof. They are devoid of inherent nature. The way that they appear corresponds to the how and the what of them such that it does not conflict with either direct perception or nonobservation.

The Guhyamantra System

According to the Guhyamantra system, given that there is no ultimate thing, conventions are just appearances to the confused mind. The manner in which a thing appears corresponds to how it exists. The apprehension of existential and predicative statements regarding such things are totally imagined and have no basis in reality. Since they appear to confused consciousness, it is not possible for the apprehensions to actually be in accordance with appearances. Take, for example, an appearance that is generated by causes and conditions in a dream: all of the following—the harvest being the result of plowing the field, drinking poison leading to illness, and recovery being the result of taking medicine—appear to arise because of causes and conditions. In fact, dynamic appearances do, too. Furthermore, in a dream, a vase's form appears capable of retaining water, and the image of a vase appears incapable of retaining water. Thus, even in the context of just a dream, given that appearances like that do not require any proof, there is nothing at all to actually distinguish them [that is, dream appearances from waking appearances].

Similarly, outer and inner things that appear to be generated through causes and conditions, and these distinctions between appearances capable and incapable of performing functions, too, are possible in terms of mere appearance, for skilled *paṇḍitas*, foolish women, elephant herders, and everyone in between. Varieties of appearances, such as the experience of consistent appearances with respect to one's karma, totally pure and totally impure appearances, and so on, are all consistent in the sense that they are all said to appear. No proof is needed on this point because appearances are the basic criteria upon which the various characteristics of phenomena are posited. Characteristics are proven in accordance with their appearance, though they have not even the minutest particle of reality.

Therefore, all presentations of things in term of their own character ineluctably characterize what is totally imagined. Thus, since the possibility of proving the how and the what of something empty of the totally imagined that has its own characteristics is nonimplicatively negated with respect to everything that is knowable, there is nothing at all left over upon which to base the teaching of the totally imagined. Given in terms of appearance alone, those inconsistent experiences that vary with respect to one's karma do not seem to be posited as something real. Yet for those with even the slightest conceptual activity, they seem to be posited as something totally imagined.

These explanations that correct conventions exist defined by their generation by causes and conditions and their ability to perform functions, which are given here only as brief explanations used by scholars of the past, according to the system of Guhyamantra, pertain to the character of the totally imagined. In the Madhyamaka system, beginning with the assertion that since these outer and inner things arise interdependently, they cannot be ultimately produced, conventions are said to arise and cease because of the influence of causes and conditions and are thus impermanent and changeable. All these are said to "arise and cease to be via the mode of interdependent origination; there is no cause and effect akin to a burned seed producing a sprout: there is no nonexistent nothing arising from nothing."[12]

If that is the case, what is the character of appearance as cause and result? It has been proclaimed in extensive detail in texts that "given that the mind as such fixates on things and conceptualizes causality, it appears as cause and condition."[13] Thus, in the system of Guhyamantra, all phenomena are totally imagined; that's it. Whatever is merely imputed, that per se is totally imagined. The inherent nature of that which is totally conceptual is the character of the totally imagined, since the character of perfected phenomena is devoid of any basis in reality.[14] Indeed, the totally imagined is itself the character of knowable phenomena—it is also the path and the fruit. Thus, yogins who persist in the system of Guhyamantra should understand knowables in terms of an awareness of just the totally imagined and objectified (*sākṣātkāra*, *mngon du bya*) result.

If that is the case and it is true that the character of phenomena is like this, why do the buddhas not teach that to be the case from the very beginning? This particular teaching pertains to the domain of experience of those with vast and extensive insight and conviction, because if it were taught to those persons troubled by pride and afflictive emotions, it would be no different than postulating a nihilism, the continua of migrators would be wasted, and all positive effort would be reversed. In deference to that fact, it not something that is to be taught to all, and it is difficult to realize—therefore, it is called *the system of secret mantra* (*guhyamantra*, *sangs sngags*).

Thus, it is necessary to bring the minds of those fixated on things to the tantric view slowly and gradually. Think, for example, of a person who, carried away by the waters of a rushing river, searches for something solid to grab on to. Having seized the tip of a branch of a tree that has fallen in the water, the person thinks, "Since this branch is unstable, I can't rely on it!" She quickly lets it go and clutches at a piece of the tree's root and gradually pulls herself closer and closer to the base of the root thinking, "I've got dry land!" But because it is an unsound or diseased root, the water carries the person away and the segment of the root itself sinks into the water while she frantically searches for it. Upon seeing the tip of another root protruding from the river bank, the person would again make an effort in that direction, thinking, "Before, the part of the root I thought stable was in fact a sinking weight. Part of the tip of the branch that I thought was unstable can support and save me. Now, I will break it up into something useful. I will lean on the branch pieces, breaking up the branches. Some can be relied on, some act as shelter in the face of the wind, some act as an anchor against the wind, and some can be made into paddles so I can get out of here!" Such a person is as if freed from the water (*chus las thar pa de bzhin*).

Similarly, those who desire the path of liberation, first clutch a worldly path. After perceiving it to be something totally imagined, they desire a path accompanied by a fruition free of the totally imagined—one that is, by its own nature, genuinely qualified as perfected. When they gradually investigate and search, they see that everything that is correctly imagined is unstable and unreal. As for how they traverse the path, if they seize "one that is genuine," what need is there to even mention their predilection for searching for something that is seized as *the* ultimate? Grasping at the correct character of conventions is, in fact, itself perceived as a sinking weight of bondage. Once the weapon of insight severs all correct theories, only awareness of the totally imagined remains. One engaged in such skill-in-means is as if free of bondage, not attached to, or dependent upon, anything. The accomplishing of whatever is desired by the one engaged in skill-in-means through play and sport is just like a bird soaring through space.

Third Objection: Concerning the Yogācāra View of Concepts

If it is the case that everything is, in the end, totally imagined, how is it that the Yogācārins do not explain conceptuality (*kalpanā, rtog pa*)[15] as totally imagined?

Response to the Third Objection

There is no one who holds their own tenets to be totally imagined. For each perspective, respectively, there are two explanations of an instrument and its activity: as independent or dependent. When they are validated as the one, they are denied as the other. Accordingly, when the instrument, for example, an ax, and the activity, for example, chopping wood into pieces, are considered as two, they are described as dependent. It is not possible to validate the statement "an ax cuts itself." If, when validating instrument and activity as dependent, we are establishing something like a lamp qua something that throws off light, the lamp is the instrument that illuminates and the activity is illuminating a darkened area. The illuminated was made into an area with no darkness. If validated as independent, the lamp is the instrument that illuminates and the illuminating activity. The actual lamp is illuminated, generating a divorce from ongoing darkness. It is possible to validate either independent or dependent views of instrument and activity. When considering the two, if an instrument is given as existent—that is, not as something negated—it is not tenable to negate its product as nonexistent. Accordingly, whether insisting upon the existence of an instrument that chops wood while denying the wood that has been chopped or insisting upon the existence of an instrument illuminating darkness while denying what has been illuminated, a proof is untenable.

Similarly, given the existence of the conceptual, a denial of its effects is not tenable. Nevertheless, the textual tradition in which instrument and activity are described as dependent is refuted. Accordingly, the totally imagined as activity and the instrument as a concept both participate in the same class of dependence. If the kinds of conceptual awareness that are actively capable of labeling conventions are posited in terms of something totally imagined, which is characterized by object and subject, it is possible to negate as nonexistent something totally imagined as distinct.

According to the procedure validating the independence of instrument and activity, just as it is not tenable to prove the nonexistence of what is illuminated—that is, the actual lamp—and given that the lamp is the instrument that illuminates and the illuminating activity, then inasmuch as the mind and mental factors associated with the three realms are false conceptions, the totally imagined as activity is not something distinct from the instrument qua mind and mental factors. Even the totally imagined, since it proceeds via causality as mind and mental factors, appears as dual, although it is in fact nondual in nature. Thus, when "totally imagined" is said in other contexts as well, because varied conceptions persistently involved in what is only imputed are perceived, it applies to everything else along the same lines.

In sum, when the character of conceptions and imputations are all given in general, conceptions comprise at least three species: conception (*kalpanā, rtog pa*), imagination (*saṃkalpa, kun du rtog pa*), and discursive conception (*vikalpa, rnam par rtog pa*). When these three terms are invoked, they are not unlike, for example, the terms *affliction* (*kleśa, nyon mongs*), *secondary affliction* (*upakleśa, nye ba'i nyon mongs*), and the *thoroughly afflicted* (*saṃkleśa, kun nas nyon mongs pa*). When the terms are used casually, there is a sizable semantic range. When the terms are used strictly, the import is consistent. These three [terms] connected to conception are similar. The term *conception* has a broad semantic range and applies to the path, fruit, and doctrinal discourses. The term *imagination* applies to the mind and all mental factors, especially those associated with the three realms. The term *discursive conception* applies to intention (*cetanā, sems pa*) and particular species of insight, some classes of which are active in labeling conventions. There are some contexts in which what is imagined is itself indicated by the term *discursive conception*. On occasions when that term is applied in connection with a buddha's emanations, the path, and the dharma that is taught, they are also called *skillful conceptions*.

What is it that those conceptions consider? It is the very nature of conception that is considered by skillful conception; and only such conceptions are considered as skillful. Further, it is stated:

> From within the domain of nonconceptual phenomena,
> Sentient beings understand objects;
> Anything that is imputed through ideas,
> Is, on that account, called a concept.[16]

There are other [such terms that signify skillful conceptions,] as well. In whatever way these [terms] are related in the tantras of the Guhyamantra and within individual conceptions, they are broadly connected not only to conception but to imputation. What is imputed by the imagination was already explained above; and what is imputed by discursive conception was already carefully explained above in the context of the individual philosophical positions concerning the self asserted by non-Buddhist extremists and Śrāvakas in connection with such conceptions as the apprehended and apprehender and so forth.

What, then, is it that appears imputed with those concepts? As in the case of what appears imputed in connection with skillful conceptions, it concerns such things as the capacity of this karmically developed body to train for the buddha ground until it is discarded by the attainment of those who secure the spiritual accomplishment that is the divine buddha body—that is, the Great Seal (*lha'i sku phyag chen*) endowed with the major and minor marks of awakening and the six types of clairvoyance (*ṣaḍabhijña*, *mngon shes drug*). Even if it does not become like that, it does become a fire-like substance that is as if ablaze, soaring through space, moving through the totally pure realms and capable of remaining for an age, and so on. In the case of the imagination, what appears imputed is all that manifests and is developed with respect to the bodies (*deha*, *lus*), environments (*pratiṣṭhā*, *gnas*), and resources (*saṃbhoga*, *long spyod*) of the three realms. In the case of discursive conception, what appear imputed are things like monks of the past who are unsurpassable companions who live together and by the force of contemplating the repulsive become objects of animosity.

What things are incapable of appearing in that way even though they are imputed by those conceptions? The things that are incapable of appearing in that way though they are imputed by skillful conceptions are such things as the syllables and symbolic gestures given in the context of cultivating the path of Guhyamantra. Though meditated upon, they are incapable of manifesting. Nevertheless, their seeds grow. What is incapable of appearing though it is imputed by the imagination is karma, the coming together of that which exists, though its total development is not capable of being drawn out by the mind and mental factors, because of the subtle nature of karma. Nevertheless, those seeds grow. What are incapable of appearing though they are imputed by discursive conceptions are such things as the self asserted by the non-Buddhist extremists. It is not real. Nevertheless, its seeds grow.

What do not appear because they are not imputed by these conceptions? What do not appear because they are not imputed by skillful conceptions are the qualities of arhats, which do not appear to ordinary beings who have not in fact cultivated the path. What do not appear because they are not imputed by the imagination are the unconditioned (*anabhisaṃskāra*, *gon par 'dus ma byas pa*)—because conscious awareness is not possessed of sufficient conditions (*pratyayavaikalyam*, *rkyen ma tshang ba*)—and the unproduced aggregates. In terms of what are not imputed through discursive conception, there are two types. [First, there is] what is not imputed because of insufficient conditions, as a result of which concepts are not generated. This type is subsumed under what was given above. Since individual insight analyzes specifically, it realizes the empty and the selfless. [Second,] as for what does not appear because it is not imputed as self or a thing, we may speak of the path of the unconditioned that is attained through practice.

The appearance of something that is not imputed is also not a contradiction because even the appearance of falling hairs is the conceptual imagination of those with cataracts. A hare's horn, too, is imagined and does not appear through imputation because there is simply no accumulation of the karma that produces a horn within a hare's continuum. Discursive conception applies to conventions described as *imputations* and *realizations*. On this view, the false perceptions connected with discursive conceptual awareness are designated *imputations*. The perceptions connected with unmistaken awareness are called *realizations*.

Here, someone might object and say that these two terms have something in common. In that case, the term *realization* applies even to perceptions that are false—just as in the phrases *not realized* or *wrongly realized*. And it might be said that the term *imputation* applies to unmistaken perceptions as well, whether it's individually discriminating awareness correctly imputing something or the so-called cessation through individual analysis (*pratisaṃkhyānirodha, so sor brtags pa'i 'gog pa*).[17] Yet this objection does not follow because even though the words *realization* and *imputation* might indicate something similar as terms, they are applied in two different contexts in connection with the action of activity and the action of the instrument, since the false perception indicated in terms of the action of activity is not applied in connection with the term *realization*. And the term *imputation* is generally not applied to unmistaken perceptions. In terms of the action of the instrument, the term *realization* may be applied to false perceptions and the term *imputation* may be applied to unmistaken perceptions. This is because in fact the Sanskrit term *kalpita* indicates something imputed; *unmistaken* indicates the action of the instrument, either through the Sanskrit term *avabodha*, meaning "understanding," or *pratisaṃkyā*, meaning "analytical." Therefore, it follows that what is "totally imagined" by a discursive conceptual awareness that is false is an object subsumed under the concept of distortion (*sgro skur*) [literally: "imposition and denial"],[18] because it is in fact an imposed object, not unlike the five bases of the eternalist view described above. Those bases are denied (*apavāda, skur 'debs*) and attacked because they are said to be without cause, without effect, without instrument, and without distinctive qualities. The designation of the convention *realization*, given an unmistaken perception by a discursive conceptual awareness, is a state of distortion since, as was already explained above, an imposed object may be unmistakenly realized. In a state of denial [or "distortion"], there is a cause—the seed—which is a cause of a sprout. That effect—the sprout—is an effect of the seed. There is an agent—a being who engages in the activity of planting the seed.

There is such a thing as a distinctive quality. Think about the three jewels (*triratna, dkon mchog gsum*): they are said to be obviously superior to all worlds and something sublime. Likewise, as long as everything is posited as either totally imagined or real, there are two types of posited object: what is set forth as imputed because it is perceived by a mistaken discursive awareness and what is set forth as really realized because it is perceived by an unmistaken discursive conceptual awareness. Whatever is itself presented as realized by unmistaken awareness by one party may be said to be established as imputed, or imagined, by mistaken awareness by some other party. Thus, in the end, something real is *not* found and the awareness that is doing the looking, which is itself said to be unmistaken, is also not found. Since it is the case that they are not found, the objects that are not found—being something posited under the influence of varying species of discursive awareness along these lines—and even the character of all subtle and coarse false conceptions that are generated, are alike. Therefore, the establishment of the cognitive nature of consciousness, especially, is something imputed that appears because there is no real perfected nature that is established.

For example, the descriptions "a person killed by an enemy" and "a person killed by a weapon" have a similar object. Being killed by a weapon is itself being killed by an enemy. In the same way, the description "all conscious awareness is produced from its own seeds" and the description "it is the imagined appearance of the conceptual mind" have a similar object. This is because by describing it as "produced from its own seeds," there is no conscious awareness that is not an imagined appearance that possesses its own nature. In that case, the two types of truth—that is, conventional and ultimate truth—would be indistinguishable. It is by realizing that the two truths are indistinguishable that one becomes capable of entering into the nonduality of phenomena. Thereby, one may be described as "abiding in the view of the Great Perfection," which is the act of simply being divorced from all clinging to views.

In this context, claims such as "the Śrāvaka realizes that there is nothing that is the person," "the Pratyekabuddha realizes that appearance, beginning with physical forms and so forth, has no apprehended object," "the Yogācārin realizes the nonduality of subject and object," "the Mādhyamika realizes that there is nothing ultimate," and "the Guhyamāntrika realizes the indivisibility of the two truths" all correspond to clinging to views. Given that the "view of Great Perfection" is designated as being divorced from clinging to theory in that way, the conventional designation *view of the Great Perfection* is also called *the great view of the timeless release* (*lta ba ye btang chen po*).

Some Supplementary Explanation concerning the Differences between the Aforementioned Views with respect to Limitations and Power

Now, let me give some supplementary explanation concerning the differences between the aforementioned views with respect to limitations and power: Śrāvakas realize the absence of any ultimate person and thereby eliminate the view of the internal transitory collection, the retinue of afflictions generated under its influence, and the karmic life that ensues from it. They are purified and some slight power is obtained. Pratyekabuddhas reduce conception in terms of both the subjective self and the apprehended object. This is achieved by realizing the absence of the objective external form aggregate qua appearance, which guarantees eliminating anything connected with karmic imprints. Such a realization obtains the great power to purify karmic life. Summing up the Mahāyāna, it is by realizing the selflessness of both phenomena and people that one obtains a gnosis free of all ideas of self and duality. Thence anything connected with karmic imprints is totally eliminated and the great power of the Tathāgata's inconceivable blessing is obtained. Such ancillary comments should suffice for our purposes.

It is this Great Perfection approach to the path, which is free of all views, that is said to be the very pinnacle of all vehicles (*yāna*, *theg pa*), the lord of all transmissions (*āgama*, *lung*), the quintessence of doctrinal discourses (*pravacana*, *gsung rab*), the general meaning of all tantras, the deepest intention of all the buddhas (*abhiprāya*, *dgongs gzhi*), and the core of all esoteric precepts (*upadeśa*, *man ngag*).

Great Perfection as a Vehicle

The term *vehicle*, corresponding to the Sanskrit *yāna*, is a term applied to a conveyance that acts on a real path, which, in context, is applied to the activity of conveying and to doctrinal discourses. Since what it indicates will emerge just below, let me just mention here that acting on the path per se conduces to the unsurpassable—the highest pinnacle of all paths. The complete liberation (*vimukti*, *rnam grol*) of the Śrāvakas is generated because of causality, and their concentration remains on a level marked by a mental object. The complete liberation of the Pratyekabuddhas is divorced from a verbalized path, and the source of their meditative concentrations is inexpressible phenomena. The complete liberation of the Mahāyāna is generated through gnosis that is devoid of discursive conceptions of subject and object ("apprehended and apprehender"). The concentrations of the Mahāyāna paths penetrate the expanse of utterly, totally, pure phenomena. In the system of Guhyamantra, when the "acquisition of the threefold diamond-like experience" emerges, complete liberation and concentration are indistinguishable; the two progress and emerge in relation. In the Great Perfection approach to the path, however, nothing is accomplished in that way, because the state of nonprogression pertains to the supreme path. For that reason, Great Perfection is said to be the highest pinnacle of all vehicles.

Great Perfection as a Transmission

The meaning of the term *transmission* corresponds to the Sanskrit term *āgama* and suggests a derivation from something else; it also suggests something fundamental and basic; and it is used to characterize the actual words of the Conqueror. Yet those kinds of teachings of the Buddha (*vacana*, *bka'*) are incapable of revealing (*ston par byed pa*) the Great Perfection approach to the path. They are also incapable of undermining it—and indeed are incapable of surpassing it. Given that the system of the Great Perfection is capable, moreover, of distinctively disclosing each of the various philosophical presentations of all of the different vehicles, it is also capable of disproving (*saṃdūṣaṇa-karoti*, *sun 'byin par byed pa*) all of them. In the context of what surpasses all the *vacana*, for example, it should be said that just as the powerful sovereign who has placed a wish-fulfilling jewel at the tip of Indra's victory banner is unrivaled and irrepressible, the Great Perfection is the lord of all transmissions.

Great Perfection as a Doctrinal Discourse

The term *doctrinal discourse* corresponds to the Sanskrit term *pravacana*. Here, *vacana* indicates verbal expression or speech; and *pra-* is a prefix (*upasarga*, *nye bar bsgyur ba*) indicating extraordinary significance, whereby it is designated *doctrinal discourse*. Worldly sciences (*'jig rten gyi gtsug lag*) are lesser issues and are described in the context of *kuvacana*. Here, the prefix *ku-* indicates something negative. Yet such is not the case with verbal expressions, or speech, that disclose the path to liberation. The twelve branches of doctrinal discourse are included in the collection of dharma teachings.[19]

There are two types of instruction given in these branches of discourse: those disclosing teachings of definitive meaning (*neyārtha*, *drang don*) and those disclosing teachings of provisional meaning (*nīthārtha*, *nges don*). Moreover, anything that espouses the definitive meaning might, by means of others, disclose a provisional meaning. Even though there are individual texts in which both provisional and definitive meaning are disclosed, within the context of the Great Perfection approach to the path, there is nothing other than exalted definitive meaning that is disclosed—the provisional teaching of the Buddha is not. In the Great Perfection approach, since there is nothing to be eliminated and nothing affirmed as corrupt, it is called *the quintessence of all doctrinal discourses*.

Great Perfection as a Continuum

The term *continuum* corresponds to the Sanskrit term *tantra*, which is used in the sense of something related, dependent—even turbulent. Actually, if in Kriyatantras and Yogatantras, the method of accomplishing unexcelled awakening, the method for accomplishing the great worldly accomplishments such as clairvoyance and others, and even all the various elaborate means employed by the practitioner for cultivating peace, and so forth, are not encompassed within the domain of the Great Perfection, they are symbolically bound. Because they are encompassed within the domain of the Great Perfection, one is not taken in by saṃsāra no matter how the ocean of conditioning behaves. For that reason, the Great Perfection is proclaimed to be the general meaning of all tantras.

Great Perfection as a Hidden Intention

When we speak of a *hidden intention*, this corresponds to the Sanskrit term *abhisaṃdhi*, a term that suggests that a verbal expression is not straightforward—that it reveals its significance in a figurative and indirect manner. This might also correspond to the Sanskrit term *abhiprāya*, which refers to when the language at use is totally at odds with what is being taught. In short, they are termed, respectively, *hidden intention* (*abhisaṃdhi, ldem por dgongs pa*) and *underlying intention* (*abhiprāya, dgongs pa*).

According to the Śrāvaka system, the basis in thought (*dgongs gzhi*) that motivates teaching in terms of existential descriptions [literally, "in terms of what exists and what does not exist] in all of the Conqueror's teachings is the underlying intention of teaching the reality of people and phenomena. According to the Yogācāra system, the basis in thought in teaching in terms of existential descriptions in all of the Conqueror's teachings is the thought to teach the reality of the three types of nature. According to the Madhyamaka system, the basis in thought in teaching in terms of existential descriptions in all of the Conqueror's teachings is the intention to proclaim the reality of ultimate and conventional truth. Indeed, all these pertain to a basis in [the Buddha's] thought, though none pertain to the deepest. The deepest of all the teachings in the Conqueror's teachings makes allusions by means of a variety of terms and is concerned to reveal the domain of nondual quality. Because of the fact no other discourse is possessed of this intimate thought of all the jinas, the Great Perfection [discourse on the path] is thus called *the most intimate of all the Buddha's thoughts*.

Great Perfection as Intimate Advice

The term *intimate advice* (or *esoteric precept*) corresponds to the Sanskrit term *upadeśa*. *Upadeśa* is a term that functions to indicate *advice* and a *resolution* on a particular point. An esoteric precept, then, is a point or object that lies outside the usual explanatory current of the day.[20]

How is an object resolved through intimate advice? When resolved decisively, the significance of the object is recognized in connection with several points: all phenomena are resolved to be empty and selfless, without inherent nature, absent production, qualitatively the same, and nondual. On occasion, the meaning of these terms may overlap. At times, they indicate there are verbal points made precisely in accord with the terms that are used to express them.

Thus, according to the Śrāvaka system, the fact that all phenomena are not their own identity and the assertion that *in* or *of* phenomena, there is *something* that is a self or something that is not, is in fact given in the context of "all phenomena being empty" and "something resolved as selfless." Nevertheless, because the Śrāvaka system insists upon the dual nature of apprehended and apprehender, it does not count as "resolving the absence of inherent existence."

According to the Yogācāra system, the insistence upon the absence of any essential nature connected to apprehended and apprehender is called *resolving the absence of inherent existence*, because at that point it is not different from the absence of inherent existence and the empty, selfless nature of phenomena. Nevertheless, because they insist upon the existence of the causal production of dependent phenomena, their system does not count as "resolving the absence of production."

According to the Madhyamaka system, the insistence upon the ultimate as devoid of conceptual elaboration is called *resolving the absence of production*, because at that point, there is no distinction between the absence of production, the absence of inherent existence, and the empty, selfless [nature of phenomena]. Nevertheless, because of their insistence upon correct conventional truth, their approach to the path does not count as "resolving qualitative similarity."

According to the Guhyamantra system, the insistence upon the indivisibility of the two truths is called *resolving qualitative similarity*. Here, there is no difference between qualitative similarity, the absence of production, the absence of inherent existence, and the empty, selfless nature of phenomena. Nevertheless, because of the existence of those who are too timid to be able to experience the practice of sameness,[21] and because of those who voluntarily take up austerities in order to swiftly nullify that timidity, their system does not count as "resolving the nonduality of all phenomena."

Regardless of those, the Great Perfection, like this fourth knowable scheme for all phenomena [Guhyamantra], is not recognized then abandoned, recognized then accepted, recognized then settled as equal, or then actualized—none of which is established. "All phenomena are resolved to be nondual" because at that point, there is no distinction between "nondual," "qualitative similarity," "absence of production," "absence of inherent existence," and "the empty, selfless nature of phenomena." Thus—and given the fact that the Great Perfection's cultivation of the resolution concerning the nonduality of all phenomena in fact pertains to the very core of all intimate advice as such, it is called *the core of all esoteric precepts*.

Here ends the third chapter, which distinguishes the perfected system of the illusory in the Great Perfection from the other vehicles that retain the nomenclature of illusion.

4. The Great Perfection Approach to the Path Is Not Undermined by Reason

When this Great Perfection approach to the path is taught in a condensed manner, it is said that the bases of all phenomena are simply included within mind and mental appearance; the nature of the mind (*citta*, *sems*) itself is awakening (*bodhi*, *byang chub*) and thus is referred to as *the mind of awakening* (*bodhicitta*, *byang chub kyi sems*). There is nothing to be taught other than this. People with faith in the Great Perfection approach realize and penetrate it through being shown this alone. People who are obsessed with (*abhiniveśa*, *mngon par zhen pa*) grammatical treatises on grammar[1] and logic[2] have abandoned the Great Perfection approach to the path, which is like a wish-fulfilling jewel. They are fixated on various trinket-like philosophical tenets and tend to think, "These philosophical tenets of ours are established through grammatical points and reason. The Great Perfection approach to the path is in conflict with reason and that which is in conflict with reason ought not to be accepted." For the benefit of such people, here I will set aside the idiom renowned in the Great Perfection approach to the path, which uses such terms as *sphere* (*thig le*) and *greatness* (*che ba*). Instead, I will explain some facets of the system of logic using a more broadly accepted nomenclature.

Bodhicitta

Regarding the term *mind of awakening*—that is, the Sanskrit term *bodhicitta*: *awakening* (*byang chub*) corresponds to the Sanskrit term *bodhi*, which itself suggests the term *avabodha*, which is used in the sense of something being exhausted and in the sense of something of conscious awareness that is not generated, of that which is totally pure of all blemishes, of unmistaken realization, or even of total mastery (*avagata*, *kun chub*). The term *mind* corresponds to the Sanskrit term *citta*, which itself suggests the term *vicitta*, whose various meanings are used in the sense of cognizing a variety of objects perceived by the mind; or, in another sense, as the seeds of karmic processes are gathered, it acts like a container, a little bag in which things are managed.[3] The Sanskrit terms *cetanā* and *citta* mean, respectively, *intention* and *mind*; and any karmic process concomitant (*samprayogataḥ*, *mtshungs par ldan pa*) with intention that thinks upon, moves toward, or engages in, various activities is for that reason called *mind*. The Sanskrit term *cittamanavidyārtha* suggests that *mind* and *awareness* are synonymous. It is called *mind* because it is immaterial and has the nature of cognitive awareness.

Conceptual Frameworks, Appearance, and Nature

The presentation here of mind and awakening as different natures pertains to the character of a conceptual framework. Their actual nature is nondual. Yet at the level of appearance, the two do not occur at the same time. In this context, a conceptual framework (*dmigs pa*) is the domain of experience qualified by cognitive discrimination. Appearance (*snang ba*) is the domain of experience qualified by sensation. The character of nature itself (*ngo bo nyid kyi mtshan nyid*) is a domain of experience qualified by stainless insight.

By virtue of a conceptual framework, such conventions as "existence" and "nonexistence" are designated. At the level of appearance, we find designations such as "correct" and "incorrect." It is in terms of nature itself that we find conventions such as "established" and "nonestablished." At the level of conceptual frameworks, the mind has no capacity to remove states of distortion. At the level of appearance, given the capacity to eliminate objective distortions, there is yet no capacity to remove confusion. At the level of nature itself, even confusion is eliminated. Therefore, awareness following after the discriminative—that is, the conceptual, propositional domain of experience—is inferior. Awareness following after sensation—that is, bare perception—is fair to middling. And awareness following after the domain of stainless insight is superior.

Take, for example, a fire-wheel: at the level of conceptual frameworks, both the fire-brand and the fire-wheel are each observed to be basically the same in being present.[4] At the level of appearance, they are coincident. Yet when the fire-wheel appears, the fire-brand does not; and when the fire-brand appears, the fire-wheel does not. At the level of nature itself, neither are real. If the fire-wheel's nature as such exists, the fire-brand would have no basis in reality. If there exists a fire-brand's nature as such, the fire-wheel would have no basis in reality. Thus, only at the point when the fire-wheel appears is the fire-brand's nature as such real. Further, it should be recognized that the nature of the fire-wheel has no basis in reality.

Mind and awakening are a similar case: at the level of conceptual frameworks, both mind and awakening are considered to be basically the same insofar as they are conceived to exist as distinct entities. At the level of appearance, they do not coincide. When there is mental appearance, there is no appearance of awakening. At the point that awakening appears, ordinary mind does not. Mental appearance, because of its deceptiveness, is confusion. Appearing as awake[5] is not mistaken since it is not deceptive. From the point of view of nature alone, when the very essence of the ordinary mind is established as something, the very essence of awakening has no basis in reality. When the very essence of awakening is established as something, the very essence of ordinary mind has no basis in reality. Thus, what appears in the ordinary mind is something delusive, because its actual nature does not exist in the manner in which it appears. Thus, the very state of perceiving [such a state] is nature as such; and it should be recognized that "the essential nature of the ordinary mind has no basis in reality."

This point is not unlike teachings that accord with the Great Perfection approach, in which the great path to total liberation is affliction as such, in which karma as such is naturally arising gnosis, and in which suffering as such is awakened. In the Great Perfection approach, "total liberation," "naturally arising gnosis," and "awakening" are taught only as specific conventions for turning back awareness that is fixated on the affliction, karma, and the discontent of sentient beings. Their very nature is in fact indivisible and unified (*gcig go*). In this context, *unified* indicates the nature of identity. Identity has three types. There may be identity in similarity (*mtshungs*), identity in number (*grangs*), and indistinguishable identity (*dbyer med*). Although they are similar in turning back pluralizing awareness, all terms for identity are separated into different species in virtue of whether they make distinctions in foundation,[6] quantitative observation,[7] or nonobservation.[8]

What is identity in similarity? In this case, a pillar is characterized by holding up a canopy and a vase is characterized by holding water.[9] When it is described as something made (*kṛta, byas pa*), the pillar qua being something made shares a common core of being with a pillar. Likewise, the vase qua something made shares a common core of being with a vase. Though each is observed by the ordinary mind as if possessed of its own reality, in terms of both being something made (*kṛtakatva, byas pa nyid*), they are observed to be the same. Yet while they are not considered as distinct in the context of that particular nature—that is, in the context of both being products that are made—a pillar cannot change into a vase, and a vase cannot change into a pillar. The reality of their respective roof holding and water holding is not lost.

In such a system as this, the hell being in Unrelenting Torment (*avīci, mnar myed*) perfectly characterizes suffering. The lord Buddha is the perfect characterization of bliss. Even though they are not perceived as distinct when considered in terms of emptiness, both sentient beings and buddhas are described as "empty of any real self and empty of their own reality." If in fact they are not really empty of nature as such, then a hell being could not change into a buddha because of simply being empty of an *I and mine*. Buddhas do not revert (*ldog*) into hell beings. The character of bliss and suffering is not lost. For example, it is not unlike when one hundred or two hundred is described as one thousand or two thousand. It is indeed true to say that a hundred and a thousand alone are both a lot, but two one hundreds are not divisible into one one hundred. Thus, the single term *one hundred* is applied.

What is identity in number? Take, for example, the phrase *rhino-like* (*khaḍgaviṣāṇakalpa, bse' ru lta bu*): it can be used to describe a leathery beast that has a single sword-like horn—not two horns growing at the same time[10]—just as the phrase *a rhino* can. Analogously, whether it is that the aggregates are said to exist, though both the person and his or her aggregates are said not to; or that the Pratyekabuddha's subject is said to exist, though the object is denied; or the Yogācāra position that one's own awareness is said to exist, though both object and subject are denied—whatever the case may be—any given philosophical perspective (*blta ba*) consists in various ways of validating something that is supposed to be real after eliminating what is supposedly totally imagined, asserting a subject and its predicate to form a single identity in what is itself real and invalidating difference between these two reciprocal phenomena as if they both pertain to a single nature. An *identity in number* is given in the context of a proof for a thing's unified [quantitative] identity. The phrase "there is not two—there is one!" is what we say in establishing a phenomenon that is unified.

In terms of an indistinguishable identity, for example, the nature of space might be described as "space itself" [or "space as such," "spaceness," "the nature of space"] (*nam mkha' nyid*). Occasionally, even though space, as a conventional object, and the nature of space, as a conventional object, are designated in terms of, respectively, a subject and its predicate, *space* is also another expression for the term *emptiness*. Calling the nature of space *space as such* is yet another expression for the term *emptiness*, though it is not at all the case here that one object is being presented as two. Along these lines, even the mind of awakening (*bodhicitta*, *byang chub sems*) would be considered in terms of identity in number at the point when awakening is brought about through the arrest (*bkag nas*) of the ordinary mind (*citta*). Inasmuch as the subject "ordinary mind" is not established, the mind of awakening that is described in dependence upon it would also not be established. Yet, just like when the nature of space is called *space as such* and there is no insistence upon any separation between ordinary mind and awakening, awakening and the ordinary mind would constitute an indistinguishable identity.

Both awakening and mind are taught in the Great Perfection approach to the path: when the greatness of the mind of awakening (*bodhicitta*) is taught, the two terms *bodhi* and *citta* are described as an identity in number. When the nature of the mind of awakening is taught, mind and awakening are described as an indivisible identity. In sum, this explains the fundamental point of significance.

The explanations given in the chapter below, which treats the textual tradition of the Great Perfection (*gzhung nyid*), do not improve upon this point.

General Systems for Such Things as the Establishment and Negation of Identity and Difference

At this point, let me explain a bit about the general systems for such things as the establishment and negation of identity and difference. All the numerous ways in which individuals assert the establishment of their own philosophical system (*grub pa'i mtha'*) and reject those of others are subsumed under two types of discourse: the establishment of something and the negation of something.

All the numerous ways in which things are negated are subsumed under two methods: nonimplicative and implicative negation. The former pertains to the mere negation of an existent in which nothing else is established in its place. The latter is used to invalidate nonunderstanding, wrong understanding, and gnawing doubt without teaching a different object. For example, the word *no vase* (*bum pa med*) does nothing other than overcome the idea that there is a vase; it does not disclose such things as a place where there is no vase (*bum pa med pa'i sa phyogs la stsogs pa ni ston par mi byed do*). Similarly, when the phrase *personless* is used, it does nothing other than overcome the idea that there is a person; it does not disclose the presence of a person's empty aggregates. Explanations along similar lines should be applied to everything.

An implicative negation is given when there is the negation of one thing while another is suggested in its stead. Just as a place without a vase is made sense of when it is described as "vaseless," the fact that the aggregates are empty of anything personal is disclosed when they are described as "personless." Therefore, a nonimplicative negation simply consists in denying your opponents' philosophical system because it is not sufficient to negate it implicatively since one's own philosophical position would then [need to] be validly established.

On the Two Methods of [Establishing] Proofs

In fact, the numerous ways of proving something are subsumed under two types of discourse connected to *establishing the existence of something* and *establishing something as an objective basis*. These proofs are qualified in terms of both *identity* and *difference*. The basis of these, in turn, is qualified in terms of both *nature as such* and *distinction*. Awareness that participates in these functions of proof are subsumed under two species: holistic awareness (*piṇḍagrāha, ril por 'dzin pa'i blo*) and anatomizing awareness (*rjes su gzhig pa'i blo*), both of which are indeed natural types of awareness. Nevertheless, when two philosophical opponents dispute, it is set forth—though it should not be—that *one's own philosophical position is integrated through a holistic awareness and cannot be broken by an opponent's philosophical position*. Since the basis of all proofs that establish something are qualified in terms of nature as such and distinction, without understanding both, there is no recognizing any proof for anything. Thus, we start with them.

What is nature as such? When the appearance of an object in awareness is undifferentiated in value and scope, it in fact appears possible to signify that undifferentiated mode as its nature. That which indicates it is the *name*, which corresponds to the Sanskrit term *nāma*. As for the term *name*, it also corresponds to the Sanskrit term *nayati*—it "leads," "brings," or "guides" said awareness to the object with which the name is made to connect, which accords with the possibility of connecting the object's nature as such to such names as *pillar* and *vase* in a narrower context and the possibility of connecting such terms as *compounded* and *uncompounded* in a broader context. No matter how many names lead the mind to an object, they connect to its nature as such.

The Sanskrit term *lakṣaṇa* suggests such concepts as cause, distinguishing mark, or indicator. Thus, once a given discursive awareness has mixed name and object, it references the object as one. Having qualified the object's distinguishing marks and indicators, the lakṣaṇas are called *marks* or *evidence* (*rgyu mtshan*). Even the excellent marks of a buddha are said to be lakṣaṇas because they are taken as distinguishing marks, or indicators, of the body of someone enlightened. Such a name and reason are asserted in accordance with those who adhere to grammatical treatises and are not affiliated with the object's nature as such, which is separate from the name and reason of the object.

What is an object's *distinctive quality*? The term *distinctive quality* qualifies whatever specifics are individuated from within an object's nature on the basis of that nature. It especially correlates with *character* since it pertains to things *describable* or *descriptions*. A distinctive quality is also referenced by the Tibetan term *chö* (*chos*), which may refer to both "quality" and the Sanskrit term *dharma*, which derives from the term *dhara*, which means "something that holds." Affixing the suffix *-ma* yields the term *dharma*, or "quality," which thus suggests that an object is something that holds its attributes. That is to say, something is termed *dharma* because of holding to an object as an attribute; or because of being apprehender and apprehended; or because of preventing downfalls;[11] or because of causing understanding; or because of holding its characteristics. At times, this distinctive quality is apprehended in terms of nature as such and, because of being based on nature as such, it is reliant upon something else; thus the term *dharma* is applied along these lines. So, any existent phenomenon is a subject (*dharmin*, *chos can*). Any characteristics present are its illustrations ["basis of indication"]. Any distinctive quality present is a basis for distinction; and in the context of nature as such, there is no difference in object between them in terms of nature as such. If there is some slight difference, awareness of an object such as nature as such, one that does not rely on another object, emerges. Such things as those qualified by a predicate, a distinguishing basis, and so forth, because they depend upon such things as a subject, bring about awareness of such things as something qualified by a predicate. Thus there is no distinctive quality here.

In fact, the classification into nature as such and distinctive quality takes nature as such to be not reliant upon any distinctive quality while taking a distinctive quality to be reliant upon nature as such. This is because a distinctive quality comprises individuated instances of differentiation. On that point, a *word* (*vyañjana, yi ge*) discloses a distinctive quality. Here, the Sanskrit term *vyañjana* is also a name for the eighty minor marks of excellence (*anuvyañjana, dpe byad bzang po*); it is also a name for spices (*tshod ma*) as well as syllables (*tshig 'bru*). In terms of the major and minor marks of excellence, so-called vyañjana: just as it is the case that while a flower's anthers (*kiñkalka, ze'u 'bru*) *as such* are the flower and the generic properties of the flower are measured[12] by the anthers, so it is the case that while the major and minor marks as such are also included within the concept of buddha character, the generic characteristics of a buddha, for example, are measured by the major and minor marks. This is not unlike the fact that phrases such as *impermanent vase* make differentiations in a vase's nature as such. Just as spices accentuate and direct the flavors of food, some distinctive words, so-called syllables, make differentiations in nature as such. This leads to a unified perspective.

In this way, after being qualified by the nature and distinction model, [there are inevitable attempts to] validly establish sameness and difference in terms of whether or not nature itself or [some particular] quality is one thing or another. In dependence upon those [types of arguments], we find attempts to validate what exists and what can be said about it (*yod pa dang yin pa*)[13] in terms of whether the very nature of something is whole or not, or whether its qualities (*dharma*) are one or many. Proving something to be (*yin par sgrub pa*) establishes something to be real. Proving something exists is to prove something to be a conceptualized object. Moreover, proving something to be establishes something [that is, attributes, qualities, characteristics] to be *in relation* to (*ltos nas*) [its basis], while proving something exists is to prove something to be *a basis for* (*rten nas*) attributes.

What are those? That is to say, what is a proof of a unified nature? It precludes (*bzlog*) multiple consistent and inconsistent types. Thus, a vase is precluded from being a pillar, which is a type inconsistent with a vase [that is, a vase and a pillar are two types of things]; and one vase is also precluded from being a second vase, though in that case, it is a consistent type [that is, both are a type of vase]; and [a proof validating a unified nature, for example] validates the vase's unified single nature as such.

What is a proof of a different nature as such? It is proven in relation to a unified nature. After [one vase is] precluded [from being another] in relation to one consistent type of vase, a second vase, and others, are proven to be distinct [vases]. Once inconsistent types, such as pillars, are collected within a category after [difference between them is] precluded, they are established as all being [pillars that are in fact] different from such things as a vase, straw (*kaṭa*, *re lde*), a horse, an elephant, and so on. All this is to say, the system for proving phenomena to be the same and different is similar to this.

Furthermore, there are two types of procedure (*tshul*) for proving something to be the same: proving sameness in terms of isolation and proving sameness in terms of consolidation. There are also two procedures for proving difference: proving difference in terms of preclusion and proving difference in terms of differentiation.

What is it that proves the existence of sameness? It is possible, in fact, to assert a universal that is a real entity. It is also possible to assert its status as an imputation. This is because from the presence of multiple natures in the same universal, the statement "This is present as a unified nature" is given. In terms of isolation, the existence of a unified nature as such is proved. In isolation, the proof establishing something to be utterly the same nature as such relies on the universal because of being established in multiple baseless natures. Once isolated through preclusion (*bzlog nas bkar te*), the statement "This pertains to the same nature as such" is validated.

In the context of consolidation, what will prove that something pertains to the same nature as such? In this case, something is proven to be utterly identical.[14] Here, when a subject and its predicate are established to have a common nature, one nature as such is validated—for example, [whether] the fact of blue on an utpala flower or the nature of a vase's impermanence—[both share a common] status [since both share in the nature of being] products. In fact, these are the criteria used to validate existential statements [that is, what we say there is] and predicative statements [that is, what we say about the stuff there is].

In the case of proving the presence of distinct natures as such, a differentiation within the universal validates [a distinction therein]. In predication, the preclusion of unity is established. When a phenomenon is established as a unity, if proven in the context of isolation, then apart from that unified nature as such, each and every other distinction—for example, "being a holder of water," "being a product," "being impermanent"—is eliminated; they are precluded in validating nothing but a unity. When proving a subject and its predicate to be a single phenomenon, each and every part of it is proven to be a unified phenomenon after its nature as such is formed as a single class.

Different natures as such are consolidated when phenomena prove to be the same. If it is claimed that they are utterly identical, that would amount to consolidation. Take, as an example, when both the nature of a pillar as such and the nature of a vase as such are "the same" in being a product. Proving the phenomena to be the same establishes either existential or predicative proofs that validate difference accordingly.[15] We may distinguish the specific color, shape, tactility, and characteristics in a vase's unified nature as such. In its character, as well, we may distinguish specific characteristics such as being something made, being impermanent, and so on.

When phenomena are validated as being different through preclusion, being a product is something other than being impermanent. A product is, on this view, characterized by the manifestation of karmic processes. Impermanence characterizes the interruption of karmic processes. Thus, production as such is impermanent. Thus, karmic processes would not manifest in the absence of impermanence as such. Along these same lines, the statement "If being impermanent is a product, conditioning would not cease" is validated.

In all these cases, establishing the character of existence and predication is disclosed in a procedure wherein other distinctions are not eliminated by existent terms and awareness. Proofs that validate in such a manner as this are qualified by two types of awareness[: an awareness that apprehends holistically and an anatomizing awareness that establishes differentiation].

An awareness that apprehends holistically elides any natural distinction between a subject and its predicates when it establishes sameness, or unity. In that case, a natural difference would not obtain between a given phenomena and its qualities. Rather than being present as a unified phenomenon, that nature as such would be a real entity whose nature as such would be qualified only in terms of instances and marks of itself. If they are taken as individuated instances of nature as such, the entity qua a whole would be nullified. In that case, nature as such, devoid of components, is established as existing as one entity or as pertaining to a unity.

When an anatomizing awareness establishes differentiation, the insistence that differentiation exists in one universal collapses the notion of a unified universal because of [this anatomizing awareness] making differentiations into multiple natures. Because, in this case, nature as such is being differentiated into multiple distinctions, the notion of *being the same nature* as such, devoid of components, collapses. Because individuated distinctions are differentiated within components, the notion of a phenomenon's individual entity collapses—it cannot be real. When phenomenal differentiation is hierarchized in this way, a mereological awareness that fabricates unchanging differentiation for as long as even an age becomes inevitable (*mi ldog du rung la*).[16] For the establishing proof that the very nature of all things exists in that way, physical form cannot be measured (*parimāṇa, bong tshod*). Form cannot be measured because it is an image of the mind and mental factors. In the end, there is no space-like reality that is an unchanging state.

In some contexts (*skabs kha cig tu*), it is even taught that the twofold classification of awareness is cast off when it is analyzed in terms of being reliant on both components—both karmic processes and their character, impermanence. After observing the fault in identity and difference, it is in fact free from both. Similarly, the character of dependent and perfected phenomena is like that. In that case, by means of all the philosophical positions that hypostasize things, one's own philosophical theory proves the existence of a unified real entity—nature as such—by means of holistic awareness, and the philosophical theories of others are dissected by an anatomizing awareness that proves the nonexistence of the opposing philosophy's ultimate entity.

Howsoever something is validated, it is thereby circumscribed;[17] and the absence of a perfect knowable is simply a scale of distortion.[18] Yet, on this view, proving nature as such and its attribute[s] to be identical or different—or free from both [identity and difference] and different [from each other]—is possible. At the point of constructing a proof for identity, one might establish qualities as identical to nature as such or establish nature as such as a unified quality. Thus, insofar as all phenomena are perceived to be characterized by their contributing to spiritual attainment, these rational attacks also appear to the mind as just so many opposing contradictions between proponents of realist theories.

These paradigms of reason do not arrive at the point of Great Perfection—just as one cannot claim to have surveyed the depth of the ocean and the extent of space by the shot of an arrow or a glance of an eye.

Grammatical Treatises

In the treatises on grammar, too, whatever conventions may be offered, there is nothing other than nonimplicative and implicative negation, given in the context of existential and predicative proofs. Proving something is mostly described through secondary derivations (*taddhitapratyaya*, *de la phan pa'i rkyen*) and primary derivations (*kṛtpratyaya*, *byed pa'i rkyen*). Secondary derivations transmit the content their respective universals, disclose something akin to the nature as such of whatever it is, and disclose what seem to be natural distinctions—not unlike primary derivations. Even with primary derivations, it follows, that there is no loss in saying "going far" discloses attributes in the existential sense with respect to something that functions to go for a distance; and there is no loss in saying "goes far" discloses attributes in the predicative sense with respect to departing for a long distance. Furthermore, given that nouns (*nāman*, *ming*) are attested only from what is unattested and are marked by grammatical case (*vibhakti*, *rnam par dbye ba*) alone, they are described as conjugated (*tiṅanta*, *yin byed*) verbal roots (*dhātu*, *khams*), suffixed/affixed qua derivation. Thus, something like "making the white of a cloth" (*ras yug gi dkar po bya ba lta bu*) does not go beyond this point—even without grammatical particles that disclose existence and predication.

Logical Treatises

In treatises on logic, refutations and proofs given in terms of the four principles of reasoning do not go beyond the two types of negation and the two types of proof discussed above. Even in the appraisal of phenomena given in terms of the four principles of reason, all we observe is that proponents of realist theories simply subvert one another's philosophical systems. Furthermore, once the reasoning itself is seen to be excessive, it is seen to be subverted once more because of the consequences of reasoning per se. As stated before [at the end of chapter 1], such does not undermine the Great Perfection approach to the path.

The Four Principles of Reasoning

In the system of the four principles of reasoning, generally, it is established that phenomena are characterized by their interdependence—that is, arising as dependent relations. The principle reasoning of reality (*dharmatāyuktiḥ, chos nyid kyi rigs pa*) comprises proofs given in terms of nature as such. The principle reasoning of efficacy (*kāryakāraṇayukti, ba byed pa'i rigs pa*) comprises proofs given in terms of result. The principle reasoning of dependence (*apekṣāyukti, ltos pa'i rigs pa*) comprises proofs given in terms of cause. The [principle] reasoning of valid proof (*upapattisādhanayukti, 'thad pa sgrub pa'i rigs pa*) comprises proofs qualified by stainless reasoning alone.

Given in each of the four principles of reasoning are their four respective eliminations: gnawing doubt about nature as such, gnawing doubt about causal instruments, gnawing doubt about manifestation, and gnawing doubt about reasoning are each, in their turn, eliminated through application of the four principles.

Regarding their objects and limits: inasmuch as the actual basis of reality remains stainless and undenied, it is possible to posit it as the principle reasoning of reality. Similarly, if explicit bases—instrument, manifestation, and knowledge—are stainless and undenied, they can be set forth as principles. That is to say, the presence of stains in the actual basis would be like a sun crystal, which is used to direct light in such a way as to start a fire itself, becoming hot to the touch. Denial of the actual basis is not unlike denying that the fire-cleansed deer is "cleansed by fire."

Another point in question is also this: what principle is to be applied? On the limits of the four principles: if one is excessive with proofs via the principle of reality, things are all undenied and eventually one becomes a proponent of nature as cause.[19] If one is excessive with proofs via the principle of efficacy, agent and effort are undenied and one becomes a proponent, in the end, of a creator as cause. If one is excessive with proofs via the principle of dependency, all power will remain undenied and one will become a proponent of Iśvara as cause. If one is excessive with proofs via the principle of valid proof, all contexts in which there is reasoning are made stainless and eventually one becomes obviously proud (*abhimāna, mngon pa'i nga rgyal*).

The Limits and Excesses of the Four Principles

When proponents of realism prove things, for the most part it is done through the principle of reality and direct perception. Therefore, the limits and excesses wrought by these two should be described.

Limits

When there is an intellectual assessment of objects,[20] then along the lines of what was described above, intellectual observations are qualified by discriminations, what appears to the intellect is qualified by sensations, and intellectual realization is qualified by stainless insight. That is to say, while they are experienced because of the inability to eliminate confusion, appearances that participate in the realms of experience associated with sensation are nevertheless comprehensible because they are not unlike a real entity. Objects of a discriminating mind are incapable of removing distortion [literally, "imposition (of what does not exist) and denial (of what exists)" (*sgro skur*)].[21] Thus, they are simply part and parcel of what it means to be an ordinary person. Realization through taintless insight is not unlike the correct appraisal of weight.

Insight is twofold: specifically discriminating insight and nonconceptual discriminative awareness. When the nature of reality (*dharmatā, chos nyid*) is assessed via specifically discriminating insight (*pratisaṃkhyāprajñā, so sor rtog pa'i shes rab*), distortions are cleared away gradually. Just as it was demonstrated earlier, for those who categorize phenomena rationally, there is a gradual clearing away of distortions related to the totally imagined. However, there is no end to distortion as long as a real basis in reality remains undenied—that is, taken as real. When realized through nonconceptual gnosis, an actual base of reality is denied. Therefore, this proof by means of the principle reasoning of reality is only a partial outline of the distortions in undenied reality that are simply settled in terms of the principle reasoning of reality.

Excesses

Here, there are excesses. The "correct convention" (*tathyasaṃvṛti, yang dag pa'i kun rdzob*) categorized in the Madhyamaka text tradition means that poison is actually lethal and medicine is actually salutary. If those potencies lie in the very nature of things, then the mind and the gnosis associated with [or presented in] the Yogācāra would ultimately exist, or transform into *dharmatā*. In such a case, the subject–object dualism of the Śrāvaka, in the end, would be nothing other than the theory of nature as cause itself, because the Madhyamaka's correct convention amounts to being a guardian of all realist theories.[22]

What is established through direct perception, too, is like this. As pointed out above, establishment via direct perception according to the Śrāvaka system is said to be refuted by some other rational systems. According to the Yogācāra system, a given object is a confusion in the actual base of reality. A stainless reality is intelligence (*vijñaptitva, rnam par rig pa nyid*) simply appearing in the inner and outer sense fields. Therefore, reflexive awareness does not pertain to something that fabricates any subject or any object. Stainless reality is established as the reality of mere reflexive awareness and characterized as nondual. This need not be proven, however, by reasoning. Further, this point is itself incapable of being subverted by reasoning.

Someone may ask: are not all mind and mental factors reflexive direct perception? If that is the case, is direct perception as such not conscious awareness of reality? In which case, what is the point of proving it by some distinct form of reasoning? Further, that authentic recognition (*yang dag pa'i shes pa*) is of greater power than a second authentic recognition that is fabricated for the purposes of philosophical conflict.[23] When everything knowable is simply mind, any other object comprehended and established by that authentic recognition is either stainless reality or stainless direct perception. As it is said, "What need is there to seek out anything else?"

On the other hand, there are also proofs that are impure. It is commonly stated that a directly perceiving awareness is either something generated along with conceptual images or is something generated without conceptual images. If generated without conceptual images, how is an object made to be directly perceived? If direct perception is generated with conceptual images, what acts as the unmistaken witness (*sākṣin, dpang po*) of such an epistemic event? Thus, there is also a refutation of direct perception, which claims it "is not a viable epistemological warrant" (*pramāṇa, tshad ma*).

According to the Yogācārins, are not all the minds and mental factors associated with the three realms *false conceptions*? If they are *conceptions*, how is it that a directly perceiving awareness is free from concepts? If they really are *false*, how is it that a directly perceiving awareness is unconfused? Insofar as it is marked by conception and thus is a confused awareness, how is it possibly an epistemological warrant (*tshad mar ji ltar rung*)? Furthermore, on this view, the negational terms *conceptual* and *unconfused* indicate, respectively, negation in *adherence* and negation in *separation*. Accordingly, just as what is disclosed by the phrase "the absence of darkness at the heart of the sun" discloses nothing at all about the source of obscuration, a faculty of awareness does not become distracted with nature as such. It is the very nature of gnosis.

If negation is subtle or slight, then, not unlike the case in which "no discrimination" is described, though there is subtle discrimination, subtle conceptions may be described as "nonconceptions." This is not unlike when a little material is described as "no material" or a little confusion is described as "no confusion."[24] In such descriptions as these, nature as such is conceptual and confused. Thus, how could it possibly be an epistemological warrant? Further, even though the dualistic nature of apprehended and apprehender is eliminated, if the cognitive state generated is something experienced through sensation, then whether such a reflexive awareness is real or not is uncertain—and still ought to be assessed because the domain of sensory experience does not interrupt confusion.

Conclusion

At this point, someone might very well state the following: "If your point is that all reasoning is corrupt (*amala*, *dri ma can*), how is it that you happen to be possessed of some distinct incorrupt reason by which you are able to explain all this?"

We do not, in fact, say there *is* an incorrupt reasoning. Nevertheless, because there are greater and lesser degrees of corruption, those reasonings of little corruption are capable of refuting those of greater corruption.

To that it may be asked: if there were one incorrupt system of reason that handled everything knowable, what would be the reason the jinas do not just present that system of reason in all the teachings of the Buddha from the very start?

In any case, none of the presentation here should suggest that a reliance on reason must be unhelpful. For example, the first glance and the first step do not complete the distance a person might intend to travel. Yet it is also not the case that these can be dispensed with. Just as such [a journey] is completed through reliance upon them, realization becomes perfect through transmission, intimate advice, and one's own awareness that is arisen from reason. As it is stated: "Previous skilled adepts, until stable, do not subsequently give up [philosophizing in the above ways]. After becoming stable, they gradually give it up, and do so without falling into the abyss of defeat because they come to realize all positive points."

Therefore, those who are devoted to grammatical treatises and logical treatises—especially those who think that they adopt their own philosophical position via incorrupt reasoning and repudiate the Great Perfection approach to the path because it is considered unreasonable—should not engage in such thinking. Rather, [they should] faithfully engage in the Great Perfection approach. For if they do not, they will come to be overly proud. This is the fourth chapter, concerning how the system of the Great Perfection is not undermined by reason.

5. Writings on Great Perfection

Here, we should disclose something of the actual writings (*gzhung nyid*) of the Great Perfection. Any and every writing that discloses the system of the Great Perfection is included under four types of teaching. That is, writings on Great Perfection teach (1) the nature of bodhicitta, (2) the greatness of bodhicitta, (3) deviations and obscurations (*gol sgrib*) connected with bodhicitta, and (4) methods for "settling" or "consolidating" (*gzhag thabs*) bodhicitta. Teachings on the deviations and obscurations, in fact, become teaching on the nature of bodhicitta. In the teaching on nature, greatness is penetrated and deviation and obscuration are eliminated. Therefore, even though there is no such fourfold organizing rubric in writings on Great Perfection as such, [the discourse in the writings] does not go beyond it.

The Nature of Bodhicitta

In sum, then, consider the nature of bodhicitta: all phenomena, outer and inner, appearance and existence, are nondual bodhicitta—the primordial nature of the quintessence of awakening (**bodhigarbha*, *snying po byang chub*) is primordially perfected (*yas nas sangs rgyas ba*), not something refined and corrected through a path, and is accomplished spontaneously, without effort.[1]

The Greatness of Bodhicitta

Concerning the greatness of bodhicitta: consider an island of gold where the word *stone* does not even exist because everything is naturally occurring gold. By analogy, given that the true nature of all phenomena in the universe is included within outer and inner, there is in the end no name for such things as saṃsāra, bad migrations, and so forth, which are imagined as faulty and imperfect phenomena. On this view, everything pertains to the very greatness of the tathāgata. It is all simply unimpeded appearance—Samantabhadra's ornament of play.

Deviations and Obscurations

Accordingly, deviations from, and obscurations to, bodhicitta pertain to all the theory and praxis associated with the lower vehicles of the worldly person who is not realized and who is misinformed. In sum, there are perhaps thirty deviations from, and obscurations to, bodhicitta.

Methods for Settling Bodhicitta

On the topic of methods for "settling" (or "consolidating") bodhicitta: after apprehending something not unlike the domain of Great Perfection just as it is by means of the vessel of great introspection (*samprajanyam*, *shes bzhin*), the superior awareness of the yogin remains within a state of great equanimity (*upekṣā*, *btang snyoms*). The words of the Great Perfection that teach in this way, as well as in a more well-known, ordinary idiom, use such expressions as *subtlety* and *peaceful* and make comparisons between phenomena and basic space. In the systems of the lower vehicles, we find discourse on subtlety and peace, too; yet they are coarse and distressed like the material aggregates.

From the Writings of Great Perfection

Thus, the Great Perfection approach to the path requires consideration by a broad, deep, and subtle awareness. To that end, below I will treat several statements that are found in the textual tradition of the Great Perfection such as (1) those that state all phenomena are to be considered awakened in the intrinsic nature of bodhicitta, which is a single great sphere (*bindu*, *thig le*), (2) those that state all confusing appearances are to be considered as the play of Samantabhadra, (3) those that state all sentient beings are to be considered as the profound field of awakening, and (4) those that state all domains of experience are to be considered to be naturally arising gnosis.

Eight Additional Rubrics

Our examination will also look at how all phenomena are described in terms of (5) being considered to be naturally perfected as the five types of greatnesses, and (6) how all phenomena are enumerated in terms of being considered to be naturally awakened as the six great spheres. Further, in this context, we shall (7) determine deviation and obscuration via the thirty deviations and obscurations, (8) remove the hindrance of doubt via the three types of being (*yin pa gsum*), (9) determine the final view (*dgongs pa'i rting gcad*) through the three great assurances (*gdengs chen po gsum*), (10) comprehend the basis of intimate instruction (*upadeśa, man ngag*) by means of three fundamental intimate instructions, (11) resolve all knowables by means of bodhicitta within a single great sphere (*bindu, thig le*), and (12) resolve how the ground of the indivisible Samantabhadra is disclosed spontaneously without effort in the present state because of the greatness that constitutes the fact that everything, everywhere, is at all times already perfect. In this context, the glorious Vajrasattva, being secondary in nature (*gnyis pa nyid yin pas*), is not unlike like a king empowered by a precious wish-fulfilling jewel, through which everything is made possible and impossible. Now, to demonstrate what I've mentioned.

All Phenomena Are Seen to Be Perfected within the Single Sphere of Bodhicitta

As I pointed out above, the term *bodhicitta* signifies the indivisibility of mind (*citta, sems*) and awakening (*bodhi, byang chub*). For, it is said,

> Mind alone is awakening;
> What is awakening is mind.
> There are not two—mind and awakening;
> Such a unity derives through yoga.

The meaning of *sphere* (*bindu, thig le*) is simplicity—that is, being "free from elaboration." Greatness naturally and totally pervades all phenomena. Their nature is perfect. Given the nature of the essence of awakening, obscuration is not removed and gnosis is ungenerated. Take, for example, the eyes of a jackal (*śivā, lce spyang*), which see clearly regardless of whether it is day or night. For the jackal, there is no need to rely on the power of appearance, since darkness need not be removed because at that moment luminosity is recognized in the nature of space. Similarly, when all phenomena are realized as the nature of the essence of awakening, there is no obscuration to remove, and there is no need to generate gnosis, because at that time, bodhicitta is recognized as naturally luminous.

All Confused Appearance Is Seen as the Play of Samantabhadra

Concerning the phrase "the play of Samantabhadra": everything is "all-good" (*samantabhadra, kun bzang*), because there is nothing at all negative or to be rejected in connection with everything known to beings wandering within saṃsāra, which are confused appearances (*'khrul snang*). Since there is not any goal to strive toward and no core point to resolve, since illusion is a state like a game, it is play (*līlā, rol pa*).[2] Totally unimpeded appearance never strays from reality and is in fact indivisible from reality itself—and thus is an ornament. Given that there is no phenomenon that is not totally perfect (*sangs rgyas*), everything, because of being the very proof of the Tathāgata's deeds, pertains to the nature of greatness. Just as it is stated in the sermons of the Buddha: "Eighty-four thousand afflictions, all causing affliction for sentient beings, are the very proof of the Buddha's deeds. Even the four types of demons establish the deeds of a buddha." This description, as primarily the play of Samantabhadra, is taught in the *Six Vajra Verses of Bodhicitta*,[3] where what determines the deviations from the nature of bodhicitta is taught through the first two verses. The unceasing ornament, the play of Samantabhadra that is the greatness of bodhicitta, is taught through the two middle verses. The last two verses disclose the resolution for settling, or consolidating, bodhicitta.

All Sentient Beings Are Seen as the Profound Field of Awakening

Regarding the phrase "sentient beings, the profound field of awakening": this phrase is not unlike one given in the *Bodhicitta Vajrasattva Great Space*,[4] which states: "greatness, which concerns actual reality (*dharmatā, chos nyid*)—supremacy itself—pertains to all sentient beings, the profound field of awakening" because sentient beings are migrating aggregates. They are awakened and they are a field. Thus they are an *awakened field* because they are a source of all the qualities that derive from the path of the Great Vehicle. It is called *a profound field* because it does not appear as such to, and is not realized by, cognizant beings wandering within conditioned existence.

All Domains of Experience Are Seen as Naturally Occurring Self-Appearing Gnosis

Consider the phrase "all domains of experience are naturally occurring gnosis appearing to itself": typically, domains of experience (*gocara, spyod yul*) comprise the sentient being's six fields of sense experience. Naturally occurring gnosis (*rang byung gi ye shes*), in fact, consists in the natural pacification of all karmic processes and thus those fields of experience. Gnosis is naturally occurring.

In fact, this system is also asserted by the Yogācārins who deny the existence of images (*nirākāravāda/anākāravāda, rnam par med par smra ba*). This is proven, moreover, in different Buddhist discourses (*sūtra*) of definitive meaning, such as when it is stated:[5] "Indeed, naturally occurring gnosis is not something collected (*gsog*); it is absent curative power (*gsob*), and foundationless; merit is not something accumulated, gnosis is not something that cures, and it is not devoid of a consecrated heart of naturally occurring gnosis" (*rang 'byung gi ye shes su dbang bskur ba'i snying po myed pa ma yin no*). Accordingly, even though all phenomena are collections and deceptive subjects, the accumulation of merit, perceived as nondeceptive, is cultivated. Similarly, such practices are curative because, while they are devoid of potency at their core (*bcud du bya ba myed*), all phenomena are made curative qua gnosis (*ye shes bcud du byas*) and therefore rendered as something that may be relied upon. Even though all phenomena are without a core, what is referred to as "a consecrated heart, or core, of naturally occurring gnosis" is something that will be perceived to be undistorted and unsullied by the nature of conscious awareness. While in accordance with the assertions of the Yogācārins, these assertions are not about real ontology—that is, they do not concern what really *is*. Thus, naturally occurring gnosis is indeed not something collected, is not curative, and is without a core essence. This is not unlike the system given in the *Gaṇḍavyūhasūtra*:[6]

> Even though some inconceivable [number of]
> Worldly realms may be burned [by fire],

> Space would not come to be destroyed [by it].
> Naturally arising gnosis is likewise.

A similar system is proclaimed in the *Great Garuḍa*:[7]

> Unsupported, without objective basis, unimaginable qualities of the path,
> Emerging from an object that is a subtle factor of dedication,
> The penetrated, cultivated dharmakāya devoid of any distinctive point
> Remains in all ways just as it is—nonconceptual, naturally arising gnosis.

Even though this [contemplative stance] is necessary in the context of settling bodhicitta, being the vital point of meditative absorption (*dhyāna*, *bsam gtan*), it is taught here as well because it is the abiding state of naturally arising gnosis. Accordingly, nonconceptual concentration is something that does not reside in a given basis, is not perceived by the mind as a given object, and does not conceptualize images just as they are. Therefore, when it is said that "it is to be practiced in that manner,"[8] it is not divorced from factors of dedication and has fallen into the extreme of bias. The dharmakāya is not a single quality particularized through dichotomizing schemes such as "acceptance-and-rejection"—that is, bias (*blang dor*)—and then especially enhanced. Though the domain of experience connected to the six sense faculties is conceptualized and distracting, it does not accept and reject objects, or even recognize them. Ordinary conscious awareness is, moreover, something luminous by nature. This system is free of bias and should be recognized as being analogous to the example of the jackal's eyes discussed above. What is not in accord with the Yogācāra assertion here, however, are teachings such as those that proclaim that naturally arising gnosis as such is indescribable.

Some people think that if naturally arising gnosis is present, there is nothing that could obscure it and therefore there is nothing to give up. Do not think like this. For example, to people's eyes, illumination is present as the elimination of darkness; because of that, even the power of illumination, the antidote to that darkness, is conditioned. Upon obtaining the jackal's eye, it is realized that there is no real entity to be rejected. If space is something naturally luminous, the presence of a primary element that depends on appearance, although recognized as an entity, would not function to remove darkness. Similarly, when the stainless eye of dharma (*dharmacakṣus, chos kyi mig*) is attained, if what is and what is not afflicted is not recognized, the nature of the ordinary mind is recognized as something luminous when it is recognized that a real entity is nonexistent. That is because, at that point, nonconceptual gnosis is not consonant with obscuration even though the character of cognitivity is perceived as a real entity. Because of that, there is no instrument that is an objective basis for the mind actively removing obscuration. In that case, whatever appears to a confused awareness as a sensed domain of experience is not comprehended as real. Therefore, the rhetoric of abandoning obscuration pertains to a child's domain of experience; it is not the domain of experience of the skilled. This point it is not unlike one made in the *Sañcayagāthā*, which states:[9]

> After a migrator understands confusion to be like a snare for
> wild beasts,
> The insightful wander like a bird in the sky.

All Phenomena Seen as Perfected within the Nature of the Five Types of Greatness

After having spelled out the meaning of the Great Perfection by means of each term in brief, now I will demonstrate it by means of enumeration. According to the phrase "all phenomena are considered to be naturally awakened as the five types of greatness," all phenomena are unmixed and totally perfected phenomena. In that context, *unmixed* pertains to diversity in appearance. *Completely perfect* pertains to what is naturally not dual.

The five types of greatness are the greatness of the clearly awake, the greatness of awakening as great being, the greatness of awakening in dharmadhātu, the greatness of awakening connected with being that, and the greatness of the nonexistence of everything everywhere as totally perfect.

The term *awakening* was already explained above. The term clearly indicates something directly perceived or immediate. *Great Being* indicates mastery. *Dharmadhātu* indicates being divorced from the character of all phenomena. *Being that* in fact indicates that there is no gnawing doubt. *There is nothing not perfected* indicates what is beyond convention. Something should be called *great* because it eclipses the lesser. At a given time, the term *great* might be used in connection with this vast and spacious awareness that overwhelms lower-vehicle intellects with its brilliance. Yet, in the presence of an awareness qualitatively superior or inferior, it is not possible to say that the nature of that awareness as such is greatness given the absence of any qualitative objectivity. Accordingly, this is not unlike what is proclaimed the *Great Garuḍa*:

> Spacious, great, supreme dharma,
> Is proclaimed to be the antidote for those lesser ones;
> For the greater ones, from the factor of equality,
> Lesser and greater are free of objective basis.

The five types of greatness that act to surpass five objects—inferior theories, nihilist theories, realist theories, doubt, and real exertion—are called *great* because they are overwhelming in brilliance. The overwhelming brilliance of being manifestly awake eclipses inferior theories because, whereas for those in lower vehicles who remove obscurations as something worthy of rejection and assert that awakening is accomplished by the transformation of appearance, here there is no phenomenon to be abandoned that is eliminated. The phenomenon that is to be transformed is absent any transmutation. The phenomenon that is to be actualized is nothing that is to be obtained. Teaching only the directly perceived—the immediate—to be the awakened is overwhelming in brilliance relative to those inferior theories—and is an antidote to them. Thus "greatness" is because of the destruction of the attitude connected with biased attitudes engaged in acceptance and rejection. It will be applied in that manner to those below. Dominion in connection with everything is the Lord of Knowledge—that is, Samantabhadra—who is autonomous;[10] the essence of enlightenment does not rely on the power of another.[11] The three remaining [greatnesses] are easily understood. Indeed, these fives types of greatness, in their fivefold iteration, reveal the one domain of Great Perfection. In dialectical terms, the first greatness is the thesis. The next two characterize that as predicates. The fourth is the rationale for that (*de'i gtan tshigs*). The fifth gives verbal expression to them.

Here, someone may ask, "On this view, how is the character of what is clearly already perfected (*mngon sum du sangs rgyas pa*) perfect (*sangs rgyas*)?" Everything is naturally occurring self-arisen gnosis without reliance upon some distinct, other nature of enlightenment essence. Gnosis itself transcends all characteristics. When it is characterized, it is characterized in terms of being something ineffable or beyond description (*bsnyad pa' thams cad dang bral ba*). Why? Even though this teaching states "because that is its nature, and, therefore, it is perfect," whether it applies to the presence of some flawless quality or the absence of a state of reality similar to that, the words "everything everywhere at all times perfect" have nothing to do with the conventional label "not totally perfect" (*sangs ma rgyas pa*). In fact, it is a conventional designation that discloses this domain, which is said to be resolved effortlessly by virtue of the fact that it transcends the domain of all exertion in conceptual construction.

The Six Great Spheres

What are the six great spheres? They are the sphere of reality, the sphere of the expanse, the sphere of the totally pure expanse, the sphere of great gnosis, the sphere of Samantabhadra, and the sphere of the spontaneous state. Concerning these: *reality* is the immutable; *sphere* signifies simplicity. For example, the reality of a mirage is that it is simply empty of water; and the very nature of mental movement and fluctuation means it is empty.

Emptiness is indeed viable, appearing as the generation of a mirage as well as appearing as its negation, because, in emptiness, there is nothing to be transformed into something else and the entity, being simple, is not encompassed by anything. The reality of phenomena is a similar case; and it was explained above in the context of "intimate advice" (*upadeśa, man ngag*). Not unlike the teachings from the empty and selfless up through the teaching of nonduality, there is no transforming something's nature into something else by means of various phenomena. There is also not an already elaborated characteristic quality of concreteness. On this view, characteristics are neither dispelled nor discarded. The nature of characteristics as such is not unlike nature as such. Thus, it is called the *sphere of reality*. That nature is the sphere of reality's expanse because it is the source of all perfected qualities *(buddhadharma, sangs rgyas kyi chos*). This itself is the sphere of the totally pure expanse because it is primordially purified of any distortion. That itself is the sphere of great gnosis because it is naturally luminous, self-manifesting, naturally arising gnosis. That nature is the sphere of Samantabhadra because it is the unceasing ornament of Samantabhadra's play. Even an object like that is the sphere of the spontaneous state because it is not reliant upon either change from the ground up (*da gzod bgrod*) or refinement. The first two are untainted by sentient beings' confusion. The middle three are not modified by antidotal means. The last pertains to a resolution that transcends effort.

Indeed, these five types of greatness and six great spheres teach the nature of bodhicitta, the greatness of bodhicitta, and the elimination of deviations from bodhicitta. In fact, the method for settling bodhicitta pertains to the actual capacity to remain free from effort and resolve the final view.

The Elimination of Deviations and Obscurations

Now, after having determined the final view in terms of various enumerations such as five greatnesses and six spheres, the method of the effortlessly spontaneous state is to be disclosed—that is to say, the elimination of the thirty deviations and obscurations. The thirty, as generally known terms, are given in terms of ten basic categories in two bases. The two bases are points of deviation and points of obscuration. In this context, an obscuration is something that works to hide great buddhahood. On this view, the accomplishment of great buddhahood is effortless.

What, moreover, are the points of deviation? The worldly, Śrāvaka, and Pratyekabuddha paths. The points of deviation comprise two types: common and special. Those called *common* deviate from internal mental yoga. They are the systems associated with the discourses connected with the Perfection of Insight (*prajñāpāramitā*), the Kriya and Ubhaya classes of tantra. *Special* points of deviation separate out four types of union (*yoga*, *rnal 'byor*) that are distinguished within a single yogic system, which, on this view, are distinguished as Yoga, Mahāyoga, Anuyoga, and Atiyoga. The lower would be deviations with respect to the higher. Thus, we have ten basic categories (*rdzas su bcu*). Regarding the thirty as terms: each of the four types of yoga has six common deviations and obscurations, totaling twenty-four. Special points of deviation number one, two, and three; we add six to twenty-four to get thirty.

Worldly

Nothing need be said on the worldly path.

Śrāvaka

Śrāvaka theory and practice finds its source in the significance of the four truths and such things as the four root transgressions (*parājika*), vows, and so forth. Remaining in the *pratimokṣa* discipline, a Śrāvaka renounces the three realms. Yet, that path forms a point of deviation from yoga, in general, because it has nothing to do with the yoga of suchness. It deviates from the Great Perfection because it ails under effort. It is a point of deviation for us, moreover, because it is explained as a path wherein a sentient being is transformed into a buddha. This path is an obscuration because it does not generate the mind as great enlightenment. As a general rule, all points of deviation also are obscurations.

Pratyekabuddha

Pratyekabuddha theory and practice finds its source in the system of interdependence; the basic vows are consistent with the Śrāvakas, and thus the two are alike in renouncing the three realms.

*Perfection of Insight (*prajñāpāramitā, shes rab kyi pha rol tu phyin pa*)*

Perfection of Insight theory and practice, along with its vows, originates after generating the mind of great enlightenment and practicing the six and ten perfections (*pāramitā*). In particular, the theory of the two truths comes to the fore. Having relied upon the pratimokṣa as the basic vow and remaining committed to the great enlightenment encompassed by the four uncommon root *parājika* vows and minor offenses, great enlightenment is accomplished in reliance upon the three precious jewels and sentient beings; or great enlightenment is accomplished by means of practicing, primarily, the great compassion that acts to fulfill the aims of sentient beings. It is a point of deviation from the yoga, in general, because it has nothing to do with the yoga of suchness. It deviates from Great Perfection because of using effort.

Kriyatantra

In the general system of Guhyamantra, enlightenment is accomplished by relying on the three precious jewels and sentient beings, and the practice consists primarily of enacting delight vis-à-vis knowledge-mantra, or secret mantra, and, more peripherally (*zhar la*), acting on behalf of sentient beings. Apart from that, the theory and practice of Kriya is to remain in bodhicitta and its three principles of reality. Knowledge mantra (*vidyāmantra*) and secret mantra (*guhyamantra*) completely gratify (*mnyes par byed pa*). The basic vow originates with the pratimokṣa and the basis of great enlightenment. Abiding in the five bases of training (**pañca-śikṣāpada, bslab pa'i gzhi lnga*), the four great root downfalls to be eliminated are abandoned. By enduring in the thirteen root *samaya* vows of tantra that are to be adopted, along with numerous subsidiary samaya vows, great enlightenment is accomplished. These basic vows are a discipline (*vinaya, 'dul ba*) of the Guhyamantra because all tantric practitioners rely on them. The vows proclaimed primarily in the teachings of Yogatantra are kept secure. Common vows are the basis for guarding what is worth protecting, and they function to consolidate what is worth consolidating. As such, they are something to rely upon (*rten pa*).

Bodhicitta and the three principles of reality, too, are the bases of all theory and practice in the Guhyamantra, and all knowables are included within them. Thus, I will explain a little bit about them because they are essential to the work of Guhyamantra yoga. Here, bodhicitta is something generated by a mind composed from insight and compassion. The three suchnesses are suchness of the self (*bdag gi di kho na nyid*), suchness of the deity (*lha'i gi di kho na nyid*), and suchness of the recitation (*bzlas brjod kyi de kho na nyid*). The suchness of the self comprises the nature of conditioned phenomena, just as they are. The suchness of the deity comprises the character of unconditioned phenomena. The suchness of the recitation comprises the character of the means to accomplish that.

The "self" referenced here pertains to the domain of the five psychophysical aggregates, not something simply distinguished by the intellect. The suchness of it becomes three types under the influence of the three doors. According to the Śrāvakas, this collection of five psychophysical aggregates is empty of such things as the self that is imagined by non-Buddhist extremists and what is predicated of that self, eternalism, and nihilism and so forth; and the aggregates are empty of being imagined. The impossibility of rejecting the character of these aggregates, elements and sources as utterly nothing (*chos tsam myed*) is the suchness of the self.

According to the Yogācāra, the suchness of this collection of five aggregates is not only empty of self and what is predicated of that self, it is also empty of the imagined Śrāvaka notion of subject and object. Mind and mental factors, being simply one's own awareness, pertain, on this view, neither to the apprehended (that is, the object) nor the apprehender (that is, the subject)—and that is their suchness. Further, when untainted by notions of subject and object, if there is no difference here from the state of buddhahood (*buddhatva, sangs rgyas nyid*), then because of being tainted, such a difference is thus distinguished. In accordance with the Madhyamaka, the suchness of this collection of aggregates is, further, empty of being the ultimately existent nonconceptual gnosis imagined by the Yogācārin; this complete pacification of conceptual elaboration is, on the Madhyamaka view, the suchness of the aggregates.

From this, it follows that anything tenable as one of the three suchnesses is asserted to be infused with the suchness of the deity, because meditation on the commitment being (*samayasattva, dam tshig sems dpa'*) causes the gnosis being (*jñānasattva, ye shes sems dpa'*) to be perceived by the mind to be present, thereby achieving a distinctive quality through the performance of the accompanying recitation.

In that connection, the deity is called *divine* because of being beneficent and distinctively sublime. The suchness of the deity is included under eight qualities (**aṣṭadharmā, chos brgyad*) and six deities (*saḍdeva, lha drug*). The first four of the eight qualities are as follows: the totally pure dharmadhātu, nonconceptual gnosis, its nondual concentration, and conceptual gnosis. These four, along with the four variations in the appearance of form[12]—that is, appearance as sound, appearance as name, appearance as form, and appearance as seals (*mudrā, phyag rgya*)—comprise the equal eight qualities. These are infused by the deity.

Both the pure reality of the deity and the impure reality of the self are in fact realized to be without any difference in nature. Meditating along those lines, [one realizes] that both divine gnosis qua pure natural awareness and the impure self-awareness of egoic conscious awareness are likewise indistinguishable. Given that, the distinctively sublime appearance as the deity's body and speech should be recognized as being similar to the appearance of the egoic body and speech, which are not distinctively sublime. Because of that, one will be transformed into a deity and that generation is cultivated (*bhāvanā, bsgoms*). Therefore, the phrase *infused with the deity* is used because one accomplishes the deity.

Given such an object as this, some might say, when cultivating such things as syllables (*akṣara, yi ge*), *mudrās*, buddha bodies (*kāya, sku*), and so on, that these are "something imagined, cultivated only with an antidotal purpose." This constitutes slander that accumulates very onerous karma. After considering that the suchness of the self is nature as such, there is the thought that the suchness of the deity pertains to the totally imagined. This is not unlike, for example, a fool who takes a trinket to be a precious jewel and takes a precious jewel to be a mere decoration.

The suchness of the deity, which, according to the system of Guhyamantra, encompasses absolutely everything, is nothing other than different systems of consolidating (*bsdu*), combining (*sbyor*), and considering (*lta*). One could elaborate here at length. Even this teaching as such—Kriyatantra—deviates from yoga in general because of the external and primary activities it enacts. It deviates from the Great Perfection through the construction of effort.

Ubhayatantra

Ubhayatantra is the same, because it does not dispense with activities.

Yogatantra

The four types of yoga are in general agreement because they primarily engage in yoga of the internal mind. In terms of internal distinctions, given that yoga is connected to acceptance and rejection—that is, biased attitudes—ordinary thought dualizes the deity and the self.

Mahāyoga

Mahāyoga is the opposite of this.

Anuyogatantra

Anuyoga is called *subsequent yoga*. In one moment of awareness of the nonduality of the expanse of basic space and gnosis, theory and practice are asserted to be complete. Thus, it accords with Atiyoga; but because it is not free from slight effort, it is called *subsequent yoga*.

Atiyogatantra

These internal divisions within Guhyamantra assert the indivisibility of the two truths, beginning with Kriya and ending with Great Perfection. Because of this, from Kriya through the Great Perfection, the suchness of the self and the suchness of the deity are considered to be equal in nature. Insofar as the view of equality waxes, the view of inequality wanes. In short, the view of equality slowly diminishes fixation on realist views.

A view such as this wherein the suchness of the self is the same nature as the deity is present in those sets of discourses that are definitive in meaning (*nges pa'i don kyi mdo sde*). Nevertheless, there is not much explanation other than this concerning how equality is accomplished. This is not unlike, for example, the bodhisattva's *Jātakā Tales* in the Śrāvaka system,[13] which are simply teachings on the accomplishment of enlightenment through practicing for the benefit of sentient beings over a long period of time, with no explanation of the means to accomplish bodhicitta.

These deviations and obscurations have been explained in dependence upon *The Indestructible Being of Great Space Tantra*. In the injunctions of past scholars,[14] it is well known that, in the *Undiminished Victory Banner Great Space Tantra*, each specific deviation and obscuration is revealed like the sun in the sky.[15] Those deviations and obscurations are only explained as simple parameters, beyond which one should not go. When deviations and obscurations, as a category, are broken down and set into fundamental groups, there are twenty-three points of deviation and seven obscurations—totaling thirty.

Twenty-Three Points of Deviation

In connection with the twenty-three points of deviation, the first set of ten comprises three points of deviation concerning the essence of enlightenment (*bodhigarbha/bodhimaṇḍa, byang chub kyi snying po*), three points of deviation concerning concentration, and four points of deviation concerning the path of actual reality. The second set of ten comprises one point of deviation concerning attachment to the types of bliss associated with great gnosis (**mahājñāna, ye shes chen po*), two points of deviation concerning the source of limits for hopes and aspirations, three points of deviation concerning scriptural transmission (*āgama, lung*), one point of deviation concerning cause, and three points of deviation concerning the fruit of attaining concentration. There are three points of deviation concerning dharma: the nonemergence of dharma from dharma, plus the dharma of not relying upon dharma, plus not realizing dharma through dharma equals three points. Thus, the above constitute the twenty-three points of deviation.

The Seven Obscurations

Concerning the seven obscurations, there are three obscurations that are not encompassed within the domain of yogic activity because there is corruption in the nature of the essence of awakening. There are three more obscurations that take hold through the illness of the bondage of affliction, making six. There is one more obscuration that takes hold by means of distortion—that is, various types of imposition and denial (*sgro skur*)—concerning scripture. That makes seven.

Three Deviations from the Essence of Awakening

Concerning the three points of deviation concerning the essence of awakening, the first concerns the nature of actual reality, bodhicitta and the essence of awakening, which has nothing to do with all the phenomenal characteristics of appearance. Here, it is stated that exertion, resulting from (*bas*) desiring to generate actual reality (*dharmatā*), pertains to a deviation. Therefore, it is stated:[16]

> Actual reality, devoid of appearance,
> Is meditation setting forth noneffort;
> Analogously, when the former is sought in the latter,
> Reality cannot thereby emerge.

The meditation pertains when there is no exertion at all because the nature of the essence of awakening has nothing to do with the character of phenomenal appearance.[17] Once there is desire to generate actual reality, a deviation through effort is present.

The second deviation concerning the essence of awakening is given in connection with the essence of awakening, which is unchanged through the power of something else. It is stated:[18]

> When there is a congruence of features,
> The term *karma* is designated;
> Anything under the influence of karma
> Is not present within naturally arising gnosis.

However various instantiated conceptions may appear, given that they are of the same character—that is, indivisible in nature from the essence of awakening—virtuous and negative karma are totally imagined only by confused beings wandering in conditioned existence. Such a system is also propagated in *The Illuminating Web of Illusion Tantra*:[19]

> This dharma is naturally pure.
> Ignorant sentient beings, in their delusion,
> Act like fools entangled in the web of concepts;
> The virtue and wickedness they do,
> Is labeled into two heaps—*virtuous* and *negative*.

This is not unlike what is stated in *Stainless like Space* (*Nam mkha' lta bur dri myed*), which states:[20]

> Sentient awareness proliferates,
> Thus, the process of karma varies.

Such statements like these are in agreement. Inasmuch as this is the case, at the time of conceptual construction as such, naturally occurring gnosis is something self-arising. In a different moment, however, this may not be the case. This is because when karma is grasped as a real entity, naturally arising gnosis has no basis in reality and cannot be resolved. Take, for example, the radiance of a spinning fire-brand: if the character of the circle's radiance is itself a real entity, there is no basis in reality for the fire-brand's natural brilliance.

The third deviation concerning the essence of awakening is given in terms of the essence of awakening not being causally produced. In the desire to establish awakening causally, effort constitutes a deviation; it is stated:[21]

> The cause as such is not unlike an indestructible (*vajra*) condition,
> Because it is unborn, it is indestructible;
> In the primordial awakening essence,
> The expanse of basic space remains unmoved by the force of thought.

The reality of what appears as causes and conditions is like a vajra, indistinguishable in nature. Thus, it is devoid of arising and ceasing and absent any state of movement because of causal force.

Three Deviations from Concentration

Concerning the first deviation from concentration, it is stated:[22]

> The concentration on great qualities,
> Being a state of concentration, is not thought;
> Unthought and untrained, just as are phenomena,
> Gnosis emerges from a state of conceptuality.

The unceasing formation of all merits in the heart of equality and, especially, the automatic abatement of impure karmas, happens in accordance with the concentration on great qualities. If not penetrated in this way, because of one's wanting to purify afflictions and accomplish spiritual qualities, one resides in a state of concentration encompassed by the ailment of bias—that is, attitudes structured around notions of acceptance and rejection. When, however, not reliant upon thought and effort in training, one remains in an unfabricated state (*ma bcos pa'i ngang la gnas*), conceptuality becomes as luminous as gnosis. Concerning the second, it is stated:[23]

> After labeling the door of subtlety,
> Seeking the path with a mind secluded [from discursive activity],
> And constantly remaining in the isolation of the wilderness (*araṇya, dgon pa*),
> Then, if sought, the meditation becomes conceptual.[24]

In this case, the term *subtlety* is used in two senses: [first,] there is the association given along the lines above wherein something is subtle because of some kind of corruption. After a nonexistent object is conceived as an object, the mind, isolated (*vivikta, dben pa*) from the distractions and busyness (*saṃsarga, 'du 'dzi*) of the body, is perceived as the path to liberation. When awareness is carefully analyzed, that is conceptual meditation. [Second,] if the term is applied within a horizon of contexts, in the traditions of nonconceptual meditation (*rnam par mi rtog pa'i sgom lung*), it is stated:

> In nonconceptual meditation,
> Awareness does not construct some kind of basis;
> No object at all serves as an objective basis;
> The meditation does not conceive any image whatsoever.

Subtle attitudes of bias are present where there is the desire to actually obtain the natural condition devoid of three faults. Thus, isolating the ordinary mind from things and their characteristics is asserted to be a path. And, here, isolation from the distractions and busyness of the body, if analyzed by a discerning intellect, is nothing other than meditation on conceptuality.

Three Deviations Associated with Causality

These subsequent tendencies pertain to points of deviation from the Great Perfection. It is stated:[25]

Proclaiming that the affixing of names to cause and result
And the eradication of both virtue and negativity
Occur in this world
Is a bias born of extraordinary pride.

Because of perceiving causal phenomena and karmic notions of virtue and negativity as ultimately real, this oceanic world of conditioned discontent amounts to nothing but a grievance. For that reason, one thinks, "I need to get out of this ocean of discontent to the dry land of liberation." This is an attitude of bias. This, in fact, constitutes engaging in the smaller vehicle.[26]

The phrase *the eradication of both virtue and negativity*, in one sense, signals the extinction of both virtue and negativity. That constitutes the annulment of karmic life according to the Śrāvaka and Pratyekabuddha systems. On their view, the cessation of karma is really accomplished with the cessation of life. The cessation of afflictions is accomplished when karma halts. When afflictions are halted, the aggregates of suffering are said to depart from this [oceanic] world of discontent to the dry land beyond sorrow (*nirvāṇa*).[27] This system is biased and emerges from extraordinary pride.

Four Deviations from the Path of Reality

In connection with the first deviation from the nondual path, seeking a middle way, it is stated:[28]

The lord of beings (*jagannātha, 'gro ba'i mgon po*) proclaimed
Attachment and nonattachment to be just a way of talking
(*vākyapatha, tshig gi lam*);
Like the Middle Way, it is akin to an echo;
Happiness and suffering share a common cause (*niṣyanda, rgyu mthun*).

It is taught that attachment is a state of desire and thus worldly. Nonattachment is being freed from that and is thus nirvāṇa. But the binary of saṃsāra and nirvāṇa is verbal signification and is thus just a way of talking about things. Verbal significance is the province of convention. The province of convention contains no essence. On this view, if the binary extremes of saṃsāra and nirvāṇa have no essence, then neither does the middle way between them. Therefore, the phrase *like the Middle Way* was used. Being devoid of an objective referent, the Middle Way is merely a way of talking about things and is therefore proclaimed to be *akin to an echo*. Thus, the glorious Vajrasattva, guru to all,[29] proclaimed it so, given the inseparability of the suffering of attachment and the happiness of nonattachment in the context of causality or nature.

The second deviation from the nondual path obtains after considering the characteristic marks of phenomena that are associated with the six sense faculties' domain of experience to be imperfect. It is stated:[30]

> E-ma-ho! This primordially perfected (*sangs rgyas*) domain of experience
> Is not a place found when sought;
> Like the teaching of the six perfections, no object is present.
> Those who search for it are like a blind person clutching after empty space.

The domain of experience of a tathāgata is not sought as something different from the domain of experience of a sentient being's six sense faculties. The very nature (*de nyid*) of the domain of experience of the six sense faculties, in its nature just as it is (*ji ltar gnas pa*), is indeed the domain of experience of a tathāgata. Given such a nature, because of which a sentient being's domain of experience is false, it is not an object upon which one should meditate. The object of meditation is the domain of a tathāgata's experience—actual reality (*dharmatā*)—where characteristics have abated. When one thinks "*that* should be meditated upon," this is similar to a blind person clutching at empty space, which is a deviation from the path's own nature. For example, because of the cultivation of the Field of Infinite Space,[31] form is eclipsed (*abhibhūya*, *zil gyis mnan*). And while in such a state, one that goes beyond cognitive discrimination of form and material resistance, one recedes from experience and is not free from the bondage of form since one's predilection toward form has not been eliminated.

If, after realizing that the nature of form as such and the nature of space as such are indistinguishable, concentration is attained, that is liberation from the bondage of form. Similarly, after one has seen the appearance of characteristic marks as imperfections, if one cultivates peace as the absence of characteristic marks, characteristic marks are indeed eclipsed. Yet this is not freedom from the bondage of characteristic marks. When one realizes everything that appears as a characteristic mark has nothing to do with its nature as such, which is free of characteristic marks, one has not seen characteristic marks as imperfections and has not eliminated them. If one obtains a concentration that is devoid of characteristic marks by virtue of becoming familiar with characteristic marks through understanding, then one becomes free from the bondage of characteristic marks.

In connection with the third deviation, which concerns deviation from the untraversed path because of desiring to traverse the progressive path, it is stated:[32]

> The ever-exalted path of purity (*brahmapatha, tshangs pa'i lam*),
> Free of activity, does not conduce to phenomena;
> When the path is traversed.
> Like the limit of space, there is no destination reached on it.

Given that the natural state of phenomena is the nature of phenomena as such, there is no traversing a path, or ground, in stages. If the ground were purified gradually and purity and liberation were gradually accomplished, then the actual reality of all phenomena would have no basis in reality. Thus, if that which is obtained is something totally different, in the end, there could be no acquisition.

In connection with the fourth deviation, given that the nature of awakening essence is without division or bias, the deviation from the path of equality is because the path is partially grasped. It is stated:[33]

> Such a complete path as that
> Emerges with its support, like the moon;
> Given the equality of everything,
> A partial view of one accomplishes nothing.

The nature of essence awakening is suchness (*tathatā, de bzhin nyid*). And like suchness, essence awakening is whole. Since sentient beings and buddhas constitute a shared path, the phrase *complete path* is used. Here, *path* and *ground* have a similar meaning. The *Sañcayagāthā* states:[34]

> This vehicle, like space, is an inconceivable celestial mansion.

It is not that one is creating something different to traverse; one simply acts within the natural state of the awakening essence (*bodhigarbha, snying po byang chub*). It is said that it *emerges with its support, like the moon* because [the nature of essence awakening] is analogous to the moon reflected in water. Wherever the water, as support, is, the moon is present, reflected in that water, and the moon is not present in one part [of the water] and not another, although people say that, having glanced from wherever they stand; rather the moon [reflected in] water is seen to be in each place. Because of that, people subsequently think "This moon in water appears here, and it appears over there." Similarly, given that the nature of essence awakening is without division or measure and because it is the nature of all phenomena, people who apprehend it only in part deviate from equality (*mnyam pa nyid*). These constitute the first set of ten deviations.

Connected to the second set of ten deviations is the point of deviation concerning attachment to the types of bliss associated with great gnosis. It is stated:[35]

> Bliss in the present and the future
> Emerge in the immediate and subsequent, respectively;
> Yet even that pertains to a flaw and therefore
> Should not be relied upon.

Bliss in the present is immediate (*pratyakṣa, mgnon sum*) and is nonconceptual gnosis. Bliss that emerges in the future is pure worldly gnosis. These two types of great bliss are seen, respectively, as the path of buddha and worthy of taking up, and something discordant that ought to be eliminated. But due to being an awareness bound by images, [pure worldly gnosis] is also said to signify something that is not resolved as the basis of awareness.

Connected to the two points of deviation concerning the source of limits for hopes and aspirations, first, there is the point of deviation that consists in making aspirations for high status (*abhyudaya, mngon par mtho ba*) in the world. It is stated:[36]

> Even the purification of the three conditioned states (*tribhava, srid pa gsum*),
> Manifests as illusion in name only;
> Even the great abode of a cakravartin
> Is a hermitage (*āśramapada, bsti gnas*) for purifying illusion.

Three conditioned states indicates the three realms of saṃsāra (*tridhātu, khams gsum*). Even the various states of higher status are merely labels that appear as illusion. Thus they are not a suitable state to hope for and aspire toward. The attainment of a cakravartin ruler is indeed a state of higher status in this human world; and because the human world is a hermitage of mere illusion, something to be purified and restrained, it is not "a source of hope and aspiration."

The second point of deviation concerning the source of limits for hopes and aspirations is connected to the point of deviation concerning investing hopes and aspirations in the fruits that emerge at a later point in time. It is stated:[37]

> The fruits of practices, which are temporally contingent,
> Do not emerge in the time they are practiced;
> Proclaiming the absolute reality of emptiness
> Is not unlike practicing without overcoming aspiration.

Those obsessed with types of characteristic marks, fixated on the reality of the appearance of fruits that arise from their causes at a later time, invest their hopes and aspirations in fruits that will arise at some other time, though they do not come to be in that way. This is not unlike the example wherein people develop faith in the word of the Buddha after the Conqueror proclaimed that "emptiness exists" because of the varying intellectual faculties of the trainees (*vineya*, *gdul bya*) present in the audience for that teaching. Yet these people subsequently seek, and do not find, the fact of emptiness. This is not unlike the nature of essence awakening being atemporal. Thus, investing in hopes and aspirations at a point in time is a deviation.

The first of the three points of deviation concerning scripture is the point of deviation consisting in making impositions upon scripture. It is stated:[38]

> The whole—the ultimate—is completely beyond typification;
> Yoga is a path that soars [effortlessly] through space;
> Given the unarisen, unborn essence of things,
> How could phenomena labeled through imposition be real?

The term *scripture* (*āgama*, *lung*) indicates something that qualifies as being reliable. There are definitive and ordinary scriptures. Definitive scriptures decisively resolve their subject matters such that they are free of any distortion of it. The nature of scripture is the domain of essence awakening itself, which cannot be taught by anyone. Therefore, the words in scriptures that do teach it are impositions that deviate from the nature of scripture.

The second point of deviation concerns concentration that is faulted for the external exertion it applies to counter internal impurity. It is thus a deviation from the concentration on equality. It is stated:[39]

> Take both internal and external: external as such is internal;
> There is no profound object realized partially;
> The mere name *conditioned existence* is a misguiding force;
> By it, equality is divorced.

External signifies a mind desiring to gain mental bliss. *Internal* signifies bliss obtained. The phrase *the external as such is internal* signifies the inversion of the outer-inner dichotomy because the [externalized] state of exertion would become internal peace. Already being bound to attachment to bliss, it is external, which does not penetrate the significance of the profound. It is because of the influence of the bondage of conditioned existence that we find statements such as "there is no profound object realized partially; the mere name conditioned existence is a misguiding force." This is proclaimed to have nothing to do with equal concentration because it is a deviation from the concentration on equality.

The third, here, is the point of deviation from the tantric vows called *samaya*. There is no internal and external differentiation in the heart of equality. Teaching internal and external samaya is said to constitute a point of deviation because there is in fact nothing to be guarded or unguarded. Just as beings wandering in conditioned existence are in the nature of the aggregates and elements and thereby have no means to transcend that reality, the natural quality (*rang bzhin nyid*) of the aggregates and elements pertains to the greatness of primordial perfection. Therefore, there is no method for transcending that reality. Because of the deviation of teaching samaya as internal and external, it is stated:[40]

> Inner and outer commitments
> Abide like the nature of aggregates and elements;
> Yet because they do not participate in past, present, and future,
> There is no "commitment" designated by name.

Concerning the one point of deviation connected to cause, it is stated:[41]

> Here, there is no state whatsoever to realize.
> If, through disciplined and fierce conduct,

> One is endowed with images of the syllables *Ah* and *Pa*,
> It is asserted by some that illusory bliss emerges.

Given that the nature of essence awakening has nothing to do with an object that should be realized, there is no basis for a state that is to be accomplished through the application and order of outer austerities (*tapas*, *dka' thub*) and disciplined conduct (*vrata*, *rtul zhugs*). Nevertheless, possessed of an awareness that is not attached to the domain of the unborn, it is said that qualities that are mere illusion appear.

In connection with the three points of deviation concerning the fruit of attaining concentration, there is first the point of deviation into effort stemming from desiring to attain bliss. It is stated:[42]

> Because the nature [of the awakening essence] remains an
> undetermined whole,
> Things are taken to exist in the manner in which they appear;
> Indeed, the bliss of the exerted mind chasing after appearance
> Is in fact a great hindrance and defect.

Given that appearance is seen in accordance with the manner in which it looks to ordinary awareness, because it is not the nature of phenomena, there is a deviation because of effort derived from the hope to obtain a bliss associated with the appearance of an authentic nature.

The second of the three points of deviation concerning the fruit of attaining concentration concerns a point of deviation connected with the subtle distinguishing marks of the limbs of enlightenment. It is stated:[43]

> All secondary entryways to enlightenment,
> Being meditations on attributes (*nepathya*, *cha lugs*),
> are like a moon reflected in water;
> Even when free of attachment and defilements;
> Such meditation is akin to a child's domain of experience.

The marks of divine attributes are a secondary entryway to enlightenment. Whatever parts may be included within totally perfected and not perfected become evident because they are untainted by obscuration. Since a phenomenal appearance is manifestly evident to ordinary awareness, it pertains to the domain of experience of a child.

The third concerns the point of deviation concerning coarse distinguishing marks. It is stated:[44]

> After taking the body of Great Heruka,
> By means of the attributes of the wrathful maṇḍala,
> Regardless of evincing the syllables,
> The state of peace is not found.

The significance of this passage is in line with what was said above. When applied in a given context to indicate actual reality, gnosis, name, and pure form, the term *syllables* connotes the nature of the divine body.

In connection with the three points of deviation concerning dharma, the first is connected to the nonemergence of dharma from dharma. It is stated:[45]

> No matter how many hundreds of thousands of
> Of practices are done, they generate only flowers;
> It is because of the influence of the signless,
> That the state of peace will not emerge from that hermitage.

Even though the entryways to the dharma are beyond count, they are all indeed for the benefit of beings, because while they indeed generate the quality of greatness, no core qualities emerge outside the enumerations of the dharmas since, in reality, there are no phenomenal characteristics.

The second concerns the dharma not relying upon dharma. It is stated:[46]

> Totally complete perfection,
> Unchanging and whole,
> Is boundless like space—
> Not a dharma contingent upon anything else.

The term *dharma*, here, refers to a phenomenon that encompasses its own quality, or character. Something reliant upon something else does not encompass its own qualities. For example, when establishing the quality of a fire crystal,[47] the light of a fire crystal does not rely upon the sun. When the character of a fire crystal's hotness is established, it is not established on the basis of its contingent nature. Fire, being hot without necessarily relying upon something else, is the established quality of the hotness of fire. There is also the case when something is validated as the quality of a nonthing; we might take, for example, the quality of a mirage, which is empty of water, the color blue, and any movement. Conventional awareness undertakes such a proof when establishing something as empty. The quality of emptiness, however, does not rely on the mirage. The mirage can exist as long as the sun shines; when the sun disappears, the mirage disappears. Within emptiness, there is nothing possessed of a distinct nature. Similarly, conventional awareness is engaged in dependence upon appearance as the characteristic mark of any subject, which is a quality that is, in the final analysis, essentially pure and that is devoid of any reliance upon anything at all.

The third deviation concerning dharma concerns not penetrating dharma through dharma. It is stated:[48]

> Apart from the power of one's own awareness
> Of incomparable gnosis
> By means of spontaneous great bliss,
> There is nothing that does not derive from something else.

Actual reality, which is the nature of essence awakening qua the great bliss of bodhicitta, essentially uncorrupted by distortions, if taken to be something besides one's own luminosity and naturally arising awareness—that is, as some objective referent penetrated by gnosis—is not plausible *as* actual reality. Thus these are the twenty-three points of deviation.

The Seven Obscurations

The first three obscurations concern obscurations connected to corruptions. The first concerns the corrupting obscuration [of fallaciously assuming] that the nature of essence awakening decays, which it does not. It is stated:[49]

> Simple, yet difficult—and difficult because of being simple,
> It is not an immediate state, though it is all-pervasive;
> But not even Vajrasattva can point it out
> By giving it a specific name.

Given that the nature of essence awakening is free from decay or effort, there is ease. Corruption obscures it, and thus it is not realized. For that reason, it is difficult. It is like the expanse of space, because it does not appear to direct perception. In that sense, it is proclaimed that it is all-pervasive. Its nature transcends conventions expressing characteristic marks. Thus not even Vajrasattva can give it a name and point it out.

Concerning the second obscuration: because of obscuration through corruption, the teaching requires clarification by spiritual guides. It is stated:[50]

> This is the all-equalizing path
> That is the abiding nature of all migrators;
> For the spiritually immature, it is corrupt,
> Not unlike [the absurd notion of] medicine searching for a doctor.

Nature is obscured because of corruptions and therefore unrecognized [as such]. For example, medicine is in fact naturally helpful with illness; but like being medicine searching for a doctor, sentient beings wandering in conditioned existence are naturally free, though corruptions prevent sentient beings from recognizing that. That is the reason why it is necessary for spiritual guides to make clarifications. You must please rely on a sublime spiritual guide!

The third obscuration concerns the fact that there are no divisions, or biases, within great bliss. The appearance of corruptions structures the physical world and biases the beings within it. It is stated:[51]

> Great bliss in the realm of discursive understanding
> Is itself worldly;
> By gathering light from all directions,
> That is, the four cardinal and intermediate directions, zenith
> and nadir,
> From the indeterminate colors of a rainbow,
> The distinctive buddha families clearly appear.

Given that great bliss has no division and bias, all biased appearance pertains to the play of great gnosis that is itself the ornament of greatness. Yet, the appearance too as the physical world and the beings within it is because of corruption. The phrase *by gathering light from all directions* connotes the way appearance in the physical world structures whatever is not real as if it is real. The phrase *colors of a rainbow* connotes the appearance of something that is without divisions that nevertheless appears as if it has divisions. The sentient beings in the world appear as the divisions.

In short, there is appearance as the totally pure and impure world within a single basis. Appearances that are impure are called *obscured* because of corruption. Systems like this are especially proclaimed in the sūtras where, among all the worlds constituted by the physical world and the beings within it, none are said not to be buddha fields. The trainees in those systems are reducible to two types: beings who are disciplined and beings who are arrogant. The former comprise bodhisattvas; the latter comprise ordinary beings and Śrāvakas.

In order to train sentient beings, there are the blessings connected with the appearance of a completely pure world and a body of perfect resource. In order to tame arrogant sentient beings, the totally impure world appears low and destitute as a blessing. When the world is destroyed in the aeon of destruction, trainees are as if blessed. Without fail, buddhas engage in enlightened activities using the eighty-four thousand afflictions that afflict sentient beings wandering in conditioned existence and the four demons (*catvāro mārā*, *bdud bzhi*). According to the common teachings of the Buddha, the physical world and the beings within it come into being because of the force of sentient beings' karma. Nevertheless, in these two systems, appearance is not different and there is no foundation for appearance. As the mere condition of appearance, compassion and karma may both be common to the system. Since emancipation (*apavarga*, *byang grol*) and bondage are equal inasmuch as appearance is the condition for both, it is possible to establish them in accordance with both systems. If a concordant awareness, which is incontrovertible, is established as true in that way, that manner of compassionate blessing would be real.

Yogic activity [proper] is not encompassed by an object. The three *obscured* [appearances are corrupt, however, and therefore said to be] encompassed by the bondage of afflictions. On this view especially, all yogic activity vis-à-vis [*the obscured*] is condensed into three types: (1) engaging in practices such as the dedicated feast offering, made to superior beings according to the maṇḍalic system of the ornament of play, (2) engaging in oceanic activity for the benefit of sentient beings, and (3) practicing the Guru Puja and generosity in order to generate the field of merit. Each of these embraces the view that merit-making practices should not be rejected because bondage is, on this view, totally unrelated to such a practice. The falsehood and goal of these three are easily recognized and thus are not arrayed here.

The last obscuration is connected with the obscuration consisting in distortions; that is, imposition on, and denial of, scripture as such.[52] It is stated:[53]

> Therefore, given the nature of scripture as such,
> Practice becomes obscuration;
> When reality is conceptualized in that way,
> There is no attaining the real.

Scripture [or *transmission*] as such is what it is because it is something fundamentally superior (*gzhi'i mchog yin pas*). This is itself the reality of bodhicitta: the nature of essence awakening. To *practice* that, one receives [the scripture or transmission] and then, in order to understand it, one generates obscurations by means of intellectual ideas and an effort to talk about what exists and does not exist. These are obscurations, not unlike winds that disturb the surface of water. Thus, when settling into the natural state of one's own nature, great bliss is present; during that state, it is said that no conception obtains [that is, no ideas come to mind]. Here water and fire, if unmodified, are each stable and clear. Inasmuch as one attempts to improve the mind, to that degree one thereby becomes a hindrance to oneself. Similarly, when the ordinary mind is realized to be without nature as such, no improvement is required because there is no activity to improve the mind and no explicit basis upon which one could make improvements. If it remains unrecognized, just as coercion can make improvements, conception simply becomes something that makes alternations. Analogously, both white and black clouds obscure the sky.

Thus, these points of deviation and obscuration, outlined as the thirty deviations and obscurations, themselves either teach the nature of bodhicitta or else teach methods for settling bodhicitta.

The Three Beings

The three beings (*yin pa gsum*) are Samantabhadra, Samantabhadrī, and the Nondual One. These three beings are the condensed esoteric precepts (*man ngag*) for the five types of greatness. This is because of the fact that, according to the Great Perfection approach to the path, whatever appears is mastered as the play of Samantabhadra and constitutes what may be called being Samantabhadra. The fact that whatever appears is itself essentially unreal constitutes what may be called being Samantabhadrī. And the fact that their respective characteristics are not established as dual is because the state of appearance is something unborn. The unborn state is given in the uninterrupted continuum of all variety of appearance. It is the uninterrupted continuum of compassion's blessing (*byin rlabs*). Indeed, the entire significance of the Great Perfection is subsumed under these three expressions.

The Three Great Assurances

The three great assurances [or certainties] are esoteric precepts for the six great *thig le* (spheres). What are these three? They are state (*nisarga, ngang*), nature (*svabhāva, rang bzhin*), and great being (*mahātma, bdag nyid chen po*). The state is unfabricated. The nature is uncontrived. Great being is spontaneous. The term *unfabricated* (*akṛta, ma byas pa*) indicates that regardless of corruptions because of sentient beings' confusion, the nature of the mind is not something transformed into something different. The term *uncontrived* (*anadhīṣṭa, ma bcos pa*) indicates that regardless of how the jinas methodically improve it, there is no refinement of the quality of bodhicitta. Being *spontaneous* (*anabhoga, lhun gyis grub pa*) means it is something that has passed beyond progression and improvement.

The Three Fundamental Esoteric Precepts

The three fundamental esoteric precepts (*upadeśa, man ngag*) are those that summarize putting an end to the points of deviation connected to the thirty deviations and obscurations. What are these three? First, there is the intimate instruction that is not based on authoritative Buddhist scripture. Second, there is the intimate instruction in which a result is not from a cause. Third, there is the dharma that does not emerge from the mind. It is because of the thirty deviations and obscurations that the nature of bodhicitta is not realized and spiritual attainment through the force of sustained effort is hindered. The point here is this: bodhicitta is the heart of all phenomena. That means that bodhicitta is the superior esoteric precept for cutting off ordinary awareness. Yet this is not voiced in scripture. Bodhicitta is indeed something naturally luminous, yet it is not a phenomenon that emerges from the ordinary mind's yoking together of insight and concentration. Bodhicitta is, moreover, something manifestly and primordially perfected (*sangs rgyas pa*) and not something established through the causal collection of merit and wisdom.

Resolution through Bodhicitta

How is it that bodhicitta, the single great sphere, resolves all phenomena? All phenomena are included within the mind. Therefore, there is nothing knowable outside of the mind. The nature of the mind as such is enlightened; and because of that, as explained above, the four activities connected to what is knowable are transcended such that doubt is nonexistent and there is perfect resolution in one's mind.

What Is Resolved in Great Perfection

The phrase "what is resolved through the nonexistent greatness of primordial perfection" resolves the absence of effort that is required to search for anything, given the fact that there is no primordial perfection and no primordial imperfection. That is what is resolved. Yogic beings are those who recognize the significance of such a point and spontaneously abide on a level that is indistinguishable from that of Samantabhadra. For them, the level that is indistinguishable from that of Samantabhadra runs through all the buddha levels. That reality is the domain of Great Perfection just as it is.

The phrase "Glorious Vajrasattva, the second" (*dpal rdo rje sems dpa' gnyis pa zhes bya ba ni*) accords with the intention of the Glorious Vajrasattva. The phrase "becoming and unbecoming"[54] refers, respectively, to the generation of sentient beings' karmic life—the life of ordinary beings and a bodhisattva. The phrase "unbecoming" refers to the interruption of said karmic life and pertains to the Śrāvakas and Pratyekabuddhas. All of these repeated statements that qualify the writings on the Great Perfection are just as worthy of honor as the wish-fulfilling gem of a powerful sovereign. Those great beings who penetrate and gain confidence with respect to the domain of Great Perfection are therefore the second Vajrasattva. Great Perfection teaches the nature and greatness of bodhicitta and the deviations from, and obscurations to, bodhicitta.

The Disclosure of Methods for Consolidating Bodhicitta

The teaching on the methods for consolidating, or settling (*gzhag thabs*), bodhicitta, when given in brief, states that all phenomena should be recognized as basically the same as an illusion, mirage, and so on, because, once encompassed by the vessel of great introspection (*saṃprajanya, shes bzhin*), so-called settling in bodhicitta is simply remaining in a state of great equanimity. It is in that respect that *illusion* and *basically the same* were explained above in chapter 1 in detail. Accordingly, it is because of the influence of views concerning the equality or inequality of illusions that mindfulness and introspection may come to be qualified. This is because proper mindfulness is applied to physical, verbal, and mental activity. This is because, when set correctly within the mind—even at the time of resting in equipoise—the mind clearly recognizes the presence of lethargy and mental agitation. It clearly recognizes that directing the mind toward an antidote for lethargy is something lauded; it clearly recognizes the fact that mental agitation is suppressed through its antidote, equanimity; and it even recognizes, along those lines, that when awareness is in a state of equipoise, it is free from the thorns of both lethargy and excitement. Like a vigilant observer (*gulmika, bya ra ba*), it most especially recognizes the state wherein there is no generation of effort upon which an antidote relies. This is not unlike, for example, guarding a vessel against tipping over, because it is filled with water. That emerges from views concerning illusion and inequality. For example, naturally haughty (*garvita, dregs*) elephants that are rutting become even more so when intoxicated by wine (*mṛdvīkā, rgun chang*). If such an elephant is not seized by a metal hook and chain, it will destroy greenery and houses, kill living beings, and so forth. Once reticence about applying remedies to the various faults is destroyed, the two instruments of mindfulness and introspection are constantly maintained. Taken and disciplined by them, the enemy host of afflictions may be destroyed, and the presence of great qualities works to stabilize the war-ravaged domain.

Thus, on this view, because of both faults and qualities, there is the awareness of hope and doubt, because of which the two instruments are maintained. Similarly, because the elephant of the mind is naturally difficult to discipline, if it is not seized by the iron chain and hook of introspection, afflictions such as attachment, lethargy, excitement, and other secondary afflictions, which are states not unlike states of drunkenness that totally perturb and afflict the mind, create only turbulent karma that is the cause of constant negative migrations and wandering in saṃsāra. Thus, by means of faults and defects, there is fearful comprehension. Yet when the mind is suffused with the instrument of introspection, it does not fall under the sway of afflictions. The presence of great qualities joined to the fruits of higher states of existence within saṃsāra and liberation is thus marked by hope. That means that, by means of introspection, the presence of both hope and doubt guard the trainee.

What is great introspection? Take, for example, the great ocean that encompasses the surrounding limit (*mahācakravāla, khor yug chen po*)[55] of our world. Although endless great rivers flow, there is no doubt that they will diminish. What of great introspection—is it disturbed by the winds of time or even scattered by the wings of a garuḍa? Just as there is no doubt about passing beyond the surrounding limits of our world, when all phenomena are recognized as being basically the same as an illusion, the fact that there is no awareness that is either hopeful or doubtful means that one has realized that there is neither guarding nor not guarding. For example, when an illusory elephant appears and is perceived, it is recognized as an illusion, and there is in fact no generation of an awareness that is doubtful about the object that is lost because of being let go. Awareness that hopes to protect an object through employing recitations and training is also not generated. All this amounts to something like not depending on the iron hook and chains at all.

In reliance upon two types of introspection, we find both equanimity and great equanimity. In this case, equanimity is a state devoid of affliction that is free from any imbalance vis-à-vis mental lethargy and agitation. Such a state is said to be "the attainment of a state of equality." It is original equanimity (*btang snyoms thog ma*). When control over the mind subsequently grows, one obtains an intermediate equanimity vis-à-vis the mind resting in the natural state (*praśaṭhatā, rnal du 'dug pa*), without any need for remedies or antidotes against the two mental thorns: lethargy and agitation. Subsequent to that, at the point of total control over the mind, there is no possibility for the two mental thorns and one obtains a spontaneous mind free of any effort to apply remedial antidotes.

What is great equanimity? It is nothing more than spontaneously remaining in an unfabricated state.[56] When the realization that appearances are basically the same as illusions is qualified by great introspection, which is indistinguishable from the antidote for discord, there is no effort to eliminate discord, no effort to cultivate an antidote—and no effort to realize an object. And when it is taught through the example of a mirage, appearance does not stir from the state of space, though it flows like a river. At the moment of the mirage's appearance, there is no water; at the moment of appearance of its blue color and its shimmering, there is neither blue color nor movement. The nature of space remains.

What is the state of space as such like? Sentient beings imagine the existence of something empty as opposed to form. Other than what simply acts as the conventional object called *space*, space has no nature as such. This is similar to the fact that phenomena, by their very nature, do not stir from an utterly pure state for any sentient beings or buddhas and their gnosis. Everything that appears to sentient beings in their state of suffering is nothing more than something empty when it appears—a variety of things imagined, like the water in the mirage. What appears to be blue and moving is nothing more than one's own ordinary awareness and gnosis, which is one's own awareness as such. Therefore, things that appear are not real. Their reality is naturally pure. Pure reality is itself not unlike space. When selflessness is taken as an object of awareness of a conventional mind, it is called *pacifying the ordinary mind's conceptual elaborations* (**prapañcā-upaśanta, spros pa nye bar zhi ba*) though it has no nature as such. This type of realization may be described as the realization that phenomena are basically the same as a mirage. This realization is not subject to any undermining doubts because of the example of the mirage, and it is not accompanied by any hope and doubt in the mind. There is no doubt that thoroughly afflictive phenomena are actually undermined. There is no effort made here because the awareness is qualified by great introspection. There is no hope for benefit by means of [some] totally pure phenomena. Remaining in an uncontrived state is said to be remaining in the state of great equanimity.

To sum up, the realization that all phenomena are basically the same as an illusion and a mirage is called the *realization*—and thus view—*of the Great Perfection*. The state that is inseparable from the realizing awareness is said to be *encompassed by the vessel of great introspection*. Because of that, no exertion connected to karmic processes is generated on purpose. This is called *remaining in the state of great equanimity*. It is indeed called *meditation*. By means of these three tropes, the view and meditation connected to the Great Perfection becomes wholly complete.

Disclosing Those Points through Scriptural Sources

Now, when those points are disclosed by means of scriptural sources, some without faith will become faithful; and some who do not understand will come to understand the Great Perfection. Thus, they are disclosed in a collection of writings (*gzhung gi tshog*).[57] In those writings, it is taught that there is no improvement in the mind through effort outside of the activities connected with the mind's introspection. And especially because both conceptual and nonconceptual are said to be equal in terms of nature, there is no need for mental improvement through effort. It is stated in the *Lamp of the Authentic View*:[58]

> Happiness and discontent in dreams
> Are equal insofar as one awakes;
> Both conception and nonconception, too,
> Are the same when recognized by awareness.
>
> Thus, all mental images past, present, and future, once recognized,
> Do not go beyond the natural state;
> When naive imposition is not pursued,
> The natural state emerges, contrivance is transcended.

The mind combined with great introspection that simply does not follow after imposition constitutes the absence of an object contrived through effort. We therefore refer to this as "actual reality." Since all phenomena are included within the mind, there is no phenomena that exists outside the mind. The mind, which is by its very nature unborn, is simply referred to as "actual reality." Now, who is it that meditates on what? It has thus been stated:[59]

> Just as space is without reality and therefore
> Space as such is not meditated upon,
> How could the mind, which is by its very nature unborn,
> Meditate on the unborn as such?

Yet, if someone asks, "Just how is it that the convention *meditation* is designated?" it is stated:[60]

All effort is eliminated after recognizing that
Problems and their remedies are indistinguishable;
Practice the simple convention we call *meditation* by
Settling within an uncontrived state of great equanimity.

That is, when it is recognized that both the class of afflictions that should be eliminated and the remedies that should be taken up are indistinguishable by nature, all effort connected to bias is eliminated and one simply settles into a state of great equanimity that is only conventionally labeled *meditation*.

How is it that under the influence of karmic imprints of the past the directly perceived experience of confused appearances of objects and the generation of various conceptually derived sensations come to be fabricated? It is stated:[61]

Since neither faults nor qualities are generated,
No matter what marks of conceptualization arise,
They are uncontrived, unfabricated, and luminous in and of themselves,
Unobstructed, naturally arising, unpursued, and naturally at peace.

When the concept that is a confused appearance, considered a fault, and the gnosis that is divorced from any conceptual appearance, considered a quality, are both realized to be indistinguishable in nature, then whatever objective images appear and whatever ideas are generated, in the view of the lower vehicles, are said to be *unobstructed* and *naturally arising*. Since ordinary sentient beings do not follow after them, they are said to be *unpursued* and *naturally at peace*. Therefore, the nature of bodhicitta is not contrived through some distinct condition or effort; and given that nobody can fabricate it, it is said to be *luminous in and of itself*. This very point is also proclaimed in *Meditation on Bodhicitta*:[62]

Thus, because the limits of phenomena are imagined and are either naturally illusive in nature—or nonexistent,
There is not any nonexistent reliant upon an existent, and the nonexistence of nonexistence is nonexistent;

> Since the limits are nonexistent, there is no center—and even the center does not constitute a point;
> Whether arising or not, intentionally not [engaging in the biased attitude that accompanies] elimination means no mental basis is entailed and [no mental basis becomes] evident.

Regarding said terms: All the totally afflictive and totally pure phenomena described above are unreal. Thus, *ultimate* and *conventional* are indeed only instructive conventions. In the context of definitive meaning, the two truths are also taught to be nonexistent in terms of real, established categories in that way. When the limits of phenomena are scrutinized by a discerning intellect, if they are not existent even as conventions, whose nature is only illusion, then how can they be considered to be really existent? And in that case, inasmuch as all of the objects connected to the meaning of current conventions are not real, that which relies upon them are also not real, not actual. Further, the significance of teaching in terms of no self-nature (*svabhāva-virahita, rang bzhin myed pa*) and being unborn (*anupalambha, ma skyes pa*) is said to be that discursive elaborations are established as something at peace—or nonexistent. Thus, the nonexistence of nonexistence, too, is described as nonexistent. Accordingly, if there is no limit, there is no center—and the center is not a real point. Having realized that perspective, a method for settling awareness in that manner was proclaimed: "Whether arising or not, intentionally *not* rejecting, no mental basis is entailed, and it is not evident."[63] This was proclaimed because once one realizes that afflictions and their antidotes are indistinguishable, there is no need to eliminate characteristic marks, and the conceptual mind is ungenerated. There is no basis maintained for what remains ungenerated and no object is evinced. There is also a teaching on the reasoning that sets forth the absence of acceptance and rejection: "That which does not pertain to Mañjuśrī, which stirs even slightly, is not reality and is not real."[64] Even the sense that the misunderstanding of the equality of reality itself is undermined just a bit, that itself is reality as such because no exertion is made to eliminate the characteristics of phenomena and concepts. It is stated:[65] "Since there is no nature as such in reality, there is no dwelling within it." Given that the conceptual mind does not arise, no conceptual framework is maintained. There is not even a realization of an object. It is stated:[66] "Since the ground of meditation is not found, there is nothing found through meditation." And conventionally, though the mind names actual reality "meditation," the unreality of the mind is described as "actual reality." Thus, regardless of meditation upon whatever by whomever, is there something attained? No, there is no object that is realized.

How is it that under the influence of previous karmic imprints the directly perceived appearances within the domain of experience connected to confused appearance and the generation of various conceptual processes are fabricated? Since flaws are devoid of nature as such, it is taught that when the nature of appearance is recognized, there is no removal of imperfections. It is stated:[67] "Actual reality belongs to phenomena in the conscious awareness that constitutes the domain of mental experience." In the unmistaken conscious awareness, a domain of mental experience, no matter what appears, the phenomena themselves are actual reality, undecaying, and therefore incapable of being grasped.

If there is no imperfection in what appears, what deceives sentient beings, causing them to revolve in conditioned existence? Sentient beings revolve in conditioned existence because they are fixated on the appearance of things and because they continually grasp at the characteristics of phenomena. Realizing that there is no thing connected to the appearance, within the context of the teaching that such appearances accompanied by conceptual images are unpursued, it is stated:[68] "Meditate on this supreme path that is supreme, devoid of images, and without end." When appearances are not pursued, it is because of the realization that appearances are devoid of things. Similarly, whatever mental conceptions are generated are also devoid of imperfect phenomena. They are thus unsuppressed (*mi dgag*) and unpursued because they are naturally arising. Their own nature is unreal, which is the point of their being proclaimed to be naturally at peace. It is stated:[69]

> Ungenerated karmic processes, unoriginated phenomena, and
> phenomena utterly beyond sorrow,
> Are all unreal (*abhāva*, *dngos myed*)—recognized as dharmadhātu.
> When that happens, one becomes like the arhat Subhūti.

Since all conceptually constructed phenomena are unborn by nature, no phenomena ever arises. At the point that things are conceived in this manner, if all conceptual appearances are also recognized as the dharmadhātu, that conscious awareness is said to be comparable to "the awareness of the arhat Subhūti." Here, the following analogy is given: "Space, which has no objective basis, is simply a name, without differentiation into virtue and nonvirtue—and it is unborn." In the analogy, what is simply described by the name "space" is devoid of any objective basis and has no nature as such. Similarly, given that virtue, nonvirtue, and the like are also devoid of any nature as such, they are thus unsuppressed and unpursued. Inasmuch as that is the case, when such an awareness as that is set in meditative equipoise, it is proclaimed to be qualified by its separation from conceptual frameworks. It is stated:[70]

> In the absence of any mental exertion or effort, there is no mental volition, nothing of understanding and ignorance;
> No mindfulness, no discrimination, and no bias at all; no joy or comparison, and no support;
> The state of equality—nondual, ineffable, devoid of activity and inactivity, and so on—is undiminishing.

The unreality of faults and qualities means that there is no biased mental exertion. The unreality of manifest phenomena means that there is no mental volition at all. Since the mind as such is indeed unreal, it is not cognitive in nature. Since [the mind as such] is not characterized by physical matter, it has nothing to do with understanding and ignorance. Being devoid of differentiation between afflictions and their respective antidotes, there need be no antidote to be recalled and no application of bias. Both being equal, there is not even a comparable classification and there is no objective basis whatsoever. The absence of desirable and undesirable marks a state of equality. Not being separated by distinctions, there are no dualistic analyses. The state of equality is thus beyond conventional expression—it is ineffable. Since there is nothing to aspire toward, there is no activity. Given that the three types of karma are not considered to be flawed, there is in fact no absence of activity. There is no acting to complete the two accumulations; nor is there acting to diminish obscurations. This is not unlike the statement in the Prajñāpāramitā that "nothing is diminished; nothing is added."[71] This point itself is also proclaimed in the *Great Garuḍa*. On this point, it is stated:[72]

> Rejection and acceptance are natural; yet ultimately
> Nothing is asserted and nothing is in fact accepted—

Not even a trace of delight is generated,
Like a great garuḍa, soaring effortlessly through space, leaving not
a trace.

Without any expansion or even contraction,
There is no need for evasion, or for keeping anything fixed;
All variety of phenomena issue forth
In an oceanic primordial state.

Nothing is to be established and thereby rejected. Nothing is to be rejected and thereby established. There is no object to objectify; therefore nothing is asserted. Since the very nature of things is unreal, nothing is adopted. There is no joy, and thus not even a trace of mental delight is generated. Analogously, for example, a garuḍa, soaring through space, does not flap its wings, yet it traverses the whole of space in one fell swoop. It conquered space and thus is not reliant upon anything and cannot fall into the abyss. Being unreal and not frightening (*bhayānaka*, *'jigs pa*) means that there is no need to avoid anything. Because of that alone, there is not even an object of fixed reference. Nevertheless, there is nothing that causes fear. Emptiness removes all fears. In fact, taking things to be real has not protected anyone or freed anyone from conditioned existence.

How so? Even the Śrāvaka, freed through realizing selflessness, considers subject and object to be real. Therefore, the Śrāvaka is not free. The Pratyekajina, freed through realizing the nonexistence of the object, is not free because of considering the subject to be real. The Yogācārin, freed through realizing the nonexistence of subject and object, is not free because of considering the mind to be real. Even the Mādhyamika, who should be free (*sgrol gyis*) through realizing that nothing is ultimate, is not free because of considering conventions to be real. If that is the case—if things are not considered to be even slightly real—would not the continuity of skillful practices be severed and divorced from compassion? With no union of insight and compassion, how could there be liberation? Sentient beings are the basis upon which compassion is developed. Nevertheless, it is not necessary to consider sentient beings to be real entities. Since sentient beings are unreal, when we consider all the mere illusions that appear as the joys and sufferings of sentient beings, we see that benefit occurs within the context of mere illusion. Thus, a pure great compassion in which there is no obsession and no exhaustion may come to be. Thus, there is no need to consider things to be real in connection with skillful practices. Therefore, the emptiness that dispels all fears is nothing to be afraid of.

> All variety of phenomena issue forth
> In an oceanic primordial state.[73]

Just as the waves undulating in the ocean are the ocean, characteristic marks appear variously from within emptiness without wavering from the nature of emptiness. Appearance as such is empty and thus is unobstructed and naturally arising, unadopted, and naturally at peace. Moreover, it is also stated in this text:

> Entering on to this pure path in the vast heart, immediate and
> Totally nonconceptual, sovereign equality is attained.

Given that conceptual appearances indeed manifest within direct perception, both the reality of appearance and conceptual appearance are unreal and therefore without bias. Given that in the mind there is nothing real, there is nothing real about a concept. The phrase *the vast heart* (*yangs pa'i snying po*) is used because there is nothing to be inherently objectified. One may remain on a pure path when free from all mental grasping. When endowed with just such an awareness as that, there is a sovereign equality that becomes the attainment of primordial perfection (*sangs rgyas*). It is proclaimed that it cannot be something attained through a biased awareness structured by attitudes of acceptance and rejection. This same system is in fact proclaimed in *The Dynamic Consummation of Potential*, where it states:

> The foremost domain of reality is spontaneously perfect, without
> aspiration;
> It is unaccomplished dynamic potential (*rtsal sprugs*), free of
> activity,
> In the natural bliss purified of conceptual engagement;
> How can childish misunderstanding work to beguile?
>
> In the behavior of all sentient beings, the nondual great bliss is
> Confused and thus is the construction of an imperfect path.
> Yet it is also nothing other than the superior path taught above;

> The lord of all awakened ones is evinced by recognizing that equality.[74]

Since sentient beings and buddhas are indistinguishable in nature, liberation is not something that is contrived through a path—and therefore *there is no accomplishing it*. Given that conscious awareness and knowables cannot be enhanced, they are *dynamic*. Insofar as there is no progressive movement along a path via qualitative distinction, it is *aspirationless*. Afflictions and their antidotes are indistinguishable, and thus there is *no activity*. Given that all qualities of a buddha abide primordially and are *spontaneously perfect*, they are the *foremost domain of reality*. When tainted by confused awareness, such an object remains something unchanging in nature. This is the reason that we find the statement "In the natural bliss purified of conceptual engagement; how can childish misunderstanding work to beguile?" If the conceptual mind as such is essentially unreal, how can the unsettling perturbations of karmic processes be real? For that reason, the mind as such is the nondual bodhicitta great bliss.

In that case, how can it be tainted? Aggregates, like a mirage, are similar to space, which is untainted. It is appearance-as-if-tainted that is the great path of purity. Therefore, just as a mirage and space are indistinct and indistinguishable in terms of nature, both the construction of a conditioned path by one who is confused and the construction of a liberatory path by one who is not confused are also indistinguishable. Thus, realization of, and confidence with respect to, that point on the part of yogic beings and their remaining in that state of awareness stand in agreement with the profound attitude and state of Samantabhadra-Vajrasattva. Thus it is proclaimed that "the lord of all awakened ones is evinced by recognizing that equality."[75] This system is itself taught in *The Six Vajra Lines* (*Rdo rje tshig drug pa*):[76]

> Since it is already (*zin pas*), the spontaneous state is settled
> When the illness of effort is abandoned.

Since the nature of all phenomena is already perfected within the great indestructible bliss of Samantabhadra's body, speech, and mind, afflictions and their antidotes—that is, the bias that constitutes the illness of mental fixation on what is to be accepted and rejected—is eliminated. Thus, from this spontaneous state of great equanimity, is the goal of settling into equality. Indeed, in *The Indestructible Being of Great Space* it is stated:[77]

Indestructible being qua great space is
The all-good (*kun bzang*) expansive dharmadhātu;
Since it is the pure, great path liberating all,
It is unborn, unceasing, and nothing at all intended.

The nature of bodhicitta is *indestructible being* (*vajrasattva*, *rdo rje sems dpa'*) that is uncompounded in the three times—past, present, and future—and is devoid of any point of transition. Since it is totally unwavering, it is termed *indestructible being*. The term *being* (*sattva*, *sems can*) especially applies to realization of just such an object consecrated through naturally arising great gnosis, something naturally luminous and therefore termed *indestructible being*. Space is an example of something all-pervasive yet unreal. The quality of bodhicitta is great; and, along with *indestructible being*, it constantly abides and is marked by the five types of greatness. The point, to sum up, is this: just as the nature of all physical form is equal to the very nature of space, the nature of all phenomena is primordially perfected as the nature of indestructible being.

The term *bodhicitta* qua indestructible being signifies the primordially perfected nature of all phenomena. In the phrase "all-good (*kun bzang*) expansive dharmadhātu," the term *all* refers to all phenomena as unmixed and a totality; *unmixed*, here, signifies the variety of appearance. *Totality*, in this context, suggests something without a bifurcated nature. Since none of these are something negative, something to be rejected, they are *all-good* (*samantabhadra*). That is the nature of all phenomena as such. Take, for example, space: it also abides in the nature of everything physical and is something open. Yet it is not something real in the proper sense. At the same time, since it is neither something *in* or *of* the nature of Samantabhadra, it is *expansive*—it is the "sphere of reality" (*dharmadhātu*, *chos dbyings*).

To summarize, we may ask if all phenomena are naturally bodhicitta, indestructible being. They are enlightened, of the nature of Samantabhadra, and totally great and expansive. Thus, *indestructible being* (*vajrasattva*) and *the all-good* (*samantabhadra*) are similar in meaning; *greatness* and *expansive* are also similar in meaning because "the sphere of all-good indestructible being . . ." and "the expansive, great, the supreme dharma"[78] are also similar.

That domain alone is the goal of this great path. Training on a different path in accordance with the lower vehicles (*theg pa 'og ma*) does not attain a different fruit. It is in the context of this nature that remaining in a state of liberation that is natural to all sentient beings is called *the great path*. When yogic beings realize and gain confidence with respect to reality, they become equal to the Glorious Vajrasattva ("indestructible being") or Samantabhadra ("all-good"), which is also called *liberating freedom*. Further, it is also called *awakening*. It is stated:[79]

> Not unlike the fact that objects do not ultimately proceed,
> Liberating freedom is ultimately because of inactivity.

And it is proclaimed in *The Occurrence of Astonishment* (*Rmad du byung ba*):

> Realizing this marvelous enlightenment,
> The quintessential nature of indestructible being, too,
> Is awakening on the indestructible seat (*vajrāsana*).

To sum up: it is through the writings on the Great Perfection that both the nature of bodhicitta and the methods for settling bodhicitta are given in the same system vis-à-vis simply remaining in a state of awareness consonant with the realization of that nature. Because it is said to be unborn and unceasing, and because it lacks causal conditions, bodhicitta is devoid of any generative and dissipative nature as such. Given the absence of a generative and dissipative nature as such, there is no state of conceiving it. Thus, it is said to be *nothing intended at all*. In the same text, it is taught:[80]

> Actual reality devoid of appearance
> Is cultivated through settling the mind effortlessly.

This path, which is settled without any bias and process of improvement, is also taught in *The Lamp Eliminating the Darkness of Extremes* (*Mtha'i mun sel sgron ma*):[81]

> A mental continuum in migrators is not held to be dual;
> It is unborn and as such is not an objective referent;
> Yet apart from that, since there is no other mind,
> What manipulation of, or settling within, can there be?

Beings migrating within saṃsāra do not possess a dual continuum of conscious awareness. Its single nature is unborn. When confused faculties appear to be generated as cognitive awareness, it is not itself an objective referent. For these reasons, the ordinary mind has no essential nature that is manipulable or even improvable.

Yet if that is the case, insofar as it is not improvable, is it not unblemished by the imperfections of characteristic marks? It is stated:[82]

> As long as it is conditioned by conceptual confusion,
> The ordinary mind appears like a mirage;
> When its nature is recognized, there is nothing to modify;
> When not recognized, it is like something that conjures a mirage.

As long as the condition of conceptual confusion is not exhausted, conscious awareness that is deceptive and connected to appearing objects will be generated without interruption—even though there are no such objects. When its nature as such is recognized, there is nothing to improve. The nonexistence of something is contrived, vis-à-vis manipulation of the mind for the sake of supposedly improving its condition, not unlike the desire to construct a mirage. This means that there is no improvement of unceasing conceptual appearance. Furthermore, teaching that conceptual appearance is not sought after, it is stated:[83]

> The nonconceptual and uncharacterized mind as such,
> Does not work to remain even within the uncharacterized;
> If it does not remain even within the uncharacterized,
> What need is there to mention that it does not remain within the
> characterized?

Inasmuch as an awareness that seeks out things is not generated, conceptual images are not conceived. The *uncharacterized mind*, in this connection, is one divorced from fixation upon, and grasping at, the characteristics of phenomena. Since such an awareness does not construct an underlying basis associated with the uncharacterized, what need is there to mention that such an awareness does not construct an underlying basis connected to characteristic marks? *The Lamp of Correct View*[84] teaches a similar system:

> Illusory characteristics directly perceived without hindrance
> Are realized as the uncharacterized—of a single taste in the
> ultimate expanse.

This point about settling—without manipulation—into such a state is described in *A Lamp for the Method of Nonimprovement of Mind and Body*:[85]

> Just as space is uncharacterized,
> Divorced from efforts to either observe or not observe objects,
> Just as space is considered to be naturally so,
> The mind as such is to be considered naturally so.
>
> Even the body and so forth are similar:
> Rootless and therefore considered in the same manner.
> Insofar as there is no remaining in that which is remainderless,
> There is no conflict at all.

Space, for example, is devoid of its own characteristics as an object. Therefore, there is no effort to observe or not observe it as an object. Similarly, the mind, too, is devoid of its own character as such and thus is not an object of effort. All the karmic processes of body and speech, moreover, are similar. That is the point made above.

On Critical Impediments to Concentration

Now, let me give just a bit of explanation concerning critical impediments to concentration. In general, even if the nature of the thirty deviations and obscurations explained above pertain to critical impediments connected to both theory and meditation, here I briefly explain them as something else: critical impediments to intimate instruction (*upadeśa*, *man ngag*)—subtle points to grasp that are themselves difficult to identify as impediments. In *The Bodhicitta That Discloses All Objects*, a text that primarily teaches the critical impediments to concentration, it states:[86]

> The nonabiding, nonconceptual dharma path with no object
> of observation
> Emerges from a subtle point of transmutation (*pariṇāmanā*,
> *bsngo ba*);
> The dharmakāya contemplated is absent any objective attribute,
> Thus, naturally arising gnosis is nonconceptual, ubiquitously,
> actually present.

And in the transmissions associated with nonconceptual meditations,[87] the following is asserted:

> When in nonconceptual meditation,
> There is no underlying, abiding mental state at all,
> The meditation in which no images whatsoever are conceived
> Is the path to the dharmakāya.

Once appearance and ideas concerning mental states, objective referents, and conceptual images are seen to be obscurations and imperfections and are transcended, that itself is asserted to be the unmistaken path. It is not divorced from subtle points of transmutation; and it derives from total dedication to a desired aim, because it signifies what is termed *explicitly conceptual meditation*. In that context, the phrase *subtle consideration* is defined in terms of wishes and aspirations. Although it does not pertain to remaining in a state accompanied by an objective referent in accordance with the Śrāvakas, the phrase *subtle points* does suggest a conceptual state of awareness that has fallen into the extreme of biased attitudes of acceptance and rejection.

If that is the case, one might then ask, "how does one rest the mind?" When it is proclaimed that "the dharmakāya has no objective attributes," the term *dharmakāya* refers to nothing other than the sublime object that is specifically evinced from the confused appearances of sentient beings. That which is the very essential nature of confused appearance as such, termed the *buddha body of nature as such* (*svābhāvikakāya*, *ngo bo nyid kyi sku*), is simply called the *dharmakāya*. Given that even confused appearance is the mind as such, because the mind's own nature is not real, its ideas cannot inherently exist. Thus, whatever objective images appear or whatever mental ideas are generated, the nature of a conceptual appearance itself is naturally luminous and thus is naturally arising, self-occurring gnosis. Moreover *The Indestructible Being of Great Space* states:[88]

> Space is conceived as unborn and
> The idea of it is itself not unlike space;
> Through dispassionate space-like dedication,
> The space that is of immense benefit to oneself emerges.

For example, when one uses the expression *a hare's horn*,[89] the phrase doesn't refer to an object. It is a fiction (*brdzun*) because it has no basis in reality.

Therefore, both the meaning of *a hare's horn* and the phrase *a hare's horn* are useless (*don myed pa*), and the thing that is expressed is not something experienced. For that reason, it is akin to an unreal object. Similarly, both "space" and the idea that it calls to mind are basically the same in being unborn, because space, being devoid of any nature as such, is unborn, and the idea that it calls to mind, being devoid of an object, is unborn. Thus, the idea that thinks space to be an objective referent (*dmigs pa*) is similar to the nature of space insofar as it is not generated in experience for even a single moment. It is similar to the way in which all conceptual appearances are generated contingent upon an objective condition (*ālambanapratyaya*, *dmigs pa'i rkyen*), because there is no objective condition in the object. Thus, a dispassionate awareness like space—not desiring or rejecting anything—is called *space-like dedication*. Remaining within that and gaining confidence is becoming a buddha and thus is said to be *the space that is of immense benefit to oneself*. This manner of proceeding is itself especially proclaimed in *A Lamp for the Method of Nonimprovement of Mind and Body*:

> One should recognize that the mind does not observe anything at all
> And does not abide in anything at all;
> In the mind is the subtle mental grasping connected to what is
> removed,
> The imperfections abiding in and observed by the mind.
>
> If, like a mirage, there is no mind,
> What is the instrument of nonabiding and nonobservation?
> To state that space does not abide in itself
> Is an instruction without any marked meaning.

For example, if the nature of a mirage is like the nature of space, the mirage, too, is considered as something that has no abiding objective basis at all. It does not make sense for someone else to decree that "it is a something unobserved in any object." It is observed in connection with space. It does not make sense for someone else to decree that "space is something that does not abide even as its own nature." Similarly, because confused mental appearance is itself similar to a mirage, it is said that it has no underlying basis and is not observed in any object at all. Given that it is unreasonable that the mind should be refined through some distinct mode of conception, the nature of the mind, like space, is devoid of any nature as such. Thus, it is said that it is not even reasonable to improve it. This system is itself also found in *Meditation on Bodhicitta*, which, among other things, states:[90]

> Once grasping at form, characteristics, and aspiration is eliminated,
> Even meditation on the three doors of liberation becomes the work of Māra;
> The nature of form is empty.

On this view, when meditating on the concentrations associated with the doors of liberation, three things—realist views, grasping at characteristic marks, and fixation on aspiration—should be eliminated. Their antidotes—that is, the door of liberation qua emptiness, which is characterized by isolation; concentration on the signless, which is characterized by pacification; and aspirationless concentration, which is characterized by the cleansing of discontent—are all asserted to be meditations. Nevertheless, they fall into the extreme of biases and interrupt the generation of the awareness of the equality of phenomena and therefore they are *the work of Māra*.

If that is the case, someone might ask, "How, then, should one act?" It is proclaimed that "form as such is empty"; and what is called *the liberation of those skilled in method* consists in realizing that the afflictions and their antidotes are indistinguishable. The *liberation connected to natural luminosity* consists in the realization that affliction is devoid of any real entity that can be eliminated. What is termed *the unconditioned* (*anabhisaṃskāra*, *mngon par 'dus ma byas pa*) *liberation* consists in the realization that nothing has its own essential nature. It is said that the significance of this should be embraced. Furthermore:

> Eliminating the three samsaric paths and even meditation upon the path of nirvāṇa are themselves activities of Māra;
> Those alone do not pacify, do not cultivate, and do not eliminate nature.[91]

Once one has perceived attachment (*raga/kāma*, *'dod chags*), aversion (*dveṣa*, *zhe sdang*), and delusion (*moha*, *gti mug*) as samsaric paths and eliminated them, the meditation on the fundamental virtues of being dispassionate as a nirvanic path is indeed [seen to be] the activity of Māra. This is because it falls into the extreme attitudes of acceptance and rejection. Thereby, there is no perception of the significance of the fact that all phenomena are naturally at peace. For this reason, the nature of phenomena is found neither in cultivation nor elimination.

Admittedly, the following is stated in the teaching of Vimalakīrti:[92] "Regarding liberation, it is asked, 'Is it not the case that liberation is the result of eliminating attachment, aversion, and delusion?'" In fact, arrogant people are the ones who say that the elimination of attachment, aversion, and delusion effects (*pas*) liberation. For the unselfish, the very nature (*rang bzhin nyid*) of attachment, aversion, and delusion as such pertain to liberation, which is consonant with Mañjuśrīmitra's teaching in *Meditation on Bodhicitta*. And in that text it is said, "In this way, there are arhats who think pompously, 'I have abandoned all afflictions,' though they are not in fact truly arhats." This is a similar system, as well.

Here, someone might ask, "If that is the case, then what is the actual basis for the Śrāvaka Superior's (*ārya*, *'phags pa*) path?" Given that the object and state of accomplishment perceived by all superiors is nothing more than the nondual equality of phenomena, the path attaining nirvāṇa as well is nothing other than the nondual equality of phenomena. Thus, so long as there is no confidence vis-à-vis penetrating the nondual equality of phenomena, there is some subtle point of the awareness connected to bias. Bias is simply a source of liberation rather than being the essence of the path to it. Therefore, in all the teachings of the Buddha, it is in fact proclaimed: "There is no becoming a buddha through some path other than the realization of this path."

There is no attainment of the state of buddhahood if there is no penetration of the significance of the nondual equality of phenomena, which is the point of the phrase *the deepest of all intentions*. This system is also consonant with what is taught in the *Gaṇḍavyūhasūtra*:[93]

> I and the buddhas—all beings—
> Naturally abide in equality,
> And those who do not, who do not *get it*,
> Will yet become sugatas themselves.
>
> Form, sensation, and discriminations,
> Consciousness, intentions,[94]
> They will become a great number of buddhas—
> Tathāgatas beyond count.

Criteria for the Attainment of Mastery over the Ordinary Mind

Now, let me give some explanation concerning the criteria for the attainment of mastery over the ordinary mind after one has abided in the expanse of reality and gained confidence with respect to bodhicitta. *Meditation on Bodhicitta* states:[95]

> As long as there is mental volition, there is the activity of Māra—and a minor path;
> Moving and unmoving are terms for nonabiding and not remaining within a state;
> The sugatas call the Middle Way path devoid of appearance bodhicitta.

On this view, any conceptual appearance is considered unobstructed, naturally arising, and unpursued. That means it is naturally at peace. At the point of settling long-term into the effortless sphere of great equanimity, inasmuch as any bit of mastery is obtained, it is generated without any grasping at phenomena and their characteristics, regardless of the constant generation of conceptual appearance. As an example, we might consider dreams and the objects that appear in them, which are quite tenuous. It would be as if the objective appearances in the dream remain uncollapsed even though fixation on hypostasizing views and grasping at the characteristics of objects has collapsed. This is not unlike fixating on realist views and grasping at characteristics, which are errors even though appearance is not unreal. Then, because of that, when insight and concentration are practicable (*karmaṇyam, las su rung ba*), they are nothing more than some subtle forms of grasping at the characteristics of phenomena. Production itself is subtle, too. For example, when sleep becomes lighter, it is not simply reducible to an attenuation of the fixation on the objects that appear in dreams; appearance as such appears subtle. When someone has total mastery over insight and concentration, experience or even consideration of the mind's *movement* or its *stillness* does not go beyond these two conventions. Thus, it is called *the Middle Way path devoid of appearance* because both the experience at such a moment as that and the recognition of something like it after it ceases are not as if two sensed appearances. Something that can be conventionally labeled *some such constructed object as this* should be called *the*

Middle Way path devoid of appearance. This very system is taught especially in *The Lamp Eliminating the Darkness of Extremes*:

> To what degree does the profoundly nonconceptual
> Manifest as an object to awareness?
> The experience of the profound nonconceptual,
> Since it is experience, is not reality.

When there is no way to transmit to someone else the profound object of nonconceptuality, someone might question whether or not it is experienced by one's own awareness. Yet even in that case, since it *is* experience, it is simply something conceptual,[96] and thus it should not be referred to as *perceiving the real.*

On this view, what is impossible for someone to transmit to another is all one's own direct experiences, particularly of actual reality. For example, while for the most part people and animals share in the experience of tasting salt, there is nevertheless no means to transmit that experience to those who have never tasted it by saying "this is what the taste of salt is like." Similarly, though one has experienced the taste of concentration, it is impossible to transmit it to others. What does not count as profound is something that is reducible to an idea. This system is also taught somewhere else, where it is proclaimed: "The path of bliss is divorced from sensation." It is said that unexcelled enlightenment is also divorced from sensation and has nothing to do with the intellectual domain. In Vimalakīrti's teaching, something similar is proclaimed:

> Lord of Sages (*munīndra, thub dbang*), in completely subduing the powerful host of demons,
> You attained supreme enlightenment—total peace, undying bliss—
> Wherein there is nothing of mental sensation or the intellectual domain of experience.

What is spoken of here is the point at which enlightenment was attained. If the **distinguishing feature** [**that is the**] difference between perceiving the truth and this **mind of the Buddha** is also presented as a slight distinction between the proponents of the collection of eight consciousnesses and the proponents of a single consciousness, it is, in brief, as follows: *perceiving the real* is the collapse of constantly occurring conceptual appearances. Exhausting latent biases (*anuśaya, bag la nyal*) is the attainment of the state of enlightenment. The phrase *perceiving the real* is an alternative phrase for *perceiving no phenomena whatsoever*. Just as it is said in Vimalakīrti's teaching:

> If even those who perceive the real have no perception of reality as such,
> How can they perceive something fictive?

This is not unlike what is taught in the *Sañcayagāthā*:

> Sentient beings use words to say they can see space;
> Just how this space is seen is [as] an imagined object;
> Similarly, *seeing the dharma* is also taught by the Tathāgata.

As was said above,[97] the concentration of those who perceive the real is divorced from conceptuality. There is even a nomenclature about there being no difference between sentient beings and the tathāgatas, even though the term *latent bias* is used in connection with conceptuality, the subtlety of which, one is simply unaware of; it is not applied to concepts that do not waver from the ground (*gzhi*).

The Sanskrit term *anuśaya* ["latent karmic dispositions"] may [be understood in the context of a comparison with] sea dragons following after the shadows of sea birds.[98] A [sea dragon] pursues the shadow of a bird flying over the water. *Shadow* is just a term for a reflection present in the depths of the ocean as the bird soars above it. As the sea dragon, [likened here to anuśaya, "latent dispositions"] pursues the [the bird's] reflection, the bird remains unaware [that the sea dragon is pursuing it], which is a latent disposition (*anuśaya, bag la nyal*). In the sūtras, the designation *latent disposition* is used. In the Abhidharma, the term *underlying defilements* (*anuśaya, phra rgyas*) is used. When the bird descends on to the surface of the water, the bird and its reflection coalesce; and when the bird becomes aware of the fact that the sea dragon is pursuing it, it rises up (*paryutthāna, kun nas ldang ba*) off the water into space, which is referred to by the Sanskrit term *paryutthāna*. Conceptuality, in fact, is a subtle and a coarse type of volition corresponding to conscious and unconscious experiences, labeled in terms of the constantly occurring latent disposition. Neither waver from the basis. This system is also taught in the sūtras—for example in the *Sāgaramatiparipṛcchā*, which states:

> Considered from a distance, Sāgaramati, an immense body of water appears to be utterly still. Yet, upon arriving at the water's edge, one sees it is not still. Similarly, that which appears to be the utterly still concentration of the bodhisattvas is not seen to be still when viewed through the eye of a tathāgata's gnosis.

It is also said that the nature of a bodhisattva's obscurations to omniscience itself is such that, when a still mind (*cittasthiti, sems gnas pa*) is attained in meditative equipoise, a bodhisattva remains unaware of the presence of subtle conceptuality. Here, it is said:

> What constitutes the bodhisattva's obscurations to omniscience?
> It is that a still mind is not itself suchness.

A bodhisattva's concentration is like fast-moving water that appears still from a distance but not so upon approach. That is proclaimed to be the supremely subtle core of conceptuality. This is also said:

> Bodhisattvas of the ten grounds see the nature of the Tathāgata, yet they do not see it properly because [that vision] is generated through the power of the concentration of courageous progress (*śūraṅgamasamādhi, dpa' bar 'gro ba'i ting nge 'dzin*), which is a perception that makes discriminations.

This *seeing* and *not seeing* the nature of the Tathāgata, moreover, pertains only to the power connected to the nature of nonconceptual gnosis. "Seeing the nature of the Tathāgata by means of pure worldly gnosis" is not imaginable even as a convention. This is similar to what is stated in the *Mahāparinirvāṇasūtra*:

> Śrāvakas, being predominantly engaged in śamatha meditation and less so with vipaśyanā meditation, do not see the nature of the Tathāgata. Bodhisattvas, being predominantly engaged in vipaśyanā and less so with śamatha, also do not see the nature of the Tathāgata properly. Tathāgatas, being engaged in the union of śamatha and vipaśyanā, see properly.

Therefore, in the system of Guhyamantra, it is said:

> Except for recognizing appearance qua conception as actual reality, meditations on the still or unborn mind, which are referred to as presentations of mental stillness [or] nonconceptuality, are simply reducible to fixation on conceptuality, making it impossible to penetrate the nonconceptual sphere as long as one is not awakened.

Thus, this presentation of the extent to which the mind has arrived at meditative experience boils down to setting forth a temporary measure connected to the simple collapse of the continuous occurrence of conceptual appearance. The state of being aware of the collapse of fixation on conceptual appearance is the attainment of the warmth of bodhicitta.

On the Signs of Warmth

Now, let me explain a bit about the signs of warmth. In *Meditation on Bodhicitta*, we find the following:

> Recognize the unperturbed recognition of equality, in which
> there is no deliberate effort and no so-called mental application,
> No attachment to anything, and no excitement or anxiety
> concerned with objects, to be without separation or remaining;
> It is understood as four unperturbed recognitions of discordant
> classes of phenomena and the pāramitās.

In accordance with the teaching above, practice, cultivation, and signs such as these emerge. This is because when concentration arises, any image that appears is not hypostasized through the force of fixation. Here, even if the apparent object is attractive, no mental attachment or desire is generated; and even if the apparent object is not attractive, no mental fear or aversion is generated. Appearances of things in direct perception do not come to be objectified in views. They are not delusive because there is no awareness generated that either picks them apart or remains fixated upon them. That is a sign of cultivating bodhicitta. Furthermore, the path of dharma, its fruit, and everything included within great gnosis, too, are nothing more than the realization of the significance of the nonduality of phenomena. At this point, there is attainment of the signs of cultivating bodhicitta. When realized in this manner, there is no need for training on a multitude of paths.

Therefore, the unmistaken path is simply the realization of the nature of one's own mind just as it is. This is the reason for statements such as "There is no luminosity through meditation on other than this meditation on the mental sphere"[99] and "Meditation on Vajrasattva pertains to an unmistaken practice of all paths."[100]

On the Qualities of Bodhicitta

Now, a bit of explanation concerning the qualities of bodhicitta. In the lower-vehicle systems, the generation of the aspirational mind (*praṇidhicitta, smon sems*) is primarily accomplished because of the influence of the lineage[101] and a spiritual guide (*kalyānamitra, bshes gnyend*). Thus, one is moved to loving concern through the force of great compassion because of sentient beings' deluded grasping at "I" and "mine" such that virtuous qualities[102] are perfected and aspirations are accomplished spontaneously in activities in which the dharmakāya is obtained. It is a collection of qualities and thus is called *the body of qualities* (*dharmakāya*), because of which the unceasing deeds of the two types of form body (*rupakāya, gzugs sku*) emerge.

Some methods of Guhyamantra teach that an effect emerges that is exactly like the cause, and thus, from the very outset (*dang po nyid nas*), the power of great compassion rises; and after the deeds of a buddha are practiced, the two types of *rupakāya* are cultivated by means of activities that benefit sentient beings and delight the Tathāgata. It is through such activities that one engages in the accumulation of merit. Through unmistaken meditation upon the dharmadhātu, the existence of buddhahood qualified by the three resultant buddha bodies is asserted. For that reason, if the qualities of bodhicitta are not explained, a point may come where they are rejected.[103]

In that regard, the explanations given in terms of cause and effect found in the lower vehicles are not in conflict with explanations concerning the causes of fictive appearance found in the higher teachings. This is because illusory appearances result from illusory causes and conditions. Nevertheless, though objective appearances are something to be relied upon, they are also not precluded from the Great Perfection approach. Because of the inconceivable power of its [the Great Perfection's] ocean of methods, an ocean of appearances comes come forth. Even so, all the qualities of a buddha emerge without effort from the power of bodhicitta and, moreover, from the power of its nature and manifestation. In fact, the *Great Garuḍa* states:[104]

> Immediately upon manifesting the essence of awakening,
> A great ocean of concentration emerges—
> Appearance, like a great ocean—nonconceptual,
> Vast and open, like the limits of space.

On this view, immediately upon realizing the significance connected to awakening essence, all the qualities of greatness as well—ritual mnemonic chants (*dhāraṇī*), concentration (*samādhi*), power (*bala*), absorption (*niyata*), and so on—emerge as steady blessings, which are unwavering like a great ocean. For trainees, though appearances emerge without effort, like the constant flow of a great ocean, nevertheless, the essence of awakening is nonconceptual and as pervasive as the limits of space. It is therefore vast and open. This very fact is also proclaimed in *The Indestructible Being of Great Space*:[105]

> Great miracles are not something difficult;[106]
> Through the subtlety of realization,
> All qualities and powers
> Naturally occur.

Such a teaching is similar to the one above. The insistence upon an utter absence of effort eliciting the result is especially taught in sūtras of definitive meaning. It is stated:

> If this is realized by means of the unexcelled great secret,
> It is an effortless result—and thus primordial perfection.

Such a proclamation is consonant with that given above. In that very text, we also find the great compassion that acts for the benefit of migrators; it says:[107]

> Taking hold of the nonconceptual state of equality that is dharmakāya
> Is similar to grasping at a moon reflected in water—it is ungrasped.
> The play of Samantabhadra is
> Taught in depth through language.

The nature of the dharmakāya is nonconceptual and a state of equality. Thus, like space, it is all-pervasive. All the buddhas' emanations, as well, which do not waver from that state, are not nonexistents. And since Samantabhadra's play is similar to the play of illusion, *taking hold of the dharmakāya* is described as *taken hold of ungrasped*. This is not unlike the manner in which a pool of water holds the moon that is reflected in it. It is through such a nature as this that all migrators are set in the ornament of Samantabhadra. Through the profound practice of method and insight, sentient beings are set in liberation. Thus, *the play of Samantabhadra* is *taught in depth through language*. *Language* (*a li ka li*) signifies Samantabhadra, Samantabhadrī, and the nonduality through which the illusory world is purified; through it, training practices are described. In this connection, short *a* (*a*) signifies that everything is unborn. Long *a* (*ā*) signifies the continuous practice of compassionate deeds. Short *ka* (*ka*) signifies the instrument, because great gnosis has a command over everything. Long *ka* (*kā*) signifies acts that move a migrator from one state to another. *La* corresponds to the Sanskrit term *layati-trina*,[108] which signifies acceptance and grasping. When the vowel indicating the *i* sound (*gu gu*) is explained elsewhere in the context of its shape, it is said that the *i* is like an elephant's trunk (*glang po che'i sna*), which signifies that great compassion cradles sentient beings wandering in saṃsāra rather than letting them go. In the context of grammatical terms, *i* marks the Sanskrit feminine (*strilinga*), which signifies the *dhāraṇī* of insight that apprehends all phenomena. When its affixation to *la* is explained, it signifies mastery over the deeds of profound method and discriminative insight. Therefore, in regard to teaching the system of how meaning is constructed, it is said:[109]

> That is *a* adorned by *ta*,
> *Pa* is an attribute, not unlike the growth of a branch;[110]
> In the whole domain of worldly experience,
> The profound teaching of the Buddha arose.

In this context, *a* is long *a* (*ā*) and signifies the unceasing practice of the deeds of great compassion. The adorning of *ta* pertains to the deeds practiced; the adornment itself refers to the unwavering state within which insight is purified and elaborations are absent. *Ta* is the nature of insight, formed of a moon maṇḍala. *Pa* is the work of liberating all sentient beings within those two—compassion and discriminative awareness—such that they are, moreover, not external. While this alone is the common practice for beings wandering within conditioned existence, for those with a lot of positive karmic residues especially, there is, depending on one's capacity, appearance as refuge. For those karmically unfortunate beings, no refuge appears. Even if there is no appearance of refuge, the nature of method and discriminative awareness, like the growth of a branch, becomes pervasive. Thus it is stated:[111]

> *Pa* is an attribute, like an elaboration;
> In the whole domain of worldly experience,
> The profound teaching of the Buddha arose.

The *Great Garuḍa*, as well, states:[112]

> Bodhicitta is not found when sought; if settled, it will arise properly;
> It does not appear in direct perception; its occurrence totally fulfills all, regardless of comportment;
> Free of fixation on self or other, it is a precious treasury that shows the way;
> It is not an object that accomplishes all—it is taught as selflessness and compassion.

Bodhicitta is not a phenomenon that is obtained, though it fulfills all sentient beings' hopes. And while self and other are not objective referents, it works perfectly for their benefit. It is not an object to be accomplished, though it arises from selfless compassion. The mind of compassion that forms for the benefit of sentient beings is divorced from any object that one sets one's mind to—this is selfless compassion. In *The Lamp of the Precious View*, it is stated:[113]

> Insight devoid of an object is also unsullied by the dust of attachment;
> It is through compassion that sentient beings do not grieve in the conditioned realms.

And something similar to that is proclaimed in *The Lamp Illuminating Method and Insight* (*Thabs dang shes rab gsal ba'i sgron ma*):

If it is recognized that sentient beings and buddhas comprise a
 unified reality—
That one's own mind as such is primordially perfected—
There is nothing else at all to be accomplished;
Therefore, there is also nothing to be eliminated.

After recognizing just such a dharma as this,
Compassion emerges for those who don't understand;
Once compassion is generated, it is by means of an illusory
 concentration
That any and all beneficial methods of practice are disclosed.

In short, the nondual realization of the state of equality of phenomena in this way does not become minor compassion. Rather, it becomes like the compassion of the buddhas and bodhisattvas. The compassion that results from the realist theories of reality does not become great compassion. Rather, it becomes like the compassion of the Śrāvakas and ordinary sentient beings.

In the systems of the higher vehicles, it is said that the qualities of the rupakāya emerge through the power of aspirations and meditation. Not only that, the power of nondual bodhicitta is not something that simply boils down to the force of good karma. In fact, it is stated in the *Great Garuḍa*:[114]

The teaching and the buddhas are brought to mind and appear,
Not unlike the images of an illusionist;
The fluctuating perturbations of mind are something that have
 obscured the gnosis
That is the source from which the qualities of the rupakāya and so on
 emerge.

It is from the power of calling to mind the doctrinal discourses of the sublime dharma and the power of the buddha that the appearances of the qualities of greatness in fact emerge. Take, for example, the appearance of an illusion that is an image of something nonexistent: though the image that is the basis [for such an appearance] has no status or physical dimension (*mthon dman*), it may appear as if qualified by such. What appears under the influence of some obfuscating condition is an obscuration marked by objective referents and fluctuating conceptions. Thus, appearances akin to images of qualities emerge. Yet, they are not the qualities that comprise the nature of bodhicitta. More need not be said here except that in the Great Perfection approach, there are no qualities connected to awakening, no flaws or imperfections that are not already perfect.

Here ends the fifth chapter, explaining the writings of the Great Perfection.

6. Instructions on Paths Encountered through Methods Connected with Effort for Those Who Are Unable to Remain Effortlessly within the Natural State according to the Great Perfection Approach

Now, I am going to explain the cultivation of paths that employ effort for those unable to remain in the natural state as it is given in the Great Perfection, because [these paths] should be embraced via the view of the Great Perfection since the great bliss of bodhicitta is the fundamental dharma that works to alleviate all the maladies connected to the bondage of conditioned existence. As it is stated in *Meditation on Bodhicitta*:

> Any virtuous dharma possible that is not encompassed by Samantabhadrī—
> Even the practice of Samantabhadra—is the work of Māra, and thus it will eventually diminish;
> They are indeed the work of Māra, though proclaimed to be the practice of a bodhisattva.

Other Paths as Doors to Great Perfection

Even methods to improve the mind in the Pāramitā and Guhyamantra vehicles appear as many doors to the path. In these cases, a "path to liberation" emerges that is a meditative absorption (*dhyāna, bsam gtan*) consisting in the elimination of the five faults and the removal of the ten obscurations.

There is also a "path to liberation" constituted by concentration (*samādhi, ting nge 'dzin*) that is qualified by the eight applications that eliminate the five faults (*pañcadoṣā, nges pa lnga*) to śamatha.[1] There is also a "path to liberation" constituted by the concentration that overcomes grasping, imagination, negation, and differentiation with respect to the psychophysical aggregates (*skandha, phung po*), constituents (*dhātu, khams*), and bases (*āyatanam, skye mched*). There is also a "path to liberation" that emerges in terms of the six qualities of disciplined recitations and concentrations for the mind that is naturally difficult to tame. There is also a "path to liberation" that emerges in terms of concentration that takes mind, body, and deity as an objective support. While there are many methods such as these that are taught for improving the mind, all of them cannot be fully explained here—they are explained only in part. The teaching of these doors, which are accessed through the force of people's convictions (*adhimukti, mos pa*) and emerge unconnected [with them], are nevertheless explained as reinforcing each other.

Six Faults Connected with Concentration

There are six faults associated with meditative absorption, the first three of which are distraction, caused by sensation; torpor, caused by laxity and lethargy; and solidity, caused by endurance. These pertain to the inability to practice śamatha meditation. With regard to the first two, we might consider, for example, a lamp: if buffeted by an external wind, it does not become increasingly brighter. Regardless of whether the causal continuum of wind ceases, the lamp is nevertheless going to meet its end eventually. Likewise, a state of mind becomes distracted while fanned by various karmic processes; and regardless of whether the causal continuum of karmic processes ceases, that mind as such will meet its end. Thus, its own processes are not negated given the cessation of some other process. The third—the perception of reality's solidity—is qualified by previous recollections, subsequent to which that perception constantly flows like, for example, a stream of water drops that are observed by the mind as if they constitute one solid stream of water. Here, even if the objective support is practicable, given the inconceivable nature of the object of concentration, the absence of a method for engaging is obscured.

Conceptuality

[The fourth, fifth, and sixth faults connected to meditative absorption are given in terms of] three obscurations to insight meditation (*vipaśyanā, lhag mthong*). What is termed *blockage*, and is caused by an obsessive mind, is the blocking of liberation such that insight is obscured because of not penetrating selflessness and a mind always obsessed with any appearing object connected to meditative absorption.

"Corruption," which is caused by the influence of existence and nonexistence in this sense, pertains to being ignorant of interdependence such that whatever one thinks falls into the extremes of existence and nonexistence. This *corrupts* gnosis in the sense of veiling it. "Confusion" is caused by the narrow scope of conscious awareness. This narrow-mindedness occurs because of the shallow manner in which what is heard and considered is associated with insight into reality. Consequently, any object of meditative absorption that is accessed is not penetrated. Like a bird that is afraid of the dark and therefore hides itself, the mind is confused and bewildered. While these are actual obscurations, they interfere with the generation of calm abiding and insight meditation and thus are called *the six faults connected to meditative absorption* because of being rather large faults and imperfections. Only the imperfections connected to conceptual distraction, moreover, are taught as the five faults. Here, it is stated:[2]

> The mountain of coarse conceptions,
> Characteristic marks, movements (*pracāra, rgyu ba*), sensations,
> And awareness of occurrence are the five faults that are to be eliminated.
> Conceptions are twofold: coarse and subtle;
> Characteristic marks are twofold: greater and lesser;
> Movement is twofold: enduring and brief;
> Likewise, sensations are manifest or not;
> Sensation is also given as two:
> Fleeting and drawn out.

These are indeed instances of realization categorized in terms of whether or not they are coarse or subtle and whether they are distinguished by a type of image. The *types of images* are described in terms of conceptual differentiations made when seeking an objective entity; *characteristic marks* refer to differentiation through fixation and grasping; *movement* describes continual differentiation; *sensation* refers to experiential differentiation; *awareness of occurrence* refers to differentiation through fluctuation; and *coarse and subtle* refer to structure and instance, respectively.

To sum up, *subtlety* comes in two types: subtle production and subtle grasping; *the coarse* also comes in two types: coarse production and coarse grasping. The awareness of scholars is marked by subtle grasping within coarse production. Coarse production suggests that all knowables are conceived and disclosed, while subtle grasping suggests an absence of fixation on their entities, or characteristic marks. The awareness of fools is marked by coarse grasping within subtle production, which is to say: in subtle production, all knowables are unable to be conceived and disclosed; while in coarse grasping, there is no avoiding grasping at, or fixation upon, entities. Thus, at the point of nonconceptual meditation, a mind connected to coarse grasping within subtle production does not pertain to a path of liberation because it conduces to a state within which there is absorption devoid of discrimination (*asaṃjñisamāpatti, 'du shes med pa'i snyoms par 'jug pa*), which thus obscures the path.

Therefore, at first, one becomes familiar with a mind marked by subtle grasping within coarse production; and production as such is made increasingly subtle through the power of subtle grasping, after which one is finally liberated from these five types of conceptions. When the mind's self-awareness is unceasing, it is called *seeing the real* (*satyadarśana, bden pa mthong ba*). When there is a gradual coming into awareness of the pacification of these conceptions by means of conceptions grasping at objects and by means of conceptions grasping at the grasping at objects, one will seize upon the attainment of *mental warmth*. At the point at which one is aware of subtle production that is unaware of subtle grasping, there will be no grasping the *warmth of the path*.

Nine Obscurations Associated with the Path

That touches upon the nine path obscurations,[3] which I will describe here in terms of three points that are hindrances to proper effort: unwavering meditative absorption, the integrated path, and the manifestation. Here, immovable meditative absorption does not cast off a preceding path. Regardless of being unwavering, there is no effort to attain another path.

This is comparable to a baby sparrow who remains in the nest. Similarly, even on the integrated path, there is no effort. This is comparable to an arrow that has disappeared into its target.[4] Even being utterly manifest is effortless. This is comparable to a faculty of awareness holding a manifest object.[5]

The desire to generate many thoughts within the ordinary mind, the desire to attain clairvoyance, and the desire to issue forth the miraculous (*ṛddhi, rdzu 'phrul*) marks of a buddha hinder proper concentration. Take, for example, a householder who desires pure butter, but from his reliance upon dairy cows, he becomes fond of milk and yogurt and thereby hinders his ability to enjoy pure butter.

From here we consider three things that hinder proper mindfulness: thinking "I have attained the dharma that is unsurpassable—**others are below me!**" being puffed up with pride over one's own theory, and being contemptuous of others' theories. Here, proper mindfulness concerns not forgetting the meaning of definitive sūtras and hewing to the council given by spiritual guides. For when obscurations are present, these are neglected. This is akin to, for example, the wild, rowdy children of a king or minister who do not apply their minds to the advice of holy beings. The tenth obscuration is natural obscuration. The ten types of practice[6] mutually obscure one another like flat wooden planks all lined up in a row. Thus, the point is said to be this: those who abide in the great objectives such as meditative absorption and so forth do not practice the lesser objectives such as being a scribe. It is proclaimed that through these points, one enters the path to liberation by eliminating all the obscurations and defects connected with meditative absorption.

The Eightfold Concentration That Eliminates the Five Faults

What is the concentration marked by the eight applications that eliminate the five faults? The five faults are laziness, forgetting the object of meditation, the mind being either too lethargic or too restless, nonapplication [of antidotes when necessary], and excessive application [of antidotes when no longer necessary]. Laziness concerns not listening and a lack of engagement with religious injunctions. Forgetting the object of meditation concerns the weakening of deliberation such that one does not remember [the dharma] one has heard and studied. Slackness and excitement concern the [conditions] that do not allow for awareness to cultivate its object [of meditation]. Nonapplication and [over]application both create obstacles to merging śamatha and vipaśyanā.

Among the eight factors that eliminate the five faults, four—faith, aspiration, effort, and mental pliancy—eliminate laziness. Through mindfulness, one does not forget the object of meditation. Through introspection, one eliminates mental lethargy and restlessness. If there is excessive nonapplication of antidotes, intention fortifies the mind. Equanimity suppresses excessive application of antidotes. Thereafter, when calm abiding and insight meditation are in equilibrium, no effort is made to apply a superfluous antidote. Settling into a relaxed equanimity, then, creates familiarity with the object of meditation. In this system, this is the "path to liberation."

What is the concentration that overcomes grasping, imagination, negation, and differentiation? Here, it is stated:

> Even after seizing this greedy monkey,
> A thieving cat fabricates the imagined;
> After razing each and every bit of an empty house,
> All the cracks and crevices and windows are closed;
> Yet if the royal storehouse is open,
> They are always and forever perfect.

In this context, the *greedy monkey* who seizes refers to the psychophysical aggregates, elements, and sense fields of phenomena that seize on whatever can be seized on; because, in this way, mental consciousness is not unlike a greedy monkey. It is also unable to truly assess an object (*don la ni ched du gtad kyang*). Given an object that is not viable, the mind will absorb itself into it without any dissent. This type of conscious awareness, which is always wandering aimlessly, is put into the container of introspection and mindfulness such that it is perforce confined therein and not capable of shifting to somewhere else.

Similarly, there is the *thieving cat*, the designator who designates terms and concepts and experiences—whatever can be designated. A cat, for example, acting with ease and subtlety (*dal zhing 'jam pa'i spyod pas*), steals away another creature's life without the other being aware of it. Similarly, the afflicted mind, through its subtle movements, is internalized into an egoic intention under whose influence mental awareness is generated concomitant with a realist view of reality. Thus everything is transformed through its power—*consecrated* as it were—into something defiled by it. Thus, if this is not labeled by being retained in the insight that realizes the selflessness of all phenomena, the opportunity for liberation will never be disclosed. Here, the practice pertains to vipaśyanā. The aforementioned practice pertains to śamatha meditation. The phrase *razing each and every bit of an empty house* pertains to the razed empty village that is the psychophysical aggregates and the sense fields. These are all empty villages devoid of residents; and because of being something razed insofar as its own entity is unreal, there is also no empty village per se, which should be understood to be like space. This, too, is the practice of vipaśyanā. The phrase *cracks and crevices and windows are closed* refers to the five types of sensory awareness operative when the mind's power to internally consolidate those objects that come before it as natural distractions ceases and they do not scatter the mind. This, too, is the practice of śamatha. The *royal storehouse is open* is a phrase used for those schooled in the character of the fundamental consciousness. For example, there are such things as precious jewels, even priceless things, in a royal storehouse. Yet there are baser substances, too—poison and the like. In a similar way, the fundamental consciousness is the storehouse of all contaminated and uncontaminated phenomena, because it is the source of everything knowable. On that point, however, according to the explanations given in the lower-vehicle systems, because the reality of the basis-of-all endures in the essence of the cause and result of phenomena that are contaminated, and given that it is similar to ripening fruit from a seed, it is simply the basis of, and source for, the uncontaminated—like a source of medicine inside a pot of poison. According to the higher-vehicle systems, because the character of the "fundamental consciousness" [also known as the "basis-of-all"] is of the essence of awakening (*byang chub kyi snying po*), naturally pure from the very first, the basis-of-all is called the *mind of awakening*—bodhicitta. Afflictive and turbulent karmas are adventitious stains, and like gold obscured by turquoise or a precious jewel concealed in mire, not the slightest quality is evident, yet its nature is not corrupted. Just as it is stated **in the *Indestructible Array* (*Rdo rje bkod pa*)**:[7]

> Since the precious stone that blazes like a lamp
> Has qualities that naturally illuminate it
> Even while sunk in a terrible mud,
> Its light illuminates space.

Like that, the precious jewel that is the mind itself,
Even while sunk in a terrible saṃsāric body,
Is itself naturally luminous and thus
Insight illuminates the space of actual reality.

To sum up, whatever the case may be (*gang ltar yang rung*), given that all positive and negative phenomena are simply the appearance of the fundamental consciousness, appearance is caused by karmic imprints in connection with karmic processes, because the way that they appear does not accord with the way they are. Therefore if the nature of all phenomena is realized to be beyond sorrow, the royal storehouse is open, at which time even the monkey is seized, the cat is indeed something imagined, and even the empty house is razed. The windows are shut as well. There is no need to look anywhere else for the buddha's path when possessed of an awareness like this.

Regarding the six qualities that are disciplined in the mind that is difficult to discipline, it is stated in the *Dpung gzungs*:[8]

The mind is comparable to lightning, wind, a monkey,
It is similar to the waves of a great ocean;
Mischievous, always delighting in objects,
This fluctuating, wandering mind must be tamed.

The mind is similar to lightning insofar as it is something that illuminates for just a moment rather than continuously. The mind, similar to a wind insofar as it is devoid of an essentially abiding quality, is something characterized by fluctuation and distraction. It is similar to a monkey insofar as it is an actor (*karmaka*, *las can*) that naturally involves itself in everything, which takes attention away from the mind as such. The mind is similar to the undulating waves in a great ocean because it, like the ocean, is inexhaustible mental activity. It is mischievous (*dhūrta*, *sgyu can*) since it is something that always discloses a false object. It is always delighting in objects and therefore does not delight in retiring into practice (*pratisaṃlayana*, *nang du yang dag 'jog*). It is because of just such a nature that those who are difficult to discipline are trained via recitations and meditative absorption, which are thereby applied on the path to liberation.

In brief, there are also two types of method for disciplining those who are difficult to discipline: through favor (*anugraha*) and discipline (*nigraha*). Favor is holding on to trainees by means of the compassionate care that is favored by them. Discipline is when that is accomplished through restraint, subjection, or discipline—that is, the idea is to overcome trainees, and then hold on to them; or to dominate them and then hold on to them. In this connection, retaining trainees through favor works like the brief brilliance of lightning that first presents the object of meditative absorption for just a moment, yet not any longer. Like wind, it is instigated by means of disparate processes. Like a monkey, it engages in anything agreeable. Like the ocean, it acts in concert with various mental activities. It is like a trickster (*sgyu can*), which, although not entirely up front, can be reliable in the context of training. It even tends toward objects of desire while delighting in objects. In that context, consider the phrase *to drive away, then take hold of*: The opposite of *lightning* is brilliance enduring over a long time. The opposite of *wind* is that which is unmoving. The opposite of the *monkey* is something that behaves and minds its own business. The opposite of the *ocean* is waves of mental activity pacified. The opposite of the *trickster* discerns the real point. The opposite of *delighting in objects* is settling into spiritual practice.

In short, in this method for taming trainees, which is appropriate for a vulgar mind's system of dharma, there is no bias for one so-called method or another. Therefore, whatever manner of mental processes proliferate, whatever they penetrate, however many times, they are all considered afterward to be something appropriate as a possible object of meditative absorption. In the end, the extreme of conceptuality is beyond the realm of meditative absorption; so there is no other point found to which one goes. This is most likely taught in the context of the practice of śamatha meditation.

Six-Limbed Yoga

With regard to the concentration endowed with the six limbs of yoga,[9] it states in ***The Collection***:[10]

> Specific withdrawals, meditative absorption,
> Stopping, inhaling and holding the breath,
> Recollection, and concentration
> Are called the *six applied limbs of yoga*.

These limbs, which attain to the yoga of the inner mind, number six. *Specific withdrawals* pertain to abiding in a vow. Since, just as through the desire for perfect ethical discipline, the constantly restrained sense is without distractions and the stains of regret, it is a cause for attaining concentration.

In a similar way, these *specific withdrawals* are not objects to be eliminated, since, by means of the object and the sense faculty, conscious awareness has seen everything produced as flawed. Nor are characteristic marks seen as things to be pursued. Constantly seen as one's own divine nature, these two things that are to be eliminated—obsession with, and negation of, entities in practice—naturally restrain the sense faculties, which are not touched by the longing to suppress desire; and when the royal blessing grows closer, the mind becomes a receptacle for meditative absorption. Here, the phrase *specific practices* is also used to refer to resources, and *specific withdrawals* is used because distraction is eliminated through desire. Since meditative absorption is something generated in isolation from desire and wicked, nonvirtuous qualities, it stands to reason that meditative absorption becomes subsequently more stable. Further, the five limbs pertain to conception, analysis, joy, bliss, and the single-pointed mind. Even the object of meditative absorption is the nature of the three secrets because all seals are included within it. It is through the seals that the totally pure deities are in fact gathered in their objective and logical modalities. In that connection, within the three secrets, there is the secret of the buddha body (*kāyaguhya, sku'i gsang ba*)—the particular color, shape, and movement of a divine form. This is similar to the teaching that says:

> Eyebrows, eyes, teeth, and lips,
> Like bodies and limbs,
> Are the seals of the glory of Vajrasattva
> That act to accomplish one's own welfare.

What is taken to mind as an object in meditative absorption is given in terms of all the methods associated with the buddha bodies. With regard to the secret of buddha speech (*vāgguhya, gsung gi gsang ba*), it is not teachings that proclaim such things as "verbal and nonverbal analyses." **From the *Dhyānottaratantra*:** "Roar the hidden vajra teaching." According to such statements, contemplation of the characteristic marks connected with the shape and color of the dharma syllables upon the heart and tongue of a deity and, furthermore, the investigation and analysis of the actual reality of the terms and their referents are causes for attaining meditative absorption. Thus, it is not unlike the statement:

> Meditative absorption originating in sound is an instrument for attaining union (*yoga, rnal 'byor*);

> Meditative absorption originating at the end of sound confers liberation.

In this context, primarily described in terms of meditative absorption, constant verbalization may become a cause for distraction. With regard to the secret of the buddha mind (*cittaguhya*, *thugs kyi gsang ba*), the meditation on the indestructible (*vajra*, *rdo rje*) intention in one's heart and meditations such as meditation upon the gnosis being (*jñānasattva*, *ye shes sems dpa'*) are characteristic marks of the exalted mind. Its object, analyzed as bodhicitta, and the characteristics that abide in the dharmakāya as such are the buddha mind. Likewise, the goal in meditative absorption is to take the three secrets as objective supports.

The five limbs form a basis for meditation. *Conception* of them generates awareness that conceives the characteristics of the three secrets just as they are. *Analysis* is the constant preparation of awareness for penetrating its significance again and again. *Joy* is the emergence of a type of experience resembling the three secrets, which results from attaining the meditative absorption connected to both conception and analysis, at which point it is isolated from desire; and great waves of uncommon joy are generated through experiencing a previously unexperienced object. *Bliss* is the attainment of a concentrated mind, which is experienced as blissful physical and mental sensations. Once a single-pointed mind is very concentrated in this way, it is no longer generated in the subject–object duality and thereby simply constitutes one's own awareness.

Thus, given that a mind made calm by meditative absorption is aimed at totally disciplining the mind, there should be training on the breath—both to stop it and on simply breathing. Regardless of what one has studied, the multiple methods of accessing the path means (*bas*) that there is no conflict between the various methods concerning just how to train. Once the mind is tamed and the breath pacified, one ought to train on holding in the breath in order to stabilize and fortify it.

Five Signs of Mental Stability

The connection with the breath means that the mind also becomes thoroughly pacified. After that, when stability is attained, there are five signs [thereafter indicating that stability] that emerge. Here, it is stated:[11]

First is something like a mirage;
The second is the medium of smoke;
The third is similar to fireflies;
The fourth blazes like a butter lamp;
The fifth is eternal appearance,
Which is like a cloudless sky.

Further, these signs have inner and outer aspects. The external sign occurs when the breath is held in; externally, light appears in the field of vision in the space in front, which is to say: first the breath is held steadily, after which, when five-colored lights are perceived steadily over time and space, there will be the perception of something similar to smoke and the image of a mirage as signs of the experience of light. Once stable, something similar to smoke will be perceived. Once that is stable, something similar to fireflies will be perceived. Once that is stable, something similar to the light of a lamp will be perceived. Once that is stable, everything will become clear like a cloudless sky and thereby the signs will have reached their fulfillment. Here, what has been taught pertains to the context of daytime; yet when seen at night, all the similitudes of smoke, fire, and light will gradually expand.

After Attaining Such Signs of Mental Stability

Once signs of stability are obtained in that manner, one ought to cultivate recollections (*anusmṛti, rjes su dran pa*) for the purpose of attaining total pliancy of the mind. One should distill the dynamism of the mind through emanating and scattering outward and absorbing inward various magnitudes and quantities of light through higher or lower bodily apertures; these are aspects of śamatha meditation on the three secrets. After having achieved that in such a manner, we turn to training in concentration.

Through the force of such an accomplishment as described above, a gnosis that is one's own awareness (*ye shes rang rig pa*) is obtained, manifesting a nonconceptual gnosis that severs the web of obscurations. The qualities of the other limbs become the deep intention of the Sugata by means of specific purifications. In attaining meditative absorption, clairvoyance is attained. Through mastery of the breath, a luminous maṇḍala emerges.

What is the process by which body, mind, and deity are objective supports (*dmigs*)? What is an observed object in the body (*dmigs pa*) is observed (*dmigs*) through the breath and in terms of the nature of the breath, its source, domain, path, activity, methods for using it as an observed object, and its qualities. The nature of the breath correlates with the nature of the five elements such that earthy breath is hard and heavy; watery breath is relaxed and soft; fiery breath is light and warm; windy breath is light and rough; spatial breath is subtle and its movements are not sensed. The source of the breath is the cavity at the heart and the cavities connected with the lungs. The domain of the breath is the interior of the body, which is wholly permeated by the movement of the breath, predominantly from the navel up throughout the range of the body, spanning the limbs' sixteen fingers and toes.[12] The path of the breath is mainly via the throat, from the secret place up through the nostrils. The activity of the breath is dual: the action of retention and the action of producing. Retention of the breath tangibly benefits the body and indeed maintains it. The breath works as a mount for the mind; and it holds the mind, too, such that it is called the *vitalizing activity of both body and mind*. The activity of producing the breath moves both mind and body at the time of its motion. When the breath is unmoving, neither body nor mind move. There are multiple methods for taking the breath as an objective support in meditation. Thus, whichever one should take up, there is no conflict.

In short, let us speak of two types of objective supports: one in harmony with the dharma and one that does not rely upon the dharma. The former is explained in connection with the fire and wind elements moving in the right side of the body, the earth and water elements moving in the left side of the body, and the space element moving in the central part of the body. When these are differentiated, then by means of both, the whole movement of each of the five elements on the right and left sides of the body, and the rough idea that the teachings on some of the elements that are located on the right and left—phenomenal color, shape, size, and type—are each specifically taken as objective supports; the aspect that is taken as an objective support is similar to aspects of light, syllables, characteristic mark, and subtle buddha body. Not relying upon the dharma refers just to the simple movement of the internal and external breath, with no specific differentiation of the particulars such as those described above. This occurs because any possible characteristic can be taken as a single objective support. Taking a tangible object as an objective support is, however, only with the aim of setting the mind without distraction.

Consider the generally known qualities and flaws connected to physical colors and dimensions. Since the elements are characterized as harmful, when an element is taken as an objective support in meditative absorption, there are qualities and flaws. In that connection, it comes to be said that the color white is characterized by the pacification of what is harmful; the color gold characterizes apprehension of what is harmful; the color red characterizes the intensification of what is harmful; and the color black characterizes the arising of what is harmful. Indeed, tactile objects such as the elements, and physical dimensions, like hardness and thickening, bring about discontent in the body. When the parts of things are observed as smaller, subtle, and primarily like a moon reflected in water, discontent does not arise in the body.

The qualities of taking the breath as an objective support overcome monistic views (*gcig por lta ba*), views of realism (*dngos por lta ba*), and views revolving around bliss and purity—and cause insight to arise. Once that state of mind is attained, the body becomes practicable. Even when the mind is the observed object, the same applies. This is because the nature of the mind consists of the element of appearance, the element of mental conceit, and the element connected to the cognition of specific things. The mental state abides in the body that is connected to the five elements after the mind has mounted on the wind that is connected to the five elements. Like all phenomena, mental objects are appearing objects. The object of the conceited mind is the mind as such. The objects connected to cognition comprise those of the external sense fields. The mental path is the faculties. The activity of the mind is dual: the activity of grasping, which works to comprehend all phenomena, and the activity of producing, which brings about all positive and negative karmic processes.

With regard to the method for observing the mind, once the mind is made practicable through taking the breath as the objective support in meditation, mindfulness and introspection are laid hold of and thereby the reality of the mind is taken in and assimilated into experience because of observing the nature of the mind's arising.

The qualities of such an object of observation preclude any possibility for the development of views of the self, eternalist views, and all realist views, because insight arises. Once the mind is made practicable, śamatha is attained. After the body and mind qua objective supports for meditation are made practicable, one ought to use a deity as the objective support. The provisional characteristics[13] of the deity are indeed taught to be consonant with mind and body because, on this view, the nature of the five constituents are divine: pure reality, nonconceptual gnosis, gnosis's vivid exalted knowing of everything, the rupakāya connected to taming migrators, and the buddha speech of the teacher of the holy dharma in each language.

The source of the deity is a sentient being's body and the mind as such. The deity's domain is the dharmadhātu and fields of compassion. Although the divine path does not come and go, sentient beings are comprehended. The refuge for sentient beings is the deity. The deity becomes a path by means of the two relations/connections—that is, the qualities of the path, which connects a sentient being to a deity, and the qualities of transmission, which connects a deity to a sentient being. Divine activity is twofold: there is the activity of retention, which consists in having all qualities, and the activity of producing, which consists in the buddha activity that works to liberate sentient beings.

The method for taking a deity as an objective support pertains to the cultivation of the body and the mind as the deity and involves meditation on the three types of yoga; any system of which—whether the way of consecration, the way of the completely imagined, or the way of perfection—is tenable.

The two types of accumulation are perfected at one time as qualities. Thus, training progressively with the three types of objective support in this manner and this explanation by means of teaching in stages is simply so that children will enter the path at first. In actuality, the body itself is an aspect of the mind. Thus, the recognition that the very essence of any phenomenon within and without is in the nature of a deity is, first, the recognition of the deity. Next, understanding the method for deity meditation is something taught in a variety of *sadhanas* that teach methods for improvement via the scripture and mind connected to meditative absorption as described above.

Finally, on the topic of teaching the criteria for practicability, the criteria for a deity free of any characteristic marks was already described above. The criteria for meditation upon the divine buddha body with marks are revealed in the ten divine prophecies (*lha'i lung bcu*) but are nevertheless included within three principles: radiance (*bhrājate, lham me*), clarity (*tapati, lhan ne*), and brilliance (*virocate, lhang nge ba*). *Radiance* is something not solid. *Clarity* is something unwavering. *Brilliance* is something unobstructed. A lack of solid reality—a moon that is reflected in water, for example—suggests an absence of intrinsic nature. *Unwavering* suggests being unmoved by the thorns of lethargy and excitement, like the light of a precious jewel. *Unobstructed* suggests that, by being qualified by these two, there is an appearance of utter luminosity devoid of both the obscurations connected to not misunderstanding and the obscurations connected to what is confused. Utter luminosity is such that it is unbearable to gaze upon. These are explained in the context of those who desire to train properly.

Whoever is devoted but becomes distracted by practices and thus is unable to train properly should apply his or her mind to the meaning of the Great Perfection and the nature of the deity just as it is. It is also possible that ritual sequences [of the types described above] may be used for the generation through the perfection phase, in which [the generation of the deity and maṇḍala] occurs in a single moment; or through the force of karmic imprints or by means of devotion and divine pride that can be used by the undistracted to seize upon, and engage in, recitations and concentration. It's suitable to visualize the deity in front of oneself even when engaged in recitations; yet not visualizing it also works. Practices that visualize the absence and presence of light that is emanated and absorbed from oneself also works. Any visualization of the path or the result is also viable because, in general, great power and transformation flows from striving in single-pointed focus.

Generally, within the suchness of the deity, six [types of] deities are widely known. That is to say, the ultimate deity, **the deity of actual reality**, the deities connected with particular intentions, **all other** imagined deities, and the deity imagined by beings with tantric commitments are widely known.

Insofar as the sealed marks of a buddha body are known to be deities, a number of imputed types are said to be disclosed: analyzing "the particular shape of a body that is fully matured" **pāramitā system**; analyzing "the marks of great beings" **mantra system**; analyzing that "they have the capacity and power of consecrated beings"; analyzing "they are something imagined to be deities by beings who hold samaya"; analyzing that "they are an indistinguishable mix of a particular fully matured form and the blessings of great gnosis"; analyzing "that they are physically emanated as the characteristic of the state of gnosis connected to the secret buddha mind, like water becoming ice via conditions connected to cold water"; and the following: "The fact that all phenomena pertain to the nature of the spontaneous seals of enlightenment and that they appear specifically under the influence of merit and karmic good fortune. For those pure beings who have become disciplined, all phenomena appear as the buddha body of perfected resources (*sambhogakāya, longs spyod rdzogs pa'i sku*). For those sentient beings who have gone from arrogance to purity, all phenomena appear as the accoutrements of the emanation body (*nirmāṇakāya, sprul pa'i sku*) connected with renunciation. For those below that, they appear as partial seals. For those below that, they depend on ordinary form as a basis for the appearance of the seals because everything is asserted, in fact, to be no different from spontaneous seals." The five above them are explained in the context of realist views. The last two are explained in the context of being divorced from fixation upon things. What is totally understood, when engaged in just this analysis, is like what is recognized by the last. In short, all these species of *meditative absorption* become the practice of those skilled in method inasmuch as they are qualified by the significance of the Great Perfection. Inasmuch as they are not, they will become practices of the unskilled in method. Here ends the sixth chapter, on traditional methods.

Closing Verses

All phenomena are said to be illusory,
And while this is widely known in the basic doctrines,
Such tropes of illusion, a mirage, and so forth,
Work to disclose their equality.

One should practice this approach—
The approach of Great Perfection, which is definitive in meaning,
Capable of answering objections and making rational differentiations,
And thus not subverted by reasoning.

The definitive meaning of bodhicitta,
Its nature and its greatness,
Points of deviation and obscuration, methods for settling, too,
Are the teaching of a lineage imbued with method.

Stating that the effect does not manifest
While its effective conditions are present
Does not constitute the denial of anything; thus
There is no state seen here that is denied.

In the system of causal interdependence,
There is no object imposed
Outside of mere appearance,
Because causal things are not real.

Whatever other significance there is, being divorced from distortions,
I have described it here according to my own understanding,

For those working to accomplish liberation via other systems,[1]
Following the definitive word of the Buddha.

Because this simple disclosure of the Great Vehicle system,
Was composed for the benefit of a meditator in the south,
Will it be seen by migrators
Who are suitable vessels for the Great Vehicle?[2]

Even those with intellects fixed on commentarial treatises
That establish what is accepted in the world
Can perceive the truth of the Great Perfection
Through the blessings of the *real* Great Vehicle.

Penetrating the domain free of biases,
Is like a great garuḍa soaring through space:
Unbound and unmoving,
Covering great distances at ease.

Appendix: Tibetan Names in Phonetic and Transliterated Forms

Phonetic spelling	Wylie transliteration
Bangka Darchuk	Bang ka dar chug
Dö Khyungpo Hūm Nying	Mdo'i khyung po hūm snying
Gö Lhétsé	Gos lhas btsas
Gö Lotsawa Zhönnu Pel	'Gos lo tsa ba gzhon nu dpal
Gya Gyeltsül	Rgya rgyal tshul
Ju Mipham Gyatso	Ju mi pham rgya mtsho
Khépa Deu	Mkhas pa lde'u
Kyidé	Skyid lde
Langdarma	Glang dar ma
Lha Lama Jangchup Ö	Lha bla ma byang chub 'od
Lhalung Pelgyi Dorjé	Lha lung dpal gyi rdo rje
Longchenpa	Klong chen pa
Marpa Dowa	Mar pa do pa
Namdé Ö Sung	Gnam 'de 'od srung

Phonetic spelling	Wylie transliteration
Narlung Rong	Snar lung rong
Ngadak Chenpo Trashi Khorré	Mnga' bdag chen po bkra shis 'khor re
Ngadak Lhadé	Mnga' bdag lha lde
Ngari	Mnga' ri
Ö Dé	'Od lde
Pawa Désé	Pha ba lde se
Pawa Tésé	Pha ba the se
Pel Khorten	Dpal 'khor bstan
Peldéi	Dpal lde
Pelyang	Dpal dbyangs
Podrang Zhiwa Ö	Pho brang zhi ba 'od
Sétrom Gyatso Bar	Se khrom rgya mtsho 'bar
Shapkyi Yangkhyé Lama	Shab kyi yang khyed bla ma
Tsamtön Gocha	Mtsham ston go cha
Tuken Ngakwang Chökyi Gyatso	Thu'u bkwan ngag dbang chos kyi rgya mtsho
Uyukpa Da Samten	'U yug pa mda' bsam gtan
Yéshé Ö	Ye shes 'od

Abbreviations

Bka' 'gyur	*Bka' 'gyur dpe bsdur ma.* Beijing: Krung go'i bod rig pa'i dpe skrun khang, 1998–2009.
Bstan 'gyur	*Bstan 'gyur dpe bsdur ma.* Beijing: Krung go'i bod rig pa'i dpe skrun khang, 1994–2005.
P	*The Tibetan Tripiṭaka.* Peking edition. 168 vols. Tokyo-Kyoto: Suzuki Research Foundation, 1955–1961.
Tōh.	*A Complete Catalogue of the Tibetan Buddhist Canons.* Edited by Hakuju Ui, Munetada Suzuki, Yenshō Kanakura, and Tōkan Tada. Sendai, Japan: Tōhoku Imperial University, 1934.

Notes

Translator's Introduction

1. See Roerich 1976.
2. On the historical context of this work and its authorship, see van der Kuijp 2006.
3. The so-called Four Horns of Tibet (*ru bzhi*) refers to four areas in Central Tibet: the side horn of Tsang, called Rulak; the right horn of Tsang, called Yéru; the Left horn of Ü, called Yoru; and the central horn of Ü, called Uru. For an examination of the Four Horns, see Uray 1960.
4. Sources typically name the following figures: Bangka Darchuk, Dö Khyungpo Hūm Nying, Gö Lhétsé, Gya Gyeltsül, Marpa Dowa (b. 1011), Sétrom Gyatso Bar, Shapkyi Yangkhyé Lama, Tsamtön Gocha, and Uyukpa Da Samten.
5. For more details, see van Schaik (2013, 41–60). My use of scare quotes around the term *Dark Age* is meant to note that this period, between Langdarma's assassination and the so-called Tibetan renaissance of the eleventh century, wasn't so dark as the phrase suggests; intellectual life and literary composition on religion did not come to a total halt. It continued, albeit outside the reach and authority of any centralizing political or administrative powers in the region.
6. According to Lopon P. Ogyan Tanzin (2013, 367), "the six greatnesses of the Early Translations (*snga' gyur*)" given by Rongzompa are "the greatness of the patrons, the greatness of the scholars, the greatness of the translators, the greatness of the places where the translations were made, the greatness of the doctrines translated, and the greatness of the offerings made as a support for requesting the doctrine."
7. I am currently in the process of preparing a larger and more detailed philosophical study of Rongzom's *Entering the Way of the Great Vehicle* for publication, tentatively entitled "The Practice of Philosophy in Tibet." In this work, interested readers will find a more detailed analysis concerning the form, content, and context of this work. In short, it is my view that Rongzom's *Entering the Way of the Great Vehicle* was composed with an audience of elite New School translators in mind, perhaps proponents of the hallmark of the New Schools, the *Kālacakratantra*, in particular. It is my position, moreover, that the particular audience for whom this text was composed helps to explain the rather peculiar place of this text in Tibetan intellectual history.
8. On Rongzom's biographies, see Almogi 2002.
9. Precise dates are offered by Bradburn (1995, 87): 1012–1131, perhaps following

Dudjom Rinpoche (1991, 709), who gives his life as spanning 119 years. The publisher's colophon of the Chengdu edition of Rongzom's collected works gives the Iron Dragon year of the eleventh century as his date of birth—that is, 1040 (Rong zom chos bzang 1999c, 2:639). An interesting, if not decisive addition to information that can be used to date Rongzom comes from the opening lines of *The Charter of Mantrins Composed by Rongzom Chokyi Zangpo* (*Rong zom chos kyi bzang pos mdzad pa'i sngags pa rnams kyi bca' yig*). This work is a document of regulations (*bca' yig*) composed for a religious community and is included in his collected works (Rong zom chos bzang 1999a). This text is remarkable for what it represents and for what it suggests about Rongzom. First and foremost, historically, it is, as far as I am aware, the earliest Tibetan example of such a document of regulations. In sociocultural and political terms, it suggests that Rongzom was an established religious figure in his area, with his own community of disciples. The text opens with a description of a royal Puhrang wedding:

> In the dragon year, at the wedding of the prince Songtsen Bar (Srong btsan 'bar), a descendent of Pawa Désé, ruler of the region of lower Gtsang in the Four Horns of Tibet, recognized that both mantrins [that is, practitioners of Buddhist Secret Mantra or Tantra] and ordained monastic clergy—the *bandé*—were distracted from their vows and commitments and lacking in diligence with respect to a rigorous understanding of the holy dharma. Because of that, in the region of Narlung Rong, Rongzom Chokyi Zangpo gathered his committed disciples and, after putting up some representations of the three jewels, gave a discourse primarily for householders who are mantrins (*'brug gi lo yul ru lag gtsang smad kyi btsad po pha ba [lde] se'i yang dbon | rgyal bu srong btsan 'bar sku khab bzhes pa tsam gyis dus na | sngags btsun sde gnyis kyi ban de kun kyang so so'i sdom pa dang dam tshig bsrung ba la g.yel zhing dam pa'i chos legs par 'dzin pa'i rtsol ba dang mi ldan par mthong nas | yul [rnar] lung rong du | rong zom chos kyi bzang pos rang gi dam tshig pa rnams bsdus te | dkon mchog gsum gyi rten gnas bu 'ga' yang btsungs nas | dang por khyim pa'i sngags pa rnams la bca' ba bgyis pa'i mdo |*).

Dragon years in the eleventh century correspond to 1028 (*sa 'brug*), 1040 (*lcag 'brug*), and 1064 (*shing 'brug*). Drongbu Tsering Dorje, of the Tibetan Academy of Social Sciences, identifies Srong btsan 'bar as the religious name (*chos ming*) of Lha bla ma Ye shes 'od (personal communication from Steve Weinberger, January 15, 2012); Drongbu also glossed *yang dbon* as "great-grandfather" and notes that *sku khab*, rendered here as "marriage," can also indicate coronation (*rgyal po chags*). If the term does refer to that, then the phrase *great-grandfather of Pawa Désé* refers to the father of Ngadak Lhadé, a man named Ngadak Chenpo Trashi Khorré (Vitali 1996, 114). Vitali (1996, 243n345; see, by way of comparison, Sørensen 1994, 468n1751) notes Pawa Tésé [sic] settled in Khorré, in Rulak, Tsang. Pawa Désé is the middle son of Ö Dé (Sørensen 1994, 468). Ö Dé is the brother of Zhiwa Ö and Lha Lama Jangchup Ö (Sørensen 1994, 457), who are each located in the Royal Dynasty of Ngari, in the early eleventh century (Smith 2001, 193). The three, Peldé, Ö Dé, and Kyidé, based on Sørensen (1994) and Vitali (1996), seem to be siblings of Zhiwa Ö and Jangchup Ö. According to the Tibetan historian, Tuken Ngakwang Chökyi Gyatso (1680–1736), the three Dé brothers were in fact the sons of Pel Khorten (see, by way of comparison, Sørensen 1994, 465). He was an apparently incompetent ruler who was assassinated at age thirty. According to Sørensen (1994, 438), Pel Khorten is the son of Namdé Ö sung, who, in turn, is the son of the last emperor of Tibet, Langdarma. While there does not appear to be a solid case for Rongzom's precise dates, I add this information to what is already known and presume Rongzom flourished in the late eleventh century, though I make no claim to have resolved or even further clarified the details of the issue.

10. Rongzom and Longchenpa (1308–1364) are described as the two indispensable intellectuals of the Old School by no less a figure than Ju Mipham Gyatso (1846–1912):

> Although there have been numerous scholar-adepts who have been holders of the long traditions associated with the early translations, two of particular distinction among them all are Rong and Long, who are as renowned as the sun and moon (*snga 'gyur pa'i ring lugs 'dzin pa la mkhas grub du ma byon mod kyi | kun gyi nang na khyad par 'phags pa kun mkhyen rong klong rnam gnyis zhes nyi zla ltar grugs pa yin zhing |*) (Rong zom chos bzang 1999c, 1:15).

In fact, the three—Rongzom, Longchenpa, and Mipham—have been taken to represent the Old School's "archetypical intellectual figures" (Wangchuk 2004, 173).

11. Here, I am largely following Dudjom 1991, which contains the standard biography.
12. The locus classicus for the classification of the five classical sciences (*vidyāsthāna*, *rig gnas*) in ancient India is the *Mahāyānasūtrālaṃkāra*, chap. 11, v. 60.
13. Tib. *kho bus 'di dang chos kyi gtam bya ba ga la thub ces nges par gsung skad.*
14. Tib. *smra sgo la sogs pa'i 'grel pa dang bstan bcos kyang mang du mdzad | blo gros kyi mthu bsam gyi mi khyab pas.*
15. Tib. *phan gdags pa'i dgongs pa zab mo mnga' ba.*
16. Tib. *bstan bcos.*
17. Griffiths 1994, 30.
18. As is well known, according to the Buddhist worldview, the very nature of life is said to be *duḥkha*, a word most often translated as "suffering." This English rendering, however, is a bit misleading. While in the Buddhist worldview, even pleasant experiences are said to be duḥkha, in English we typically don't describe pleasant experiences as "suffering." Thus, although *duḥkha may be* accurately translated as "suffering" in some contexts, a better translation, generally, is something like "dissatisfying" in order to emphasize the fact that even pleasant experiences ultimately leave us wanting in the end.
19. *de ltar chos thams cad sgyu ma lta bu'i mtshan nyid yin par rtogs pa ni | theg pa chen po'i tshul la 'jug par nus pa yin la | chos thams cad sgyu ma lta bur 'go mnyam pa rtogs pa tshad du chud cing mthar phyin pa ni rdzogs pa chen po'i tshul yin no |* (Rong zom chos bzang 1999c, 1:458).
20. *theg pa chen po'i tshul la 'jug pa mdo tsam brjod pa* (Rong zom chos bzang 1999c, 1:417).
21. *theg pa chen po'i tshul la 'jug par 'dod pa rnams kyi | nyon mongs pa rnams la spang bar bya ba'i rdzas myed par shes par bya zhing | chos thams cad sgyu ma lta bur 'go' mnyam par bstan pa'i skabs te | dang po'o || ||* (Rong zom chos bzang 1999c, 1:435).
22. According to the Theravada traditions of Buddhist discourse, the conditioned realm of saṃsāra is an impure realm of dissatisfaction and suffering that one should

escape by entering a pure unconditioned realm of peace, termed *nirvāṇa*. With the development of the Great Vehicle traditions, however, this radical bifurcation was relaxed vis-à-vis Nāgārjuna's doctrine of emptiness (*śūnyatā, stong nyid*), itself an expansion and elaboration of the doctrine of no-self (*anatma, bdag med*) emphasized in the Theravada tradition. According to Nāgārjuna, and his Middle Way school of philosophy (*madhyamaka*), the real difference between saṃsāra and nirvāṇa is one of perception. Here, the attainment of the truth of nirvāṇa—including its salvific content—is not unlike recognizing that what we had formerly recognized as a snake in a dark corner is just a coiled rope: the moment we recognize the reality of the situation, the conditions that facilitate our fear simply disappear. On this view—the Mahāyāna view—there is no natural or actual difference between saṃsāra and nirvāṇa except the purity of one's perception.

23. Rongzom's philosophical method is one that may be described as an integrative inclusivism. That is, he seeks to show that differing philosophical systems are not so much in conflict with one another as they are part and parcel of an increasingly refined philosophical journey along the paths, all of which are likened to streams flowing into the same ocean of Great Perfection: enlightenment. On inclusivism in Buddhism, see Kiblinger 2005.
24. In addition, Rongzom does also, at times, discuss non-Buddhist systems. Throughout his various works, Rongzom does not always treat the same systems as touchstones for his analyses. See, by way of comparison, Almogi 2009.
25. The section in chapter 1 concerning the five exemplars of illusion contains images and language drawn from the collection of tantric songs called *Acintyamahāmudrā* (*Phyag rgya chen po bsam gyis mi khyab pa*) found among the Indian canonical commentaries (Tōh. 2035). I am currently preparing a more detailed study of Rongzom's work, which will include a detailed analysis of the influence of Tilopa, an important figure in the tradition of *Kālacakratantra*, within Rongzom's text.
26. The term *lakṣaṇa* is used in Buddhist philosophy (Abhidharma) to refer to the primary qualities of phenomena (*dharmā*); that is, it refers to "the principal characteristic or defining quality of something" (Buswell and Lopez 2013, 463) and means "mark," "characteristic," "attribute," and "definition," among other things. For example, heat is a characteristic, or attribute, of fire and, in part, defines it. Thus, the lakṣaṇa of fire is hot and burning (*tsha zhing sreg pa*). In the Yogācāra doctrines of the Mahāyāna, all phenomena are qualified by three characteristics (*trilakṣaṇa*). According to the Madhyamaka school of the Mahāyāna, a lakṣaṇa, or mark of inherent existence (*rang bzhin gyi mtshan nyid*), is indicative of the ignorance (*avidyā, ma rig pa*) that qualifies conditioned existence. According to the tradition's seminal text, Nāgārjuna's *Mūlamadhyamakakārikā*, the binary "character-characterized" (*lakṣaṇa-lakṣya*) forms one of the (many dichotomous) avenues by which he critiques the notion of inherent existence (*svabhāva, rang bzhin*). In Indian and Tibetan logico-epistemological discourse (*pramāṇa*), *lakṣaṇa* refers to the phenomenal marks of an object. Outside of Buddhist discourse, this polysemous term is employed in a variety of contexts. In Pāṇinīan grammar, *lakṣaṇa* refers to grammatical rules (Matilal 1990, 10). According to philosophers of the Nyāya, one of the six orthodox (*āstika*) schools of classical Indian philosophy, *lakṣaṇa* refers to linguistic signification (ibid., 22); for the Indian polymath, Abhinavagupta, the term refers to the indicative power of words to invoke metaphor (ibid., 168).

27. A general doctrine of affliction is given in chapter 5 of the *Abhidharma-kośabhāṣyam*, attributed to Vasubandhu (fl. fourth/fifth c.), and treated in the context of its synonym, a *proliferating tendency* (*anuśayaḥ, phra rgyas*). An English translation of Vasubandhu's text can be found in La Vallée Poussin 1990, 767–868. According to the dharma theory of the Sārvastivāda school of Indian Buddhism, which maintained one of the largest, most elaborate Abhidharma canons in all of Buddhism and was an inspiration for the "Mahāyāna Abhidharma of the Yogācāra school" (Buswell and Lopez 2013, 780), there are six fundamental (*mūla, rtsa ba*) or broad (*mahābhūmika, chen po'i sa*) defilements or afflictions (*kleśa, nyon mongs*) known as *outflows* (*āsrava, zag pa*) that accompany every afflicted mental state: delusion (*moha, gti mug*), heedlessness (*pramāda, bag med*), indolence (*kausīdya, le lo*), lack of faith (*aśraddhya, dad med*), sloth (*styāna, rmug*), and restlessness (*auddhatya, rgod*).
28. Tib. *'byams chos sde lnga*. These five Mahāyāna works are attributed to the bodhisattva, Maitreya: (1) *The Ornament of Clear Realization* (*Abhisamayālaṃkāra, Mngon par rtogs pa'i rgyan*), (2) *The Ornament of the Mahāyāna Sūtras* (*Māhayānasūtrālaṃkāra, Theg pa chen po'i mdo sde rgyan*), (3) *Distinguishing the Middle and Extremes* (*Madhyānta-vibhāga, Dbus dang mtha' rnam par 'byed pa*), (4) *Distinguishing Phenomena from Actual Reality* (*Dharmadharmatāvibhāga, Chos dang chos nyid rnam par 'byed pa*), and (5) *The Sublime Continuum* (*Uttaratantraśāstra, Rgyud bla ma*).
29. One fascinating part of this mostly logical discourse is Rongzom's use of what may be described as "myth as argument." Here, Rongzom turns away from rational and propositional discourse toward the use of mythic stories to make his point. I am preparing a detailed study of the form, content, and context of this text for publication that will treat this facet of the author's work in detail.
30. Critically, the Old School tradition today does *not* interpret Rongzom as denying gnosis on the buddha ground. See Almogi 2009, 193–99.
31. There were no "Hindu" people in the eleventh century. The term "Hindu," Doniger (2009, 30) writes, is not a "native [Indian] word, but comes from a word for the 'river' (*sindhu*) that Herodotus (in the fifth century BCE), the Persians (in the fourth century BCE), and the Arabs (after the eighth century CE) used to refer to everyone who lived beyond the great river of the northwest of the subcontinent, still known locally as the Sindhu and in Europe as the Indus."
32. This position, however, must still explain how, or in what sense, a buddha can "know" the needs of sentient beings and therefore continue to act in the world in their best interests, spiritually.
33. According to Dudjom Rinpoche (1991, 477), Mañjuśrīmitra (Tib. 'Jam dpal bshes gnyen) was born in a village in western India called Dvikrama. According to *The Princeton Dictionary of Buddhism* (Buswell and Lopez 2013, s.v. "Mañjuśrīmitra"), some accounts claim his birthplace was Siṅghala (Sri Lanka).
34. *kun nas nyon mongs pa dang rnam par byang bar tha snyad btags pa tsam ma gtogs pa || 'di la bsal bar bya ba'i rdzas sam | gzhag par bya ba'i rdzas kyi ngo bo gang yang myed de | 'on kyang ma shes pa'i dus na 'khrul snang gi tshul de ltar snang ba tsam yin no.*
35. According to the locus classicus found in the *Mahāyānasūtrālaṃkāra* (chap. 9, vv. 68–75), attributed to the Maitreya-Asaṅga complex, the view of equality

is embodied in one of the four types of gnosis (*ye shes bzhi*) championed by the Mahāyāna. See Limaye 2000, 139–43.

36. To be clear, the term is not *people with good karma* (*las 'phro can*), it is *people with faith* (*dad pa*) in Great Perfection.
37. *Vigrahavyāvartanī* 29: *yadi kācana pratijñā syān ma tata eṣa me bhaved doṣaḥ | nāsti ca mama pratijñā tasmān naivāsti me doṣaḥ* ||. An English translation of this text is found in Lindtner 1987, 70–86.
38. See, by way of comparison, Wittgenstein's *Tractatus Logico-Philosophicus* (1988, 4.003, 6.54) and his *Philosophical Investigations* (2001, secs. 119, 464, 524). On Wittgenstein and the nonsense of philosophy, see Pitcher 1965.
39. In his critique of Nāgārjuna as a philosopher, Robinson (1972) writes, "'Light illuminates itself' and 'Water makes itself wet' are pseudo-transitives, better expressed by 'Light is inherently bright' and 'Water is inherently wet.'" *Pace* Robinson, but a lamp lighting itself is more analogous to a pain hurting itself than it is to light being inherently bright. "Light is inherently bright" and "Water is inherently wet" are akin to "My pain naturally hurts!"—an absurd thing to say.
40. *de ltar stond pa'i rdzogs pa chen po'i tshul 'di yang mdor bsdus te bstan na | chos thams cad kyi rtsa ba nī sems dang sems snang ba tsam du'dus la | sems kyi rang bzhin yid byang chub yin pas byang chub kyī sems zhes bya'o || bstan par bya ba ni 'di tsam las myed la | rdzogs pa chen po'i tshul la dad pa'i gang zag rnams kyang | 'di nyid bstan pa tsam gyis rtogs shing 'jug par 'gyur ba yin na | 'on kyang sgra'i bstand chos dang | rigs pa'ī bstan chos la mngon par zhen pa'i gang zag dag 'di snyam du | bdag cag gi grub pa'i mtha' 'di dag ni | sgra'ī don dang rigs pas grub pa' yin la | rdzogs pa chen po'i tshul nī rigs pa dang 'gal te | gang rigs pa dang 'gal ba de ni blang bar bya ba ma yin no snyam du sems te | rdzogs pa chen po yid bzhin gyi nor bu rin po che dang 'dra ba 'di lta bu spangs nas | nor bu 'ching bu dang 'dra ba'i grub mtha' na tshogs la zhen pa'i gang zag la* |.
41. About the term *yuktiśāstra* (*rigs pa'i bstan chos*): we find, for example, the phrase *'gran zla med pa'i bdag nyid chen po phyogs glang yab sras kyis mdzad pa'i rigs pa'i bstan bcos* in Gyeltsep Chöjé's (Rgyal tshab chos rjes) *Rje'i drung du gsan pa'i tshad ma'i brjed byang chen mo*. See 'Jam mgon bla ma Rtsong kha pa chen po'i gsung 'bum, vol. 10, pha (Mtsho sngon: Mi rigs par khang, 1985), 679.3–4. On the authorship of this text, which was composed in perhaps 1404, see van der Kuijp 1999. A concise historical survey of the use of *pramāṇa* (logico-epistemology) in South Asia is found in Steinkellner 1993. The impact of this tradition in Tibet is studied in van der Kuijp 1983 and Dreyfus 1997.
42. *Mahāyānasūtrālaṃkāra* 11.60 famously states that while nirvāṇa is possible for those unschooled in the traditional Indian Buddhist sciences, no such person may attain bodhi. See Limaye 2000, 204: *vidyāsthāno pañcavidhyo yogamakṛtvā sarvajñtvaṃ naiti kathaṃcit paramārthaḥ | ityanyoṣāṃ nigrahaṇānugrahaṇāya svājñārtha vā tatra karoteyeva sa yogam || rig pa'i gnas lnga dag la brtson par ma byas na || 'phags mchog gis kyang tham cad mkhyen nyid thob mi 'gyur || de bas gzhan dag tshar bcad rjes su gzung phyir dang || bdag nyid kun shes bya phyir de la brtson bya* ||.
43. On the use agent, activity, and object (*las*) in classical Tibetan, see Tillemans, Frank, and Herforth 1989.
44. *rdzogs pa chen po'i tshul las grags pa'i thig le dang che ba la stsogs pa'i skad rnams bzhag ste | spyir grags pa'i skad kyis rigs pa'i tshul phyogs 'ga' bshad do* ||.

45. According to David Germano (1992, 878), the etymologies of this term in the writings of "Longchenpa tended to emphasize the etymological roots of this term, which correlate directly to the basic dyad of 'original purity' [*ka dag*] and 'spontaneous presence' [*lhun grub*]."
46. *da ni rdzogs pa chen po'i gzhung nyid la 'jug par bya ste | de la rdzogs pa chen po'i tshul ston pa'i gzhung ji snyed pa thams cad las kyang | don mdor bsdu' na rnam pa bzhir 'dus te | 'di ltar byang chub sems kyi rang bzhin bstan pa dang | byang chub sems kyi che ba bstan dang | byang chub sems kyi gol sgrib bstan pa dang | byang chub sems kyi gzhag thabs bstan pa'o || de la che ba dang gol sgrib bstan pas kyang rab bzhin bstan par 'gyur | rang bzhin bstan pas kyang che ba rtogs shing gol sgrib chod par 'gyur te | de bas na gzhung rnams las kyang lhag par 'di ltar gud du phye zhing bstan pa'ang myed la | 'di rnams las 'da' ba'ang myed do.*
47. As mentioned above, I am currently in the process of compiling a study of the detailed form, content, and context of this text, tentatively entitled "The Practice of Philosophy in Tibet," which will explore such issues in greater detail.
48. Since I am an amateur birder, Rongzom's analogy hit me at once. Birds are strikingly absent, or obscured, during the night, in which, for the most part, they avoid movement once settling to roost safely out of reach of predators.

Chapter 1: The Reality of Affliction

1. Skt. *duḥkhadharmajñānakṣānti*, Tib. *sdug bsngal la chos shes pa'i bzod pa*. This term refers to one of the sixteen aspects of gnosis on the path of seeing, also known as the sixteen moments of gnosis (*ṣoḍaśacittakṣaṇa*, *ye shes bcu drug*). It also refers, in some sense, to what is known to those who can "bear" the truth of discontent.
2. This section is a critique of the idea that afflictions and their antidotes are real entities. Here, Rongzompa employs the logic (*hetu*, *gtan tshigs*) known as "the neither one nor many reasoning" (*ekānekaviyogahetu*, *gcig du bral gyi gtan tshigs*). On this view, one in which it is assumed that the hearers postulate a distinction between suffering (first Noble Truth) and its origin (second Noble Truth), if it is said that one single entity of suffering is manifest in each and every instance of suffering, making them what they are, then the distinction between suffering and its origins would collapse; and if it is said that they are different, distinct entities, that would contradict their putative assertion that suffering and its origins are different. For the Great Vehicle, the two are coextensive. Whatever is suffering is an origin of suffering and vice versa.
3. This section is an expansion of Rongzompa's critique of the idea that each affliction is a distinct and real entity. On this view, if one asserts that afflictions are real entities, then the scheme of twelve links of interdependent origination, each of which is characterized by four Noble Truths, would mean that each link and its subdivisions would be multiplied in such a way that "there could be no decisive reckoning of afflictions."
4. What underlies both incorrect and correct perceptions, here, is that supposition that the ground-of-all (*kun gzhi*), represented by the earth element which is dependent phenomenon, would be included in both. See, by way of comparison, *Mahāyānasaṃgraha* 2.29 (Tōh. 4048), Bstan 'gyur, vol. 76, pp. 47.18–48.2.
5. When a fire-brand, which is glowing red and thus "luminous," is tied to the end of

a rope and whirled in a circle quickly enough, it will produce the appearance of a wheel of fire. That is, spun quickly enough, it appears the fire-brand is a fire-wheel; the faster it is whirled, the more complete the illusion of a fire-wheel.

6. Perception of the fire-brand, which is likened to a perfected phenomena, is correct. Perception of the fire-wheel, which is likened to an imagined phenomenon, is incorrect. And the luminosity, which is included in both, is a dependent phenomenon. The problem is if the fire-wheel is not a real entity, luminosity would pertain only to the fire-brand; and if the fire-brand were not a real entity, the luminosity would pertain only to the fire-wheel. By analogy, conceptuality, which is dependent, cannot pertain to both imagined and perfected phenomena or both would be real entities, since the Yogācāra maintains that what is imagined is not a real entity and only the mind is real. Rongzom's example works to show that in order for the Yogācāra to claim that the ultimate—a reflexive, self-illuminating awareness (*rang rig rang gsal*) free from subject–object dualism—is present underlying all awareness, dualistic and ultimate awareness would both have to be real entities.
7. Skt. *bhavadṛṣṭi*, Tib. *dngos por lta ba rnams*. By "realist," or "realist views," I mean to refer to a theorist, or a theory, that asserts the real or objective existence of entities (*dngos por smra ba*). The term *realist* is, in the words of Sara McClintock (Dreyfus and McClintock 2003, 131), used to refer to "a philosopher who accepts unassailable reality in any form, whether objective or subjective."
8. See, by way of comparison, *Satyadvayavibhaṅga*, v. 12 (Tōh. 3881), Bstan 'gyur, vol. 62, p. 756.12–14.
9. A view perhaps best described in doxographical terms as being close to the position of the Sautrāntika-svātantrika, *mdo sde spyod pa'i dbu ma rang rgyud pa*.
10. The representation of the vase, devoid of the whole of what comprises a physical vase, is merely phenomenal since it does not fully participate in the *personhood* of a real vase. On this view, a physical object's tactility, along with, for example, its taste and smell, cannot comprise any part of strictly visual perception in the ordinary sense, whereas a physical object's shape and color can—and *must*.
11. *Sum cu' rtsa gsum kyi gnas*, a heavenly realm located, according to Abhidharma cosmology, on top of Mount Meru.
12. Tib. *las kyi bgo skal la spyod pa mthun pa dang mi mthun par snang ba dag.*
13. Tib. *yongs su dag pa dang yongs su ma dag par snang ba dag.*
14. Tib. *ye bar spyod pa dang bcas pa dang nye bar spyod pa dang ldan pa ma yin par snang ba dag.*
15. Tib. *phyin ci log du snang ba dang phyin ci ma log par snang ba.*
16. Tib. *gnyi ga'i cha dang ldan par snang ba rnams.*
17. Tib. *phyin ci log du snang ba mthong ba phyin ci log dang bcas pa.*
18. Tib. *phyin ci log du snang ba mthong ba phyin ci ma log pa dang ldan pa.*
19. Tib. *snang ba rten gzhi yod pa dang | rten gzhi myed pa dang | rten gzhi yang dag pa ma yin pa dang ldan pa rnams |.*
20. Tib. *bya ba byed nus pa dang nus pa ma yin par snang ba dag.*
21. Tib. *rdzas su yod pa dang btags pa'i yod par snang ba dag.*
22. Tib. *kun tu btags pa dang mtshan nyid par snang ba.*
23. Tib. *ri dwags me'i gtsang sgra can.*
24. Skt. *pretī*, Tib. *yi dwags ma.*
25. Skt. *devarṣi*, Tib. *lha'i drang srong.* Such figures are exemplified by Nārada and

cited, for example, in the collection of stories describing the Buddha's previous lifetimes, the *Jātakamālā*.

26. This example appears to paraphrase the *Vimalakīrtinirdeśanāmamahāyānasūtra* (Tōh. 176), Bka' 'gyur, vol. 60, pp. 471.21–474.20.
27. In the *Śrāvakabhūmi*'s discussion of seclusion (*pravivikta*, *rab tu dben pa*), for example, we find that among a list of the five qualities for a perfect place of seclusion is being a place without physical or geographical undulations (*shang shong med pa*).
28. Skt. *paranirmatavaśavartinaḥ*, Tib. *gzhan 'phrul dbang byed*. One of the twenty-eight types of divine beings of the Desire Realm (*kāmadhātu*, *'dod khams*).
29. Skt. *smṛti ca samprajanyam*, Tib. *dran pa dang shes bzhin*.
30. This example recalls the triad of epistemological errors traditionally given in terms of a mistake with regard to the *yul* or "object" (for example, the fire-brand), the *rten* or "basis" (for example, diseased eyes), or the *gnas* or "site" (for example, the boat).
31. A member of the Solanaceae family, *Datura* is a genus of poisonous (and psychotropic) vespertine plants that flower.
32. The sovereign's host beats their drums until they come face-to-face with the enemy host, at which time their drumming halts, thus signaling their arrival. The sovereign, who has sent his host in search of the front at which the battle will occur, thus hears the drums cease from a safe distance. My thanks to the Venerable Sean Price for discussing this passage.
33. This is another term for *vajrayāna* (Tibetan: *rdo rje theg pa*), referring broadly to the tantric Buddhist path.
34. Skt. *yakṣa*, Tib. *gnod sbyin*: a type of nonhuman demonic deity (*mi min lha 'dre'i rigs*).
35. Skt. *rākṣasa*, Tib. *srin po*: a general term indicating a malevolent (*gdug pa can*) demon (*gdug 'dre spyi'i ming*).
36. Sa'i me tog.
37. Mi 'chi ba.

Chapter 2: Objections and Replies

1. Here, the illusory is described from the Śrāvaka perspective.
2. Here, the illusory is described from the Yogācāra perspective.
3. Traditional Tibetan doxographies maintain that the Śrāvakayāna does not teach the selflessness of phenomena, but only that of persons.
4. Here, the illusory is described from the Madhyamaka perspective.
5. Skt. Bhadramāyākāra, Tib. Sgyu ma mkhan bzang po. His story is found in the eponymous *Bhadramāyākāravyākaraṇanāmamahāyānasūtra*.
6. Tib. *byin gyis brlabs*. This term is often translated simply as "blessing." In this context, *byin* is rendered according to the definition *gzhan gyi bsam pa dang snang ba sogs bsgyur thub pa'i nus pa'am mthu*.
7. The final line makes a play on words by dedicating the merit "for good" or "the good one" (*bzang po la*), which may also be rendered "for Good [Illusion-Maker.]"
8. This example appears to draw on the stock of characters associated with the Ramkathā tradition. I am preparing a larger study that examines this passage and its origins.
9. According to Khenpo Gaden of Serlo Monastery, the virtue of the weaver's choice

lies in the fact that the finest kind of wood was not chosen to do the work of weaving (*thags cha tsam*). While some kinds of wood are finer than others, the finest is simply not proper for the job.

10. The broad outline of this story calls to mind the myth of Arachne, in which a skilled weaver in Lydia—a region of western Asia Minor, between Mysia and Caria in modern day Turkey—named Arachne challenged the goddess Athena to a contest. In the end, Athena destroyed Arachne's work and Arachne tried to hang herself, but Athena changed her into a spider. This work is recorded in Latin hexameter in the first-century work called *The Metaphorphoses* (*Metamorphōseōn libri*), chap. 6, by the Roman poet Ovid. The similarity of this passage in Rongzom's text to the Greco-Roman myth was first noticed by James Gentry.
11. The Tibetan cry "Kyé-ma" expresses grief, pity, or concern, not unlike the word "alas."
12. This term is generally defined as an equal setting of the mind during single-pointed meditative absorption (*samādhi, ting nge 'dzin*), which is set (*bzhag*) in equanimity (*mnyam*) through having brought to mind (*dmigs nas*) the emptiness that is a selflessness of persons and phenomena (*cha mnyam par bzhag pa ste | ting nge 'dzin sgom skabs gang zag dang chos kyi bdag med pa'i stong pa nyid la sems rtse gcig tu dmigs nas mnyam par bzhag pa*).
13. The term *pure worldly gnosis* is one traditionally said to refer to the gnosis attained subsequent to the path of seeing (*pṛṣṭhalabdajñāna, rje thob yes shes*) as much as is possible to know (*ji snyed pa'i mkhyen*). The idea that a buddha has a "pure worldly gnosis" appears to be given in the Yogācāra-Madhyamaka text tradition, which draws so heavily on Alīkākāravāda and Nirākāravada interpretations of Yogācāra philosophy. See Almogi 2009 and 2013.
14. The term typically refers to twelve literary representations of the Three Baskets (*tripiṭaka, sde snod gsum*) of the Theravada and Mahāyāna traditions: that is, prose discourses (*sūtra, mdo*), a mixture of prose and verse (*geya, dbyangs kyis bskyad pa*), explanations (*vyākaraṇa, lung du bstan pa*), stanzas (*gāthā, tshigs su bcad pa*), pithy sayings (*udāna, ched du brjod pa*), narratives of beginnings (*nidāna, gleng gzhi*), tales of heroic deeds (*avadāna, rtogs pa brjod pa*), short speeches (*ityukta, de lta bu byung ba*), birth stories (*jātaka, skyes rabs*), questions and answers (*vaipulya, shin tu rgyas pa*), reports of miracles (*adbhutadharma, rmad du byung ba*), and instructions (*upadeśa, man ngag*).
15. This rendering is found, with slight variation, in the *Āryasaddharmānusmṛtyupasthāna* (Tōh. 287), Bka' 'gyur, vol. 71, p. 537.2–3.
16. This rendering is found in the *Āryapratītyasamutpādahṛdaya* (Tōh. 981), Bka' 'gyur, vol. 88, p. 187.3–5.
17. *Mahāsaṃnipātaratnaketudhāraṇīsūtra* (Tōh. 138), Bka' 'gyur, *vol. 56*, pp. 513.20–514.2.
18. This passage is found in the *Pratītyasamutpādahṛdayakārikā*, attributed to Nāgārjuna (Tōh. 3836), Bka' 'gyur, vol. 57, p. 403.1–2.
19. This passage is also from the *Pratītyasamutpādahṛdayakārikā* (Tōh. 3836), Bka' 'gyur, vol. 57, p. 403.3–4.
20. Rongzompa explores this issue in a text called *The Great Buddha Ground* (*Sangs rgyas kyi sa chen mo*). For an English translation and study of this work, see Almogi 2009.

21. This term also means "extreme." As Buddhist philosophy seeks to articulate a "middle way between extremes," Rongzompa's play on words connotes both the innocuous phrase *edge of the path* and the rather loaded philosophical term, an *extreme* (*ānta, mtha'*). Whatever is an extreme is by definition not the middle way.
22. As stated above, the term *realism* is used throughout as a generic term for a doctrine, or postulate, that assumes objects of perception have real existence that is not reducible to, or dependent on, a perceiving subject. The words translated here as "splinters" and "torment" could also be understood in terms of "a thicket" and "being stabbed, poked," respectively.
23. This recalls the famed simile of the raft givin in the Pali canonical text, the *Alagaddūpamasutta*, found, among other places, in the Majhima Nikāya collection, sutta number 22.
24. Similar passages are found in the *Śrīvajrahṛdayālaṃkāratantra* (Tōh. 451), Bka' 'gyur, vol. 82, pp. 114.16–115.1; and the *Caturmudrādhyāna* (P 4778), Bstan 'gyur, vol. 44, p. 550.9–14.
25. A remarkably similar passage is found in the *Pradīpodyotanodyotanāmapañjikā* (Tōh. 1790), Bstan 'gyur, vol. 16, which claims to cite Tōh. 443(?), 387.12–16.
26. Skt. *kalpāgni*, Tib. *bskal pa'i me*. This term refers to the all-consuming blaze that occurs at the end of an aeon, according to the Abhidharma cosmology that is accepted in both the Theravada and Mahāyāna. Rongzompa perhaps draws this example from *Pañcaviṃśatisāhasrikā-prajñāpāramitā* (Tōh. 3790), Bka' 'gyur, vol. 26, p. 407.2–7; a similar passage is also found in *Pañcaviṃśatisāhasrikāprajñāpāramitopadeśaśāstrābhisamayālaṅkāra-vṛtti* (Tōh. 3787), Bstan 'gyur, vol. 29, pp. 133.20–134.4.
27. A similar idea is found in the *Āryakāśyapaparivartasūtra* (Tōh. 87), Bka' 'gyur, vol. 44, p. 365.11–17.
28. Köppl (2008, 159n268) lists *bdag tu lta ba'i bag chags* among four types of *bag chags* found in the work of Rongzompa.
29. The phrase *fully matured* (*rnam par smin pa*) connotes karmic conditioning, which buddhas are traditionally said to have transcended.
30. Here, Rongzompa argues against the position that nonconceptual gnosis arises by virtue of a transformation of mental consciousness vis-à-vis the *ālayavijñāna*.
31. My thanks to Khenpo Chönam for his help on this passage.
32. Perhaps critically, Rongzompa understands sensation to be something entailing (ordinary) experience.
33. Tib. *chos nyid kyi bag chags*. Such a view is found for example in *Śrīsarvatathāgataguhyatantrayogamahārājādvayasamatāvijāyanāmavajraśrīparamahākalpādi* (Tōh. 453), Bka' 'gyur, vol. 82, p. 351.8–10.
34. *√sgo* might also be rendered in the sense of "contamination."
35. This is one of four principles of reasoning (*yukti-catuṣṭayam, rigs pa bzhi*).
36. This passage is found in the *Māyājālamahātantrarāja* (Tōh. 466), Bka' 'gyur, vol. 83, p. 386.5–10, as well as the *Nāmasaṁgītivṛttināmārthaprakāṣakaraṇadīpanāma* (Tōh. 2092), Bstan 'gyur, vol. 25, p. 27.13–16.
37. This appears to gloss a line found in the *Āryaprajñāpāramitāṣṭasahasrikāvyākhyābhisamayālaṁkārāloka* (Tōh. 3791), Bstan 'gyur, vol. 51, p. 1108.16–19.
38. A similar passage is found in the *Mahāparinirvāṇasūtra* (Tōh. 119), Bka' 'gyur, vol. 83, pp. 370.20–371.1.

39. Rongzompa's *Entering the Way of the Great Vehicle* names the text as *Smon lam gyi mtha' bstan pa*, which appears to be another name for the *Āryabhadracaryapraṇidhānarājā* (Tōh. 4337), Bka' 'gyur, vol. 13, which is commonly known in Tibetan as *An Aspiration for Good Conduct* (*Bzang spyod smon lam*).
40. Some of the texts Rongzompa cites under the rubric of definitive scriptures are named as the *Vajracchedikā*, the *Sarvabuddhaviṣayāvatārajñānālokālaṁkārasūtra*, and the *Ratnakūṭa*.
41. *Vajracchedikāsūtra* (Tōh. 16), Bka' 'gyur, vol. 34, p. 333.14–15.
42. Attributed to *Bhadramāyākāravyākaraṇasūtra* (Tōh. 65), Bka' 'gyur, vol. 43, p. 68.8–10.
43. *Buddhāvataṁsakanāmamahāvaipulyasūtra* (Tōh. 44), Bka' 'gyur, vol. 35, pp. 539.15–17, 540.4–6.
44. These lines are found, with slight variation, in the *Āryasarvabuddhaviṣayāvatārajñānāloka-ālaṅkāranāmamahāyānasūtra* (Tōh. 100), Bka' 'gyur, vol. 47, p. 748.9–11, and in the *Vairocanābhisaṃbodhitantrapiṇḍārtha* of Buddhaguhya (Almogi 2009, 265n74).
45. *Vajracchedikāsūtra* (Tōh. 16), Bka' 'gyur, vol. 34, p. 354.4–7.
46. The *Gaṇḍavyūhasūtra* is one of two names used by Tibetans to designate the forty-fifth section of the voluminous *Avataṁsakasūtra*.
47. This is a slightly altered list of the five psychophysical aggregates (*pañcaskandha*, *phung po lnga*), which is typically given in terms of form (*rūpa*, *gzugs*), sensations (*vedanā*, *tshor ba*), discriminations (*saṃjñā*, *'du shes*), karmic processes or compositional factors (*saṃskāra*, *'du byed*), and consciousness (*vijñāna*, *rnam shes*).
48. A similar view is described, for example, in the *Sarvabuddhasamayogaḍākinīsambharamahātantrarājanāmamaṇḍalavidhisarvasattvasukhodaya* (Tōh. 1679), Bstan 'gyur, vol. 14, p. 766.12: *phung po rgyal ba lngar brjod do*.
49. Tib. *rgyags shing myos pa*. The metaphor at work here is from the study of elephants (*hastividyā*). The Tibetan terms *rgyags* and *myos* suggest an elephant in musth (*mada*). The term *rgyags pa* translates the Sanskrit *mada* ("musth"). The term *myos pa* translates the term *unmāda* ("frenzied, crazy"). The term *myos rdul can* ("dredged with *unmāda*") is a term for an elephant. Since the subject is a child—one can hardly expect a palace servant to address a grown prince as *boy* (*bu*)—I do not read the use of the term *mada* as referring to the prince's drunkenness or lust; he is too young. It refers, rather, to his recklessness.
50. Tib. *gdams ngag gi gnas*. Note the dual nuance here—that is, *gdams ngag* can mean both "advice" in the ordinary sense and "secret instruction" in connection with tantric teaching.
51. Tib. *gdod ma nas dri ma dang bral bar shes nas*. Note the dual nuance: *gdod ma nas* can refer to both the fact that the food and drink were never contaminated and the "originally pure" nature of mind referenced in such texts as *Bodhicittavivaraṇa*, *Ratnagotravibhaga*, and others.
52. Here, the interlocutor is trying to get around Rongzompa's view that there is nothing real (actual/objective basis) restraining beings by stipulating that while karmic manifestations might not be real, the process might be. If that is the case, the interlocutor is arguing, the problem alluded to by Rongzom goes away because, according to the interlocutor, there is then no need to account for some ontological basis. One response from Rongzom is to state that any philosophical validation of a

process qua particular attribute or quality or fundamental basis is a consequence of having a philosophical stance. This is what he means just below when he writes: "the validation of a distinct factor that is an actual basis and the validation of its qualitative factors each flow from a philosophical insistence upon a personal entity."

53. This example is found in the *Vimalakīrtinirdeśanāmamahāyānasūtra* (Tōh. 176), Bka' 'gyur, vol. 60, p. 534.3–6.
54. That is, *Bodhicittabhāvanā* (Tōh. 2591), Bstan 'gyur, vol. 33, p. 811.5–8, which is attributed to Mañjuśrīmitra. This is the most-cited text in *Entering the Way of the Great Vehicle.*
55. This citation is found in *Bodhicittabhāvanā* (Tōh. 2591), Bstan 'gyur, vol. 33, p. 811.9–11.
56. To be *filled with bones* (*rus pas gang ba bzhin*) is a phrase that calls to mind the effects of meditating on the unpleasant nature of the body (*mi sdig pa bsgoms pa*).
57. According to this view, the ordinary mind appears in the form of external objects, including one's own physical body and its faculties of perception, cognition, and so forth. Just how these appear to an individual's mind in particular depends upon one's karma and conditioning. Here, Rongzompa offers three examples: the falling hairs that are perceived by those with cataracts, the sound of drums for the ruler of an army, and a pile of bones that a meditator uses to generate an antidote to attachment to this body. Cognition of the first, a false object that does not in fact exist, depends upon a medical condition; the second, a conditioned basis of *inference* (which Rongzom often refers to as "nonobservation") for particular individuals only, depends on one's education as a ruler; the third, a psychological attitude toward the body cultivated in the long term in dependence upon one's receiving proper instructions on the meditation. Consider, for example, the ruler leading an army. For him or her, the sound of the drums is heard and thereby understood differently than most people. For the ruler, the continued sound of the drums is nothing other than inferential knowledge: "no enemy present." That is, the sound of the drums is, for him or her, an epistemological sign (a basis for correct inferential knowledge) that the enemy has not yet been encountered. That the sound of the drums functions in this special way for the ruler is a result of his or her conditioned socialization as the leader of an army in a culture where the drums are used in this way.
58. *Bodhicittabhāvanā* (Tōh. 2591), Bstan 'gyur, vol. 33, p. 811.11–12.
59. *Bodhicittabhāvanā* (Tōh. 2591), Bstan 'gyur, vol. 33, p. 811.12–13.

Chapter 3: Distinguishing the Perfected System of the Illusory in the Great Perfection from the Other Vehicles That Retain the Nomenclature of Illusion

1. Tib. *sman sten*. The medical language calls attention to the fact that this model of the Buddhist path is built on "acceptance and rejection" (*blang dor*), or bias; one diagnoses an affliction the cause of which is abandoned, and takes up the cause of its antidote. The healing metaphor is one of Buddhism's most prominent; it has a long pedigree in South Asia drawing on Āyurveda. Buddhism's own long use of this

metaphor can be traced to the *Mahāvagga* section of the Pali *vināya*, specifically two chapters: the *Bhesajja-kkandhaka* and *Cīvara-khandhaka*. For a discussion of healing in Buddhism, see Covill 2009, 99–183. This model, with its recognition of faults/ailments to be eliminated and qualities/antidotes to be taken, which is based on bias (*blang dor*), is overcome or overturned in Great Perfection.

2. Tib. *bag yangs su spyod*. This term has the sense of "easygoing behavior," "acting relaxed," "going with the flow," and the like.
3. See, by way of comparison, *Mūlamadhyamakakārikā* 15.3.
4. Skt. *pūrvānta/pūrvakoṭi*, Tib. *sngon gyi mtha'*: The Tibetan *sngon gyi mtha'* is generally defined as the foremost point in time for the emergence of the physical world and the sentient beings within it (*snod bcud 'jig rten sogs thog mar 'byung dus kyi ya mtha'*).
5. See, by way of comparison, *Brahmajalasutta*, *Dīgha Nikāya* 1.1–46.
6. Regarding the origins of such a view, the Old School luminary, Longchenpa (1308–1364), writes:

   > At the time when the Buddha was about to pass into nirvana, a teacher of the tradition of Naked Ascetics approached him. With the words, 'Come here,' the Buddha ordained him, and he became a shravaka. This teacher, Vatsiputra, then asked the Buddha whether the individual self is the same as the mind-body aggregates, or distinct from them, or both, or neither. The Buddha's answer was to say nothing at all, which Vatsiputra interpreted to mean that the self does exist but is indescribable. Although he had embraced the dharma, he accepted the existence of an indescribable self. (Longchen Rabjam 2007, 68–69)

7. Skt. *naga*, Tib. *klu*. Here, inexpressibility pertains to the relation between the self and the aggregates. In the case of the nagas, their self is somehow both of the water as well as in it; and that *somehowness* is something not particularly amenable to description. This view calls into question the nature of the skandhas: what, exactly, are they?
8. In Tibetan intellectual traditions, the Vaibhāṣika are divided into three camps: the Kashmiri (*kha che*) Vaibhāṣika, the Western (*nyi 'og*) Aparāntika Vaibhāṣika, and the Central Region (*yul dbus*) Vaibhāṣika. I am unsure as to the specific referent of this latter term. It is important to note that Tibetan intellectuals maintain that the Vaibhāṣika schools all assert that the ultimate is a real entity (*rdzas yod*).
9. Tib. *yod pa dang yin pas*; that is, the how of something's existence and what it pertains to. We might also consider the two, respectively, in terms of existential and predicative statements. As is well known, for Vaibhāṣika, ultimate truth, or reality, and real entity are synonymous (*don dam bden pa dang rdzas yod don gcig*).
10. Skt. *maraṇabhava*, Tib. *'chi ba'i srid pa*. This term is generally defined as one of the four types of becoming; it is the moment just after one has lost the physical body of this life or [being] just about to die (*srid pa bzhi'i sgras shig ste | tshe 'di'i lus rten bor ma thag pa'am 'chi kha ma'o*).
11. *Existential* refers here to ontology—what stuff there is in the world. *Predicative* refers to what is attributed to that stuff—that is, what we say about stuff in the world.
12. *Bodhicittabhāvanā* (Tōh. 2591), Bstan 'gyur, vol. 33, p. 812.13–14.

13. *Bodhicittabhāvanā* (Tōh. 2591), Bstan 'gyur, vol. 33, p. 812.14–15.
14. Thus, for Rongzompa, the three natures of Yogācāra theory are all subsumed equally under the category of the totally imagined.
15. Rongzompa glosses this term below.
16. *Sarvakalpasamuccayanāmasarvabuddhasamāyogaḍākinījālasaṃvarottarottaratantra* (Tōh. 367), Bka 'gyur, vol. 77, p. 552.5–7.
17. The Tibetan term plays on the verbal element, which can be rendered either as "to impute" or "to analyze." Both render the Tibetan verb √*rtog*.
18. The Tibetan dyad *sgro skur* refers to two ways that ordinary beings distort the objects in their awareness: imposing (*sgro 'dogs*) something where it is not and denying (*skur 'debs*) something where it is (*med pa la yod par sgro 'dogs pa dang yod pa la med par skur ba 'debs pa*).
19. This term is said to refer to twelve types of literature corresponding to the Three Baskets (*tripiṭaka*) of the Theravada and Mahāyāna. The twelve types of doctrinal discourse are *sūtra* (prose discourses), *geya* (a mixture of prose and verse), *vyākaraṇa* (explanations), *gāthā* (stanzas), *udāna* (pithy sayings), *nidāna* (narratives of beginnings), *avadāna* (tales of mythic deeds), *ityukta* (short speeches), *jātaka* (birth stories), *vaipulya* (dialogues), *adbhutadharma* (descriptions of miracles), and *upadeśa* (intimate spiritual instructions).
20. Tib. *don gyi kha brgyud pa dang bral ba la man ngag ces bya'o.*
21. Tib. *mnyam pa'i spyod pa*. The practice of sameness is one of austerity, in which one practices sameness in making no distinction of any kind between pure and impure (*de la brtul zhugs mnyam pa'i spyod pa ni | gtsang rme'i rnam pa ci la'ang bye brag mi bya bar mnyam pa nyid du spyad do |* (Nubchen Sangyé Yeshé 1974, 258.03–258.04).

Chapter 4: The Great Perfection Approach to the Path Is Not Undermined by Reason

1. Skt. *vyākaraṇaśāstra/śabdhaśāstra*, Tib. *sgra'i bstand chos.*
2. Skt. *yuktiśāstra*, Tib. *rigs pa'i bstan chos.*
3. Tib. *chun pa'i sgye'u snod ltar gyur pa*. According to Samten Karmay (1998, 326n69), *sgye'u* means "small bag." Jonathan Silk (2008, 164) suggests that the term might intimate managerial or administrative functions. The Tibetan √*'chun* also suggests a sense of control in the context of taming a horse and the possibility of taming malevolent people (*rta rgod po bcun nas 'chun pa | mi ngan rang bzhin gyis 'chun mi yong*).
4. That is, when a fire-brand at the end of a rope is whirled around in a circle quickly enough, it will produce the illusion of the fire-brand being a fire-wheel.
5. Tib. *byang chub du snang*. In another work, Rongzompa supposes his interlocutor to ask, "Are there appearances, especially confused appearances, within the domain of a Tathāgata's gnosis?" In response, he writes, "Since appearance in nonconceptual gnosis is nonconceptual, it is not appearance as such" (*de yang mi rtog pa'i ye shes kyi snang ba ni snang ba nyid ma yin te | mi rtog pa nyid yin pa'i phyir ro |* Rong zom chos bzang 1999c, 2:121.20–121.22).
6. Tib. *rten gzhi'i bye brag*. For example, the fact of being made (*byas pa*), which is shared by a pillar and vase. Thus, they pertain to a coincident identity due to their shared foundation as products (*byas pa*).

7. Tib. *du ma dmigs pa dang | gcig dmigs pa dang.* Here, perspectives dominate and one member of a binary is rejected while the other is superordinated.
8. Tib. *mi dmigs pa.*
9. Note each describes a subject (*chos*) and predicate (*chos can*).
10. According to the Tibetan dictionary *Dag yig gsar bsgrigs* 2003, rhinos are mammals, whose shape is a bit like a cow, whose body is almost totally devoid of hair and has lots of wrinkles, and who grow horns on top of the nose. In India, they only have one horn; on the African continent there are those with two horns (*nu ma nu ba'i srog chags sug bzhi'i rigs shig ste, dbyibs phal cher ba lang dang cha 'dra la, lus na ha lam spu gcig kyang med cing, gnyer ma mang la, sna mgor rwa skyes yod pa zhig yin. Rgya gar na yod pa la rwa gcig ma gtogs med pa dang, a hphe ri ka'i gling na yod pa la rwa gnyis yod* | 852 s.v. *bse ru*). Perhaps he is distinguishing rhinos from some of the two-horned beasts familiar to Tibetans; perhaps I have misunderstood Rongzompa; perhaps, in eleventh-century Tibet, he was unaware that African rhinos can have two horns.
11. That is, the Buddha's teaching, the dharma, prevents ethical and practical transgression of Buddhist precepts.
12. I think that here "measure" is another word for "assess." The fact that Rongzompa uses the Tibetan term *tshad* makes it seem to me like a bit of a pun, playing on the ordinary sense of "measure" and the philosophical/epistemological sense of assessing an object in propositional terms.
13. Tib. *yod pa dang yin pa* is a combination of two Tibetan nominalized verbs. As a phrase, it refers to what there is (for example, *nam mkha' yod* or "space exists") and what can be said about it (for example, *nam mkha' chos can | yod pa gang zhig rtag pa yin par thal | nam mkha' kho rang 'dus ma byas pa yin pas phyir* "The subject, space, exists (*yod*) and is (*yin*) permanent because space itself is (*yin*) uncompounded").
14. Tib. *gang dang gang gcig gang du gcig pa.*
15. That is, when proving two things to be the same, one starts off with two ontologically distinct things as the bases of comparison.
16. That is, this type of unhelpful philosophizing could go on, as it were, forever. This is the folly of philosophy and those who insist on philosophical precision as a criterion for efficacious soteriological discourse.
17. Tib. *ji ltar bsgrubs pa de ltar tshad zin cing.*
18. Tib. *dri ma che chung tsam du zad do.* That is, any attempt to theorize about phenomena other than the perfectly pure dharmadhātu, whose nature is beyond words and description, is an exercise is distorting what there really is.
19. That is, a proponent of the Sāṃkhya view.
20. Tib. *don la blos 'jal ba.* Assess in the sense of sizing up the character and dimensions of something (*'jal byed yo byad kyis dngos rdzas kyi lci yang ring thung mang nyung sogs brtsis pa'i don te*).
21. The term *sgro skur* refers to two distortions in which the ordinary mind participates directly in generating misknowing (*avidyā, ma rig pa*) about the nature of things: imposing (*sgro 'dogs*) something that is not there and denying (*skur 'debs*) something that is there (*med pa la yod par sgro 'dogs pa dang yod pa la med par skur ba 'debs pa*).
22. Tib. *dngos por lta ba thams cad kyi srungs mar 'gyur ro.* In Tibet, the Madhyamaka is

most often recognized as constituting a critique/refutation of realist theories (*dngos por lta ba*).

23. Skt. *dūṣaṇa*, Tib. *sun 'byin pa*.
24. The first ad hoc examples that come to mind are, respectively, walking on to a construction site to build a home, finding nothing but 1" x 6" planks, and exclaiming "why are there no building materials here?"; and an overwhelmed maître d' assuring an increasingly impatient crowd that he was unprepared for, "There is no confusion. I will have you all seated shortly!"

Chapter 5: Writings on Great Perfection

1. The term *snying po byang chub* (essence of enlightenment), sometimes written as *byang chub snying po* (quintessence of awakening)—Rongzompa uses both terms in *Entering the Way of the Great Vehicle*—is an early counterpart to more well-known terms used to refer to buddha nature (*tathāgatagarbha, de bzhin gshegs pa'i snying po*). According to David Higgins (2013), this term is particularly prevalent among theorists of Great Perfection between the eighth and eleventh centuries.
2. The trope of "play" or "sport" (*līlā, rol pa*) is best understood in the context of what stands opposed to it: karma. Bodily, mental, and physical actions that are conditioned are karmic actions, whereas play or sport refer to action that is not originated or implicated within such conditioned activity. This kind of activity is compared to child's play in that is it is not directed at some particular (karmic) aim and does not generate new effects (*phala, 'bras bu*) that come to fruition as suffering.
3. The *Six Vajra Verses of Bodhicitta* (*Rdo rje tshig drug ma*) is considered an important early work, one of the earliest available, on the Great Perfection.
4. *Bodhicitta Vajrasattva Great Space* (*Byang chub kyi sems rdo rje sems dpa' nam mkha' che*) is an early Great Perfection discourse found in the later compilation of Mind Series (*sems sde*) Great Perfection discourses entitled Kun byed rgyal po, which is itself considered the root tantra of one of the three types of Great Perfection tantra: Space Series (*klong sde*), Mind Series (*sems sde*), and the Intimate Instruction Series (*man ngag sde*). In the *Dpe bsdur ma* catalog of the Tibetan Buddhist canon, this text is given the Sanskrit title *Sarvadharmamahāsantibodhicittakulayaḥrājā* (Tōh. 828), Bka' 'gyur, vol. 101. On this text, see Norbu and Clemente 1999.
5. *Vimalakīrtinirdeśanāmamahāyānasūtra* (Tōh. 176), Bka' 'gyur, vol. 60, p. 592.1–2.
6. *Buddhāvataṁsakanāmamahāvaipulyasūtra* (Tōh. 44), Bka' 'gyur, vol. 5, p. 675.16–18.
7. The *Great Garuḍa* (*Khyung chen*) is an early Great Perfection tantra of the Mind Series (*sems sde*) and found in the root tantra of that series, the Kun byed rgyal po (Tōh. 828), Bka' 'gyur, vol. 101, p. 495.8–11.
8. This line perhaps refers to one found in the *Thabs shes sgron ma*, an early Great Perfection work attributed to Pelyang (Dpal dbyangs, fl. ninth century).
9. *Āryaprajñāpāramitāsañcayagāthā* (Tōh. 13), Bka' 'gyur, vol. 34, p. 15.2–3.
10. That is, the first greatness.
11. That is, the second greatness.
12. Tib. *gzugs kyi bye brag du snang ba bzhi*.
13. The 108 stories of the Buddha's past lives.

14. Perhaps a reference to such figures as Nubchen Sangyé Yeshé (Snub chen sangs rgyas ye shes, b. 844 CE), the author of *Bsam gtan mig sgron* (Nubchen Sangyé Yeshé 1974).
15. *Rdo rje sems dpa' nam mkha' che* and *Mi nub rgyal mtshan nam mkha' che* are both considered early Mind Series (*sems sde*) tantras. Both are included in the later collection of Mind Series tantras called Kun byed rgyal po.
16. *Sarvadharmamahāsantibodhicittakulayaḥrājā* (Tōh. 828), Bka' 'gyur, vol. 101, p. 79.2–4, chap. 30, entitled *Undiminished Victory Banner* (*Mi nub rgyal mtshan*). It is also sometimes referred to as *Indestructible Being Great Space* (*Rdo rje sems dpa' nam mkha' che*).
17. Any mind involved in phenomenal characteristics is a mind of discrimination and, thus, bias.
18. *Sarvadharmamahāsantibodhicittakulayaḥrājā* (Tōh. 828), Bka' 'gyur, vol. 101, p. 79.8–10, chap. 30, entitled *Undiminished Victory Banner* (*Mi nub rgyal mtshan*).
19. *Māyājālamahātantrarāja* (Tōh. 466), Bka' 'gyur, vol. 83, p. 393.17–20. Rongzompa identifies this text by the name *Vairocana-Māyājālatantra* (*Rnam par snang mdzad sgyu 'phrul drwa ba'i rgyud*). This text has been described by scholars as the single most important text in Old School (*Rnying ma*) intellectual history.
20. This verse is found, albeit with slight variation, in the seventh chapter of the *Māyājālamahātantrarāja* (Tōh. 466), Bka' 'gyur, vol. 83, p. 386.21.
21. *Sarvadharmamahāsantibodhicittakulayaḥrājā* (Tōh. 828), Bka' 'gyur, vol. 101, p. 79.10–12, chap. 30, entitled *Undiminished Victory Banner* (*Mi nub rgyal mtshan*).
22. *Sarvadharmamahāsantibodhicittakulayaḥrājā* (Tōh. 828), Bka' 'gyur, vol. 101, p. 79.10–12.
23. *Sarvadharmamahāsantibodhicittakulayaḥrājā* (Tōh. 828), Bka' 'gyur, vol. 101, p. 79.15–17.
24. My thanks to Khenpo Lama Chönam of Amdo, Golog, for his explanation of this verse.
25. *Sarvadharmamahāsantibodhicittakulayaḥrājā* (Tōh. 828), Bka' 'gyur, vol. 101, p. 79.16–18, chap. 30, entitled *Undiminished Victory Banner* (*Mi nub rgyal mtshan*).
26. Tib. *theg pa chung ngu*. Here, the Śrāvakayāna is described not in psychological terms, as an approach for selfish people driven by their concern for their own suffering alone, but in theoretic and cognitive terms: the approach of people with a particular interpretation of the Buddha's teaching that the nature of reality is illusory and a particular resulting perception of reality as a consequence. It is interesting that nowhere do we find in Rongzompa's work any mention of a "lesser vehicle" (*hīnayāna*, *dman theg*).
27. That is, freedom from the waves of birth, old age, sickness, and death that roil the ocean of saṃsāra.
28. *Sarvadharmamahāsantibodhicittakulayaḥrājā* (Tōh. 828), Bka' 'gyur, vol. 101, pp. 79.18–20, chap. 30, entitled *Undiminished Victory Banner* (*Mi nub rgyal mtshan*).
29. Tib. *kun gyi bla ma*; alternatively, "guru of all," "superior to all," "all-supreme one," and so forth.
30. *Sarvadharmamahāsantibodhicittakulayaḥrājā* (Tōh. 828), Bka' 'gyur, vol. 101, p. 80.7–9, chap. 30, entitled *Undiminished Victory Banner* (*Mi nub rgyal mtshan*).
31. Skt. *ākāśānantyāyatana*, Tib. *nam mkha' mtha' yas skye mched*; the first level of the formless realm (*ārūpyadhātu*, *gzugs med khams*).

32. *Sarvadharmamahāsantibodhicittakulayaḥrājā* (Tōh. 828), Bka' 'gyur, vol. 101, p. 80.9–11, chap. 30, entitled *Undiminished Victory Banner* (*Mi nub rgyal mtshan*).
33. *Sarvadharmamahāsantibodhicittakulayaḥrājā* (Tōh. 828), Bka' 'gyur, vol. 101, p. 80.14–16.
34. *Āryaprajñāpāramitāsañcayagāthā* (Tōh. 34), Bka' 'gyur, vol. 101, p. 401.14–15,
35. *Sarvadharmamahāsantibodhicittakulayaḥrājā* (Tōh. 828), Bka' 'gyur, vol. 101, p. 80.15–17, chap. 30, entitled *Undiminished Victory Banner* (*Mi nub rgyal mtshan*).
36. *Sarvadharmamahāsantibodhicittakulayaḥrājā* (Tōh. 828), Bka' 'gyur, vol. 101, p. 80.20–21, chap. 30, entitled *Undiminished Victory Banner* (*Mi nub rgyal mtshan*).
37. *Sarvadharmamahāsantibodhicittakulayaḥrājā* (Tōh. 828), Bka' 'gyur, vol. 101, pp. 80.21–81.2, chap. 30, entitled *Undiminished Victory Banner* (*Mi nub rgyal mtshan*).
38. *Sarvadharmamahāsantibodhicittakulayaḥrājā* (Tōh. 828), Bka' 'gyur, vol. 101, p. 81.2–4, chap. 30, entitled *Undiminished Victory Banner* (*Mi nub rgyal mtshan*).
39. *Sarvadharmamahāsantibodhicittakulayaḥrājā* (Tōh. 828), Bka' 'gyur, vol. 101, p. 81.4–6, chap. 30, entitled *Undiminished Victory Banner* (*Mi nub rgyal mtshan*).
40. *Sarvadharmamahāsantibodhicittakulayaḥrājā* (Tōh. 828), Bka' 'gyur, vol. 101, p. 81.6–8, chap. 30, entitled *Undiminished Victory Banner* (*Mi nub rgyal mtshan*).
41. *Sarvadharmamahāsantibodhicittakulayaḥrājā* (Tōh. 828), Bka' 'gyur, vol. 101, p. 81.11–13, chap. 30, entitled *Undiminished Victory Banner* (*Mi nub rgyal mtshan*).
42. *Sarvadharmamahāsantibodhicittakulayaḥrājā* (Tōh. 828), Bka' 'gyur, vol. 101, p. 81.13–15, chap. 30, entitled *Undiminished Victory Banner* (*Mi nub rgyal mtshan*).
43. *Sarvadharmamahāsantibodhicittakulayaḥrājā* (Tōh. 828), Bka' 'gyur, vol. 101, p. 81.15–16, chap. 30, entitled *Undiminished Victory Banner* (*Mi nub rgyal mtshan*).
44. *Sarvadharmamahāsantibodhicittakulayaḥrājā* (Tōh. 828), Bka' 'gyur, vol. 101, p. 81.17–19, chap. 30, entitled *Undiminished Victory Banner* (*Mi nub rgyal mtshan*).
45. *Sarvadharmamahāsantibodhicittakulayaḥrājā* (Tōh. 828), Bka' 'gyur, vol. 101, pp. 81.21–82.1, chap. 30, entitled *Undiminished Victory Banner* (*Mi nub rgyal mtshan*).
46. *Sarvadharmamahāsantibodhicittakulayaḥrājā* (Tōh. 828), Bka' 'gyur, vol. 101, p. 81.3–5, chap. 30, entitled *Undiminished Victory Banner* (*Mi nub rgyal mtshan*).
47. Tib. *me shel*. That is, a crystal that can be used to concentrate the sun's light in order to make fire. It is traditionally said that these crystals, and some other stones, have some luminous properties of their own. Rongzom stipulated as much above when describing the red jewel's illuminating light in the metaphor of the rowdy boy.
48. *Sarvadharmamahāsantibodhicittakulayaḥrājā* (Tōh. 828), Bka' 'gyur, vol. 101, p. 81.5–7, chap. 30, entitled *Undiminished Victory Banner* (*Mi nub rgyal mtshan*).
49. *Sarvadharmamahāsantibodhicittakulayaḥrājā* (Tōh. 828), Bka' 'gyur, vol. 101, p. 81.7–9, chap. 30, entitled *Undiminished Victory Banner* (*Mi nub rgyal mtshan*).
50. *Sarvadharmamahāsantibodhicittakulayaḥrājā* (Tōh. 828), Bka' 'gyur, vol. 101, p. 82.11–13, chap. 30, entitled *Undiminished Victory Banner* (*Mi nub rgyal mtshan*).
51. *Sarvadharmamahāsantibodhicittakulayaḥrājā* (Tōh. 828), Bka' 'gyur, vol. 101, p. 82.13–16, chap. 30, entitled *Undiminished Victory Banner* (*Mi nub rgyal mtshan*).
52. The Tibetan term *lung de nyid* can also be translated as "transmission."
53. *Sarvadharmamahāsantibodhicittakulayaḥrājā* (Tōh. 828), Bka' 'gyur, vol. 101, p. 83.10–11, chap. 30, entitled *Undiminished Victory Banner* (*Mi nub rgyal mtshan*).
54. Tib. *srid pa dang mi srid pa*. Alternatively, "existence and nonexistence" or even "possible and impossible."

55. This description of an ocean surrounding our world is found in the cosmology of the Abhidharma.
56. Tib. *ma bcos pa'i ngang la lhun gyis gnas pa tsam mo.*
57. This phrase is interesting. Rongzompa could have used the term *tshul,* which so often refers to established traditions. Here, the phrase is subtler: simply a collection of writings on Great Perfection.
58. *Lta ba yang dag sgron ma.* This text is attributed to the ninth-century figure Pelyang. See Takahashi 2009, 410.
59. Ibid., 411.
60. Ibid.
61. Ibid., 408.
62. *Bodhicittabhāvanā* (Tōh. 2591), Bstan 'gyur, vol. 33, p. 813.15–17.
63. *Bodhicittabhāvanā* (Tōh. 2591), Bstan 'gyur, vol. 33, p. 813.
64. *Bodhicittabhāvanā* (Tōh. 2591), Bstan 'gyur, vol. 33, p. 814.11–12.
65. Attributed to *Bodhicittabhāvanā* (Tōh. 2591), Bstan 'gyur, vol. 33, though citation not found.
66. *Bodhicittabhāvanā* (Tōh. 2591), Bstan 'gyur, vol. 33, p. 814.12.
67. *Bodhicittabhāvanā* (Tōh. 2591), Bstan 'gyur, vol. 33, p. 814.13.
68. *Bodhicittabhāvanā* (Tōh. 2591), Bstan 'gyur, vol. 33, p. 814.14.
69. *Bodhicittabhāvanā* (Tōh. 2591), Bstan 'gyur, vol. 33, p. 814.16–17.
70. *Bodhicittabhāvanā* (Tōh. 2591), Bstan 'gyur, vol. 33, p. 814.17–19.
71. *Bhagavatīprajñāpāramitāhṛdya*, also known as *The Heart Sutra* (Tōh. 531), Bka' 'gyur, vol. 88, p. 298.15.
72. *Sarvadharmamahāsantibodhicittakulayaḥrājā* (Tōh. 828), Bka' 'gyur, vol. 101, p. 66.08–12, chap. 22, entitled *The Soaring Garuḍa* (*Khyung chen lding ba*).
73. *Sarvadharmamahāsantibodhicittakulayaḥrājā* (Tōh. 828), Bka' 'gyur, vol. 101, p. 66.12–14 chap. 22, entitled *The Soaring Garuḍa.*
74. *Sarvadharmamahāsantibodhicittakulayaḥrājā* (Tōh. 828), Bka' 'gyur, vol. 101, p. 73.2–7, chap. 27, entitled *The Dynamic Consummation of Potential* (*Rtsal chen sprugs pa*).
75. Ibid.
76. *Sarvadharmamahāsantibodhicittakulayaḥrājā* (Tōh. 828), Bka' 'gyur, vol. 101, p. 83.19–20, chap. 31.
77. *Sarvadharmamahāsantibodhicittakulayaḥrājā* (Tōh. 828), Bka' 'gyur, vol. 101, p. 78.7–9, chap. 20.
78. *Sarvadharmamahāsantibodhicittakulayaḥrājā* (Tōh. 828), Bka' 'gyur, vol. 101, p. 66.4, chap. 22.
79. *Sarvadharmamahāsantibodhicittakulayaḥrājā* (Tōh. 828), Bka' 'gyur, vol. 101, p. 78.11–12, chap. 30.
80. *Sarvadharmamahāsantibodhicittakulayaḥrājā* (Tōh. 828), Bka' 'gyur, vol. 101, p. 79.2–3.
81. *Mtha'i mun sel sgron ma* (Tōh. 4448, Bstan 'gyur, vol. 20) is an early Great Perfection discourse attributed to the Dynastic figure (ca. ninth century) known as Pelyang. See Takahashi 2009, 415
82. *Mtha'i mun sel sgron ma* (Tōh. 4448), Bstan 'gyur, vol. 120, p. 963.1–3.
83. *Mtha'i mun sel sgron ma* (Tōh. 4448), Bstan 'gyur, vol. 120, p. 963.3–5.

84. *lTa ba rin po che sgron ma* (Tōh. 4451), Bstan 'gyur, vol. 120, p. 972.3–5). This text is attributed to Pelyang.
85. *Lus sems bcos myed thabs kyi sgron ma* (Tōh. 4450), Bstan 'gyur, vol. 120, p. 969.1–969.5. This text, which is attributed to Pelyang, may also be identified by the title *The Lamp of the Method of Meditation* (*Bsgom thabs kyi sgron ma*). In the *Dpe bsdur ma* catalog of the Tibetan canon (Tōh. 4450), it is listed as *A Lamp for the Method for Discerning the Domain Ascertained by the System of Yogācārins* (*Rnal 'byor spyod pa'i lugs nges pa'i don la ji bzhin sgom thabs kyi sgron ma*).
86. *Byang chub kyi sems yul kun la 'jug pa*. This text is also known as chapter 22 of the *Sarvadharmamahāsantibodhicittakulayaḥrājā* (Tōh. 828), Bka' 'gyur, vol. 101, pp. 6.20–64.2: the *Great Garuḍa* (*Khyung chen*).
87. Tib. *rnam par mi rtog pa'i sgom lung*.
88. *Sarvadharmamahāsantibodhicittakulayaḥrājā* (Tōh. 828), Bka' 'gyur, vol. 101, p. 80.1–3, chap. 30.
89. In Tibetan Buddhist philosophy, the example of a *hare's horn*—along with others such as the *son of a barren woman*, a *flower growing in the sky*, and so on—serves as an exemplar of an impossibility.
90. *Bodhicittabhāvanā* (Tōh. 2591), Bstan 'gyur, vol. 33, p. 814.5–7.
91. *Bodhicittabhāvanārthadvadaśanirdeśa* (*Byang chub kyi sems bsgom pa don bcu gnyis*, Tōh. 2578), Bstan 'gyur, vol. 33 p. 250.6–7.
92. *Vimālakīrtinirdeśasūtra* (Tōh. 176), Bka' 'gyur, vol. 60.
93. The *Gaṇḍavyūhasūtra* is one chapter in the voluminous *Buddhāvataṁsakanāmamahāvaipulyasūtra* (Tōh. 44); this citation is found in Bka' 'gyur, vol. 35, p. 30.14–18.
94. This appears to be a slightly altered list of the five psychophysical aggregates.
95. *Bodhicittabhāvanā* (Tōh. 2591), Bstan 'gyur, vol. 33, p. 814.2–3.
96. Sogan Rinpoche (Tulku Pema Lodoe of Amdo, Golog) adds that, traditionally, there are said to be two types of experience (*nyams su myong ba*): that of ordinary beings, which is marked by sensation, and so forth, and the experience within the exalted knower (*mkhyen pa*) of an arhat superior (*'phags pa dgra bcom pa*).
97. Tib. *yong ni*. This is the gloss given by Khenpo Tsultrim Dorje Rinpoche.
98. Tib. *chu srin chu bya snyegs pa' ming ngo*. Images of sea dragons are found, for example, in some thangka paintings, where they might dwell in a buddha's pure land and thus represent something auspicious. My thanks to Tashi Lama of Kathmandu and Sogan Rinpoche (Golog Tulku Pema Lodoe) for this information.
99. *Bodhicittabhāvanā* (Tōh. 2591), Bstan 'gyur, vol. 33, p. 815.2–4.
100. Ibid.
101. Sogan Rinpoche identifies the lineage (*gotra/kula*, *rigs*) here as the lineage of great compassion (*snying rje chen po'i rigs*).
102. Skt. *śukladharma*, Tib. *dkar po'i chos*.
103. Tib. *de'i phyir byang chub sems kyi yon tan ma bshad na skur ba'i gnas su 'gyur ba'i phyir ro*. According to Rongzom (see the top of chapter 4), people obsessed with and fixated on logical and grammatical precision were the same people who rejected the discourse on bodhicitta given in the Great Perfection text tradition. These logicians and grammarians, as it were, miss the warmth of the bodhicitta soteriological forest for the logically and grammatically precise philosophical trees. Chapter 4 describes

itself as a presentation of Great Perfection bodhicitta without some of the traditional terminology.

104. *Sarvadharmamahāsantibodhicittakulayaḥrājā* (Tōh 2591), Bstan 'gyur, vol. 33, p. 66.13–15, chap. 22.
105. *Sarvadharmamahāsantibodhicittakulayaḥrājā* (Tōh 2591), Bstan 'gyur, vol. 33, p. 79.1–2, chap. 29.
106. According to the Venerable Sogan Rinpoche, great miracles are not difficult for those who have realized bodhicitta as it is taught in the Great Perfection.
107. *Sarvadharmamahāsantibodhicittakulayaḥrājā* (Tōh. 0828), Bka' 'gyur, vol. 101, p. 80.3–5, chap. 30.
108. The 1999 Chengdu edition reads *la ya ti gri na*, which I cannot make sense of. The Namdroling edition used in South India reads *la ya ti phri na*. See Sanskrit √*lul*: to move back and forth.
109. *Sarvadharmamahāsantibodhicittakulayaḥrājā* (Tōh. 0828), Bka' 'gyur, vol. 101, p. 80.5–7, chap. 30.
110. Tib. *yan lag spros pa bzhin*. An alternative translation might read "not unlike an elaboration."
111. *Sarvadharmamahāsantibodhicittakulayaḥrājā* (Tōh. 0828), Bka' 'gyur vol. 101, p. 80.6–80.7.
112. *Sarvadharmamahāsantibodhicittakulayaḥrājā* (Tōh. 0828), Bka' 'gyur, vol. 101, p. 65.11–14, chap. 22.
113. *Lta ba rin po che gron ma* (Tōh. 4451), Bstan 'gyur, vol. 120, p. 972.2–3). This text is attributed to the ninth-century figure Pelyang.
114. *Sarvadharmamahāsantibodhicittakulayaḥrājā* (Tōh. 0828), Bka' 'gyur, vol. 101, p. 66.6–8, chap. 22.

Chapter 6: Instructions on Paths Encountered through Methods Connected with Effort for Those Who Are Unable to Remain Effortlessly within the Natural State according to the Great Perfection Approach

1. Traditionally, there are said to be five hindrances to achieving a calm and focused mind: (1) laziness (*kausīdya, le lo*), (2) forgetting the instructions (*avavādasammosa, gdams ngag brjed* pa), (3) mental laxity (*laya, bying ba*) and restlessness (*auddhatya, rgod pa*), (4) nonapplication of proper antidotes (*anabhisamskāra, 'du mi byed pa*), and (5) excessive application of antidotes (*abhisamskāra, 'du byed pa*). There are eight applications that eliminate these five faults. There are four applications to eliminate laziness: (1) faith (*śraddhā, dad pa*), (2) aspiration (*chanda, 'dun pa*), (3) effort (*vyayama, rtsol ba*), and (4) mental pliancy (*praśrabdhi, shin tu sbyangs pa*). Mindfulness (*smṛti, dran pa*) is applied to remedy forgetting the instructions; introspection (*samprajañya, shes bzhin*) is applied to eliminate laxity and restlessness; the nonapplication of antidotes is eliminated through applying (*abhisamskāra, 'du byed pa*) the proper antidotes; and not applying (*anabhisamskāra, 'du mi byed pa*) antidotes eliminates excessive application. Rongzompa brings these subjects up again below.

2. *Sarvatathāgatacittaguhyajñānārthagarbhakhrodhavajrakulatantrapiṇḍikārthavidyāyoganāma-māhāyānasūtra* (Tōh. 0831).
3. That is, three sets of three. There are three types of obscurations—great, middling, and lesser—each with its own division into great, middling, and lesser divisions, totaling nine obscurations.
4. Tib. *'ben thim pa'i mda' lta bu'o.* I have rendered this phrase in accordance with the Venerable Sogan Rinpoche's reading, though this phrase might also suggest such notions as an arrow whose target has disappeared.
5. That is, it does not take effort to see what is obviously in front of your eyes.
6. Tib. *chos spyod rnam bcu.* This phrase refers to ten types of practice: (1) copying the doctrinal discourse literature, (2) making offerings, (3) practicing generosity, (4) listening to dharma teachings, (5) upholding the dharma, (6) reading the dharma, (7) explaining the dharma, (8) reciting the dharma, (9) contemplating the meaning of the dharma, and (10) meditating upon the meaning of the dharma.
7. *Sarvatathāgatacittaguhyajñānārthagarbhakhrodhavajrakulatantrapiṇḍikārthavidyāyoganāma-māhāyānasūtra* (Tōh. 0831), Bka' 'gyur, vol. 102, p. 35.17–20.
8. The interlinear note in the text identifies the source for this citation as *Dpung gzungs*; and there is a text entitled *'Phags pa rgyal mtshan gyi rtse mo'i dpung rgyan zhes bya ba'i gzungs* (*Dhvajāgrakeyūranāmadhāraṇi*), but the text in which I located the citation is *Āryasubāhuparipṛcchānāmatantrapīṇḍārthavṛtti* (Tōh. 2673), Bstan 'gyur, vol. 36, p. 284.5–8.
9. Skt. *ṣaḍaṅgayoga*, Tib. *rnal 'byor yan lag drug.* These six yogas are traditionally connected with discourse on the practice of *Kālacakratantra*.
10. The interlinear note identifies the source for this citation as a work called *'Dus pa.* I have found the citation, however, in *Śrīḍākārṇavamahāyoginītantrarāja* (Tōh. 372), Bka' 'gyur, vol. 78, p. 456.18–20.
11. *Sādhananidānanāmaśrīcakrasaṃvarapañjikā* (Tōh. 1401), Bka' 'gyur, vol. 8, p. 954.14–17.
12. It would seem the two big toes and two thumbs are not included.
13. Tib. *re zhig gi mtshan ma.* Alternatively, this phrase might mean "some of the characteristics."

Closing Verses

1. This line may perhaps suggest that this text was penned for scholars of other systems such as Kālacakra, among others.
2. It is critical to understand that, for Rongzompa, the Great Perfection constitutes the consummation of the Great Vehicle.

Works Cited

This list includes only modern publications. The canonical references for Sanskrit and Tibetan works mentioned in the text can be found in the endnotes.

Almogi, Orna. 2002. "Sources on the Life and Works of the Eleventh-Century Tibetan Scholar Rong Zom Chos Kyi Bzang Po: A Brief Survey." In *Tibet, Past and Present: Tibetan Studies I, Proceedings of the Ninth Seminar of the International Association for Tibetan Studies*, edited by Henk Blezer, 67–80. Leiden: Brill.

———. 2009. *Rong-zom-pa's Discourses on Buddhology: A Study of Various Conceptions of Buddhahood in Indian Sources with Special Reference to the Controversy Surrounding the Existence of Gnosis (jñāna: ye shes) as Presented by the Eleventh-Century Tibetan Scholar Rong-zom Chos-kyi-bzang-po*. Tokyo: International Institute for Buddhist Studies.

———. 2013. "Yogācāra in the Writings of the Eleventh-Century Rnying ma Scholar Rong zom Chos kyi bzang po." In *The Foundation for Yoga Practitioners: The Buddhist Yogācārabhūmi Treatise and Its Adaptation in India, East Asia, and Tibet*, edited by Ulrigh Timme Kragh, 1330–61. Harvard Oriental Series 75. Cambridge, MA: Harvard University Press.

Bradburn, L. 1995. *Masters of the Nyingma Lineage*. Berkeley: Dharma Publishing.

Buswell, Robert E., Jr., and Donald S. Lopez Jr., eds. 2013. *The Princeton Dictionary of Buddhism*. Princeton: Princeton University Press.

Covill, Linda. 2009. *A Metaphorical Study of Saundarananda*. Delhi: Motilal Banarsidass Publishers.

Dag yig gsar bsgrigs. 2003. Mtsho sngon dpe skrun khang.

Doniger, Wendy. 2009. *The Hindus: An Alternative History*. New York: Penguin Press.

Dreyfus, Georges B. J. 1997. *Recognizing Reality: Dharmakīrti's Philosophy and Its Tibetan Interpretations*. Albany: State University of New York Press.

Dreyfus, Georges B. J., and S. L. McClintock, eds. 2003. *The Svātantrika-Prāsaṅgika Distinction: What Difference Does a Difference Make?* Boston: Wisdom Publications.

Dudjom Rinpoche, Jikdrel Yeshe Dorje. 1991. *The Nyingma School of Tibetan Buddhism: Its Fundamentals and History*. Translated and edited by Gyurme Dorje and Matthew Kapstein. Boston: Wisdom Publications.

Germano, David. 1992. "Poetic Thought, the Intelligent Universe, and the Mystery of Self: The Tantric Synthesis of rDzogs Chen in Fourteenth Century Tibet." PhD diss., University of Wisconsin at Madison.

———. 2005. "The Funerary Transformation of the Great Perfection (Rdzogs chen)." *Journal of the International Association of Tibetan Studies*, no. 1 (October): 1–54.

Griffiths, Paul J. 1994. *On Being Buddha: The Classical Doctrine of Buddhahood*. Albany: State University of New York Press.

Higgins, David. 2013. *The Philosophical Foundations of Classical rDzogs chen in Tibet: Investigating the Distinction between Dualistic Mind (sems) and Primordial Knowing (ye shes)*. Wien: Arbeitskreis für Tibetische und Buddhistische Studien Vienna, Universität Wien.

Kapstein, Matthew. 2009. "The *Sun of the Heart* and the *Bai ro rgyud 'bum*." In *Tibetan Studies in Honour of Samten Karmay*, edited by François Pommaret and Jean-Luc Achard, 275–88. Dharamshala: Amnye Machen Institute.

Karmay, S .G., 1998. *The Arrow and the Spindle: Studies in History, Myths, Rituals and Beliefs in Tibet*. Kathmandu: Mandala Book Point.

Kiblinger, Kristin B. 2005. *Buddhist Inclusivism: Attitudes Towards Religious Others*. Cornwall: Ashgate Publishing.

Köppl, Heidi I. 2008. *Establishing Appearances as Divine: Rongzom Chökyi Zangpo on Reasoning, Madhyamaka, and Purity*. Ithaca, NY: Snow Lion Publications.

La Vallée Poussin, Louis de, trans. 1990. *Abhidharmakośabhāṣyam*. Vol. 4. Berkeley: Asian Humanities Press.

Limaye, Surekha V. 2000. *Mahāyānasūtrālaṃkāra: Text, Translation and Commentary*. Delhi: Sri Satguru Publications.

Lindtner, Chr. 1987. *Nagarjuniana: Studies in the Writings and Philosophy of Nāgārjuna*. Delhi: Motilal Banarsidass.

Longchen Rabjam. 2007. *The Precious Treasury of Philosophical Systems: A Treatise Elucidating the Meaning of the Entire Range of Spiritual Approaches*. Translated by Richard Barron. Junction City, CA: Padma Publishing.

Matilal, B. K., 1990. *The Word and the World: India's Contribution to the Study of Language*. Oxford: Oxford University Press.

Norbu, C. N., and A. Clemente. 1999. *The Supreme Source: The Fundamental Tantra of Dzogchen Semde Kunjed Gyalpo*. Ithaca, NY: Snow Lion Publications.

Nubchen Sangyé Yeshé (gNubs chen Sangs rgyas ye shes, fl. 10th c.). 1974. *Gnubs chen sangs rgyas ye she rin po ches mdzad pa'i sgom gyi gnang gsal bar phye ba bsam gtan mig sgron*. Short title: *Bsam gtan mig sgron*, reproduced from a manuscript made presumably from an Eastern Tibetan print by 'Khor gdon gter sprul 'Chi med rig dzin. Vol. 74. Leh: Smartsis shesrig spendzod.

Pitcher, George. 1965. "Wittgenstein, Nonsense, and Lewis Carroll." *Massachusetts Review* 6, no. 3: 591–611.

Robinson, Richard. 1972. "Did Nāgārjuna Really Refute All Philosophical Views?" *Philosophy East and West* 22, no. 3: 325–331.

Roerich, George N., trans. 1976. *The Blue Annals*. New Delhi: Motilal Banarsidass.

Rong zom chos bzang. 1999a. *The Charter of Mantrins Composed by Rongzom Chokyi Zangpo* (*Rong zom chos kyi bzang pos mdzad pa'i sngags pa rnams kyi bca' yig*). In Rong zom chos bzang 1999c, 2:393–405.

———. 1999b. *Rgyud rgyal gsang ba snying po dkon cog 'grel*. In Rong zom chos bzang 1999c, 1:31–250.

———. 1999c. *Rong zom chos bzang gi gsung 'bum*. 2 vols. Chengdu: Si khron mi rigs dpe skrun khang.

———. 1999d. *Sangs rgyas thams cad dang mnyam par sbyor ba mkha' 'gro ma sgyu ma bde ba'i mchog ches pa'i rgyud kyi dka' 'grel*. In Rong zom chos bzang 1999c, 2:457–620.

Silk, Jonathan. 2008. *Managing Monks: Administrators and Administrative Roles in Indian Buddhist Monasticism*, Oxford: Oxford University.

Smith, Gene. 2001. *Among Tibetan Texts*. Boston: Wisdom Publications.

Sørensen, Per K. 1994. *Tibetan Buddhist Historiography: The Mirror Illuminating the Royal Genealogies: An Annotated Translation of the XIVth Century Chronicle "rGyal-rabs gsal-ba'i me-long."* Asiatische Forschungen 128. Wiesbaden: Harrassowitz.

Steinkellner, E. 1993 "Buddhist Logic: The Search for Certainty." In *Buddhist Spirituality: Indian, Southeast Asian, Tibetan, Early Chinese*, edited by Takeuchi Yoshinori, 213–18. New York: Crossroad.

Takahashi, Kammie M. 2009. "Lamps for the Mind: Illuminations and Innovation in dPal dbyang's Mahāyoga." PhD diss., University of Virginia.

Tanzin, Lopon P. Ogyan. 2013. "The Six Greatnesses of the Early Translations according to Rong-zom Mahāpaṇḍita." In *Tibet after Empire: Culture, Society and Religion between 850–1000, Proceedings of the Seminar Held in Lumbini, Nepal, March 2011*, edited by Christoph Cüppers, Robert Mayer, and Michael Walter, 367–92. Nepal: Lumbini International Research Institute.

Tillemans, Tom, Johannes Frank, and Derek Dane Herforth. 1989. *Agents and Actions in Classical Tibetan: The Indigenous Grammarians on Bdag and Gźan and Bya Byed Las Gsum*. Wien: Arbeitskreis für Tibetische und Buddhistische Studien, Universität Wien.

Tulku Thondup Rinpoche. 1989. *Buddha Mind: An Anthology of Longchen Rabjam's Writings on Dzogpa Chenpo*. Ithaca, NY: Snow Lion Publications.

Uray, G. 1960. "The Four Horns of Tibet according to the Royal Annals." *Acta Orientalia Academiae Scientiarum Hungaricae* 10, no. 1: 31–57.

van der Kuijp, Leonard W. J. 1983. *Contributions to the Development of Tibetan Buddhist Epistemology: From the Eleventh to the Thirteenth Century*. Wiesbaden: Franz Steiner.

———. 1994. "Tibetan Belles-Lettres: The Influence of Daṇḍin and Kṣemendra." In *Tibetan Literature: Studies in Genre*, edited by José Cabezón and Roger R. Jackson, 393–410. Ithaca, NY: Snow Lion Publications.

———. 1999. "Remarks on the 'Person of Authority' in the Dga' ldan pa/Dge lugs pa School of Tibetan Buddhism." *Journal of the American Oriental Society* 119, no. 4: 646–72.

———. 2006. "On the Composition and Printings of the *Deb gter sngon po* by 'Gos lo tsā ba gzhon nu dpal (1392–1481)." *Journal of the International Association of Tibetan Studies* 2: 1–46.

van Schaik, Sam. 2004. "The Early Days of the Great Perfection." *Journal of the International Association of Buddhist Studies* 27, no. 1: 165–206.

———. 2013. *Tibet: A History*. New Haven, CT: Yale University Press.

Vitali, R. 1996. *The Kingdoms of Gu.ge. Puhrang: According to mNga'-ris rgyal.rabs by Gu.ge mkhan.chen Ngag.dbang grags.pa*. New Delhi: Indraprastha Press.

Wangchuk, Dorji. 2002. "An Eleventh-Century Defence of the *Guhyagarbhatantra*." In *The Many Canons of Tibetan Buddhism*, edited by Helmut Eimer and David Germano, 265–91. Proceedings of the International Association of Tibetan Studies, Leiden 2000. Leiden: Brill.

———. 2004. "The rÑiṅ-ma Interpretations of the Tathāgatagarbha Theory." *Wiener Zeitschrift für die Kunde Südasiens/Vienna Journal of South Asian Studies* 48: 171–213.

Wittgenstein, Ludwig. 1988. *Tractatus Logico-Philosophicus*. Translated by D. F. Pears and B. F. McGuiness. London: Routledge and Kegan Paul.

———. 2001. *Philosophical Investigations*. Translated by G. E. M. Anscombe. Oxford: Blackwell.

Index

Guhyamantra system (*continued*)
capacity for, 98–99
conception and imputation in, 101–2
enlightenment in, 139–40
illusion in, 14, 53–56, 60, 218n25
internal divisions of, 142
liberation in, 106
meditation in, 183–84
resolving qualitative similarity in, 109
totally imagined, view of, 97–99

hell beings, 114
Hindu, use of term, 220n31
hope, 161–62, 163
hopes and aspirations, 143, 150–51
hungry ghosts, 49–50

identity
proving, 121
three types, 113–15, 231–32nn6–7, 232n9
ignorance, 42, 65, 83, 84, 86, 168, 219n26
Illuminating Web of Illusion Tantra, The, 144, 234n19
illusion, 42
Buddhist views on, 17–18, 19–20
character of, 53
emanation and, 59–60
etymology of term, 63
five exemplars of, 14, 53–56, 60, 218n25
as game, 132
of nonexistent things, 189–90
purification of, 187
of reality, 13
Rongzom's view of, 9–11, 209
imagination, 91, 101–2, 196–98
imagined forms, 61–62, 78. *See also* totally imagined
impermanence, 59, 91, 93, 94, 98, 120, 121
imposition, 103, 124, 143, 151, 158, 164
imprints, karmic
appearance and, 48, 51–52, 56, 85, 86, 165, 167, 198
in bodhisattva's continuum, 66
eliminating, 70
growth of seeds and, 67
Mahāyāna view of, 105
in Yogācāra, 96
imputation, imaginary, 47, 102–3
Indestructible Being of Great Space Tantra, The, 143, 171–72, 176, 186, 234n15
Indian Buddhism
Abhidharma in, 219n27
five principal philosophical systems of, 13, 218n24
five sciences of, 24
Perfection of Wisdom in, 10
and Tibetan, relationship between, 2, 9, 12
Indra, 46
inference, 91, 229n57
insight
arising of, 204
compassion and, 169, 188
concentration and, 71, 180
discriminating, 124
nonobjectifying, 86
stainless, 112
three obscurations to, 193–94
twofold, 124
integrated path, 194, 195
intellect
aggregate of, 19, 84, 85, 86
discrimination and, 124
enlightenment and, 23
gnosis and, 70, 77
grasping and, 32
intention, 101
as aggregate, 78, 179
egoic, 196
hidden, 108
indestructible, 201
karmic processes and, 112
in meditation, 196
in nonengagement, 166
interdependence, 14, 17, 64–65, 98, 123, 139, 209
intimate advice/instructions
impediments to, 175–79
three fundamental, 131, 159–60